THE WORKING WORLD OF INTERNATIONAL ORGANIZATIONS

The Working World of International Organizations

Authority, Capacity, Legitimacy

XU YI-CHONG
PATRICK WELLER

UNIVERSITY PRESS

OXFORD
UNIVERSITY PRESS

Great Clarendon Street, Oxford, OX2 6DP,
United Kingdom

Oxford University Press is a department of the University of Oxford.
It furthers the University's objective of excellence in research, scholarship,
and education by publishing worldwide. Oxford is a registered trade mark of
Oxford University Press in the UK and in certain other countries

© Xu Yi-chong and Patrick Weller 2018

The moral rights of the authors have been asserted

First Edition published in 2018

Impression: 1

All rights reserved. No part of this publication may be reproduced, stored in
a retrieval system, or transmitted, in any form or by any means, without the
prior permission in writing of Oxford University Press, or as expressly permitted
by law, by licence or under terms agreed with the appropriate reprographics
rights organization. Enquiries concerning reproduction outside the scope of the
above should be sent to the Rights Department, Oxford University Press, at the
address above

You must not circulate this work in any other form
and you must impose this same condition on any acquirer

Published in the United States of America by Oxford University Press
198 Madison Avenue, New York, NY 10016, United States of America

British Library Cataloguing in Publication Data

Data available

Library of Congress Control Number: 2017947334

ISBN 978-0-19-871949-6

Printed and bound by
CPI Group (UK) Ltd, Croydon, CR0 4YY

Links to third party websites are provided by Oxford in good faith and
for information only. Oxford disclaims any responsibility for the materials
contained in any third party website referenced in this work.

Acknowledgements

This project is about the people in international organizations: the presidents and directors general, their deputies and chiefs of staff, vice presidents and directors, ambassadors, state representatives, and executive directors. They are not only senior managers; they are also doctors, lawyers, economists, and engineers. They live the experience day by day. They all have deep knowledge of the internal operation of their organizations. To discover how these international organizations really work, we chose to ask them all to reflect on their experiences, on the challenges, the frustrations, and the exhilaration that they meet in their jobs. Over the last fifteen years, for this book and for those books and articles that have preceded it, we have talked to over 200 people, some of them three, four, or more times, with the conversations occasionally spread over a decade. We have benefited from them all.

We have talked to people at headquarters as well as country offices. We made a number of visits to the World Bank and the Intentional Monetary Fund in Washington, the World Health Organization, the World Intellectual Property Organization, and the World Trade Organization in Geneva, and the Food and Agriculture Organization in Rome. Many of our interviewees had extensive experience in the field and reflected on their experiences there. We also visited Beijing, Canberra, Dhaka, Jakarta, Kathmandu, and New Delhi to talk to the officials in the field and particularly to the locally employed staff there who bring a different perspective to the discussion. We owe our greatest debt to this wide range of people. We could not have written the book without their patience, their insights, their commitment, and their time. To them all, our thanks and our appreciation.

Over the last decade we have asked our interviewees if we could tape the interviews on a non-attributable basis. That is, we could cite the interviews and name the organization but without identifying the person who made the comments. We found that, the more senior the interviewees, the more informed they were, the more they were able to understand the breadth of the organization, the more relaxed they were and the more willing to share their insight about the organization. We would have understood if more junior staff were nervous, but few actually seemed to be. Only two of all interviewees asked us not to record their interviews.

We have therefore been able to develop a bank of interview transcripts as the foundation for our analysis. That is not to say they all agreed; there was no evident 'line' that was taken; rather, even from those within the same organization, we received a range of perspectives of various hues. Drawing them together into a coherent narrative that does not hide the differences was one of the great challenges of this project. In the text, comments drawn from these interviews appear in quotation marks, but without a footnote. We thought that to list every quotation as one based on a 'private interview' would be tedious. Although the actual quotations are, of course, from an individual, we have tried to ensure that they are representative of the broader opinion held by the groups from which the interviewees were drawn. We chose the sharpest expressed comments, because they make the point most distinctly; we did not choose atypical ones.

In our visits to the IOs we were often assisted in the arranging of interviews and were sometimes provided an office in which we could base ourselves. We would like to thank, in particular, Francis Gurry, Director General of the World Intellectual Property Organization, and Pascal Lamy, Director General of the World Trade Organization, both for supporting our research in their organizations and for finding time in their busy schedules to provide us with the benefit of their experience and insights. We would also like to thank the External Affairs Department in the World Bank, the Council and Trade Negotiations Division at the WTO, the office of the Assistant Director General, Economic and Social Development, at the FAO, and the Director General's Office at WIPO and WHO, for the facilitation of our research.

While it may seem invidious to pick out any individuals, we would like to give particular thanks to those who came to a workshop we ran in Brisbane on decision-making in international organizations. Over two days they provided continuing insights. So to Stuart Harbinson, Jim Adams, Chrik Poortman, Naresh Prasad, Luc Hubloe, David Hallam, and Andrew Cassels, our sincere gratitude. We would also like to thank Oxford University Press's anonymous referee for most useful suggestions and advice.

In Brisbane we have benefited from the research assistance of Paula Cowan and May McPhail. Our colleagues in the Centre for Governance and Public Policy have provided patient ears listening to us cogitate on the problems of international organizations as part of the political science discipline. We thank them for their forbearance.

Our research was funded by the Australian Research Council, Discovery Grant DP 110104791. We have appreciated that support.

We hope we have done justice to the wide range of information and views provided to us; that is for readers to judge.

Xu Yi-chong
Patrick Weller

Brisbane,
November 2016

Contents

List of Figure and Tables	ix
List of Abbreviations	xi
1. Understanding International Organizations	1
2. Representatives of Member States	20
3. Heads of International Organizations: Politicians, Diplomats, Managers	56
4. Secretariats and Staff	103
5. Agenda Setting	140
6. Funding International Organizations	171
7. Location	203
8. Conclusion: Authority, Capacity, Legitimacy	229
Select Bibliography	245
Index	257

List of Figure and Tables

FIGURE

5.1. FAO's turf	148

TABLES

1.1. Characteristics of the six selected international organizations	4
3.1. Modes of IO leadership (s)election	66
6.1. Shares of contribution of fifteen large countries to various IOs, 2014/2015	174
6.2. WIPO income, 2004/2005 to 2014/2015	180
6.3. Share of paid-up assessed contributions at the FAO, at 30 September, 2001–2006	184
6.4. Voluntary contribution to the WHO, by source, 2011/2012 to 2014/2015	200

List of Abbreviations

ACP	Africa, Caribbean, and Pacific
ADG	assistant director general
AU	African Union
BINGO	Business Interest NGO
BMJ	*British Medical Journal*
BRICS	Brasilia, Russia, India, China, and South Africa
CD	country director
CDC	Centre for Disease Control
CoCo	Coordination Committee of WIPO
DDG	deputy director general
DFID	Department for International Development, UK
DG	director general
EB	Executive Board
EBF	extra-budgetary fund
ED	executive director
ESMAP	Energy Sector Management Assistance Programme
FAO	Food and Agriculture Organization
GATT	General Agreement on Tariffs and Trade
GAVI	Global Alliance for Vaccines and Immunizations
IAEA	International Atomic Energy Agency
IBRD	International Bank of Reconstruction and Development
ICS	international civil servants
IDA	International Development Agency
IEE	Independent External Evaluation (of the FAO)
IEO	Independent Evaluation Office (of the IMF)
IFAD	International Fund for Agricultural Development
IFC	International Finance Corporation
IGO	intergovernmental organization
ILO	International Labour Organization
IMF	International Monetary Fund
IO	international organization
IP	intellectual property

IPA	Immediate Plan of Action
ITU	International Telecommunications Union
LDC	least-developed country
MD	managing director
MDG	millennium development goal
MIGA	Multilateral Investment Guarantee Agency
NGO	non-governmental organization
OECD	Organization for Economic Cooperation and Development
PAHO	Pan-American Health Organization
PCT	Patent Cooperation Treaty
PINGO	Public Interest NGO
PPP	public–private partnerships
SDR	special drawing rights
RD	regional director
RMB	renminbi
TRIPS	Trade-Related Aspects of Intellectual Property Rights
UN	United Nations
UNAIDS	Joint United Nations Programme on HIV/AIDS
UNCTAD	United Nations Conference on Trade and Development
UNDP	United Nations Development Programme
USDA	US Department of Agriculture
VP	vice president
WFP	World Food Programme
WHO	World Health Organization
WIPO	World Intellectual Property Organization
WTO	World Trade Organization

1

Understanding International Organizations

Since the late 1990s, studies on multilateral institutions have expanded: '"global governance" has become both a widespread and useful term for describing the growing complexity in the way that the world is organized and authority exercised as well as shorthand for referring to a collection of institutions with planetary reach'.[1] The terms 'international institutions', 'global governance', or even 'multilateralism' have, as many scholars have argued, lost their rigorous analytical capacity, as they can be applied to 'virtually anything' across state borders.[2] Amid the rising number of multilateral institutions, international organizations created around the mid-twentieth century have not only survived both quantitative and qualitative changes, but also thrived in their prominence and ranges of activities and impacts. This is a study of six of these 'old-style' intergovernmental organizations, also known as international organizations (IOs), created by sovereign states through treaty negotiations. They may not monopolize the attention of scholars any more, but they remain the backbone of international politics in the sense that all other types of multilateral institutions (state based and otherwise) try to build ties with IOs or/and work around IOs.

IOs have expanded in number, size, range of activities, and influence. Their member states take them seriously. When the World Health Organization (WHO) warns the world about health threats or pandemics, governments and health workers take actions. When the financial crisis hit the world, countries cited the International Monetary Fund (IMF) and World Bank's reports as objective approval of their policies. When the Food and Agriculture Organization (FAO) labelled rising food prices as a 'food crisis', countries took measures to prepare for it. IOs matter because on most occasions states listen to and act on decisions made by IOs and often justify their actions by referring back to IOs. They matter also because states frequently defer many difficult

---

[1] Thomas G. Weiss and Rorden Wilkinson, 'Rethinking Global Governance', *International Studies Quarterly*, 58/1 (2014), 207.
[2] Lawrence Finkelstein, 'What is Global Governance', *Global Governance*, 1995, 1/3 (1995), 368. See also the discussions of various authors, 'Controversy: Global Governance', *International Studies Quarterly*, 58/1 (2014), 207–24.

cross-border problems to IOs and expect them to manage these issues on their behalf. IOs are taken seriously, despite the insistence of states on their jealously guarded 'sovereignty'. 'States can and do disparage the United Nations, the World Bank, and other international organizations,' explained US president Obama, yet 'the giants of the 1940s knew that instead of constraining our power, these institutions magnified it'.[3] States, large or small, rich or poor, have been willing not only to 'use IOs as vehicles of cooperation',[4] but also to create more of them and then empower them.

It is not uncommon to hear substantial complaints about IOs: the WHO failed to respond to Ebola on time; the World Bank 'is unaccountable to the people in poor countries'; the IMF 'outmanoeuvred the encroaching authority of "rival" IOs',[5] or the World Trade Organization (WTO) indiscriminately pushed forward trade liberalization and deregulation. What do we mean when we talk about the FAO, WHO, WTO, or the World Bank? The popular mantra in Geneva is that IOs are member-driven organizations, and a few state representatives would like to think IOs are no more or no less than their member states. IOs *are* more than their member states. A growing number of studies have demonstrated that IOs have a life of their own and can have an independent impact on the behaviour of their member states, not only because states have delegated authority to these organizations, but also because member states are concerned about what IOs do.[6] IOs are more than passive sites of extensive consultation; they are active players in their own right. As players, IOs are neither single entities with single minds, nor a single decision-maker. They are complex mini-political systems, within which players exercise their power and influence in making decisions; their interactions affect the actions or inactions of IOs.

This study examines the interplay among three groups of players within the context of IOs—state representatives, as proxy of member states, serving on the Board of Executive Directors or the General Council, the heads of IOs serving as international' political and bureaucratic leaders, and international

---

[3] Quoted in Stewart Patrick, 'Prix Fixe and à la Carte: Avoiding False Multilateral Choices', *Washington Quarterly*, 23/4 (2009), 77.

[4] Kenneth W. Abbott and Duncan Snidal, 'Why States Act through Formal International Organizations', *Journal of Conflict Resolution*, 42/1 (1998), 4.

[5] Jeffrey M. Chwieroth, *Capital Ideas: The IMF and the Rise of Financial Liberalization* (Princeton: Princeton University Press, 2010), 189; also Ngaire Woods, *The Globalizers: The IMF, the World Bank, and their Borrowers* (Ithaca, NY: Cornell University Press, 2006).

[6] See, e.g., Thijs van de Graaf and Dries Lesage, 'The International Energy Agency after 35 Years', *Review of International Organizations*, 4/3 (2009), 293–317; Xu Yi-chong and Patrick Weller, *The Governance of World Trade: International Civil Servants and the GATT/WTO* (Cheltenham: Edward Elgar, 2004); Bessma Momani, 'IMF Staff: Missing Link in Fund Reform Proposals', *Review of International Organizations*, 2 (2007), 39–57; Xu Yi-chong and Patrick Weller, *Inside the World Bank* (New York: Palgrave Macmillan, 2009); Frank Biermann and Bernd Siebenhüner (eds), *Managers of Global Change: The Influence of International Environmental Bureaucracies* (Boston: MIT Press, 2009).

civil servants working at and for the permanent IO secretariat. What are their roles, interests, perceptions, and involvement in IO decision-making? How do they shape the actions or inactions of IOs? How is their behaviour shaped by the formal and informal rules of IOs? Who or what shapes decisions of IOs? How do these players interact in decision-making processes within an IO? How do the interactions vary across IOs? This study argues that *actions and decisions of IOs* cannot be explained just by focusing on the relationship between two aggregated units—states that delegate authority to IOs and IOs as agents that exercise the authority. They have to be examined from within, as there are many parts in any given IO, with each having its own roles to play, functions to fulfil, and capacity to make the organization work.

This study investigates and analyses the intricate relationship among these three groups of players in six IOs: the FAO, IMF, WHO, World Intellectual Property Organization (WIPO), WTO, and World Bank, all significant institutions in contemporary world politics. These six IOs have different systems of representation, from those with standing full-time state delegates, meeting several times a week, to those governed by occasional meetings of selected state representatives. They vary in size, with numbers of staff between 650 and over 10,000, scope of mandates (broad to narrow), range of activities (normative and delivery), functioning and decision-making procedures, organizational cultures, and degrees of centralization (Table 1.1). Some are mandated to make binding decisions, while others provide recommendations that require national action. They cover different professional disciplines, with a variety of claims to expertise, and hence different forms and levels of discretion might be expected.

They nonetheless are all 'global governing bodies' and enjoy a 'dash of supranationalism provided by the formal authority of the secretariat'.[7] While they are all nestled within the broader United Nations (UN) system, they are not direct departments of the UN. Five of the six are special agencies, with the WTO having a special association with the UN for historical reasons.[8] They all carry out significant economic and social functions. While their decisions and decision-making are always political, they are NOT political organizations per se, as in the case of the UN or UN Human Rights Commission. They are delegated with a functional responsibility to deal with technical issues, rather than issues concerning war and peace.

There are, of course, several ways to select and categorize IOs, but we contend these six IOs are sufficiently representative and distinct to provide a range of data and insights to tackle our central questions on the interaction of players and their comparative influence on decision-making within these bodies.

---

[7] Robert O. Keohane, *After Hegemony* (Princeton: Princeton University Press, 1984), 225.
[8] See the historical discussion in Craig VanGrasstek, *The History and Future of the World Trade Organisation* (Geneva: WTO, 2013).

Table 1.1. Characteristics of the six selected international organizations

	FAO	IMF	World Bank	WHO	WTO	WIPO
Members	195	189	188	193	162	185
Start	1946	1944	1944	1948	1944/1995	1967
Governing structure	Conference Meets every two years Elected member states Council (49) Work on personal capacity Meets three or four times every two years	Board of Governors Meets twice a year Executive Board (24) on site	Board of Governors Meets twice a year Executive Directors (25) on site	World Health Assembly Meets annually Executive Board (34) Three-year term State-based representation Work on personal capacity	Ministerial conference Meets about every two years General Council (all members represented by ambassadors) Meets six or seven times a year	General Assembly Meets once or twice a year Coordination Committee (83)
Chief officer	Director General Four-year term Term limit of two Brazil, 2012– 'appointed by the Conference'	Managing Director Five-year term France, 2007– 'selected' by a simple majority of the Board	President Five-year term 'Appointed' by US President, Endorsed by the Executive Board	Director General Five-year term Hong Kong, 2007– 'Appointed' by the World Health Assembly, with the Executive Board's 'nomination'	Director General Four-year term Brazil, 2013– 'Appointed'	Director General Six-year term Australia, 2008– Assembly appoints upon CoCo nomination
Secretariat	3,248 (1,738 professionals + 1,510 general staff) (2015) 57% at HQ 1989—a staff of 6,483 2/3 HQ; 1/3 field	2,600 Centrally located (on mission)	16,361 (2016) 11,605 full-time 4,757 consultants/temporary Decentralized 41% non-US based	7,775 (2016) 50% professional 28.6% at HQ Decentralized	677 (2012) 634 (2016) Centrally-located (on mission)	1,239 (2012) 1,402 (2016) 42% professionals Centrally located

Budget	Biennium expenditure 2014–15 US$2.56 billion Member contribution (39%) Voluntary contribution (61%) Arrear (1/3 of assessed)	Administrative expense US$532 million US$175 million loan commitment	2014–15: US$3977 million Assessment US$929 million (23%) Voluntary contribution (77%)	Assessment based on trade volumes 2015 CHF 197 million (2015)	Biennium 2016–17 707 million Swiss francs (9% is contribution)
Areas	Agriculture, forestry, and fishery	Monetary cooperation	Development	Global health issues	Trade	Intellectual property rights (copyrights, patents, trademarks, industrial designs, geographical indications)
Former heads	J. B. Orr, 1945–8 (UK) N.E. Dodd, 1948–54 (USA) P. V. Cardon, 1954–6 (USA) B. R. Sen, 1956–67 (India) A. H. Boerma, 1968–75 (Netherlands) E. Saouma, 1976–93 (Lebanon) J. Diouf, 1994–2011 (Senegal)	C. Gutt, 1946–51 (Belgium) I. Rooth, 1951–6 (Sweden) P. Jacobsson, 1955–63 (Sweden) P. P. Schweitzer, 1963–73 (France) H. Witteveen, 1973–8 J. de Larosière, 1976–86 (France) M. Camdessus, 1987–2000 (France)	E. Mayer, 1946 J. McCloy, 1947–9 E. R. Black, 1949–62 G. D. Woods, 1963–8 R. McNamara, 1968–81 A. W. Clausen, 1981–6 B. Conable, 1986–91 L. Preston, 1991–5 J. Wolfensohn, 1995–2005 P. Wolfowitz, 2005–7 R. Zoellick, 2007–12 J. Kim, 2012–16 J. Kim, 2016–	B. Chisholm, 1948–53 (Canada) M. G. Candau, 1953–73 (Brazil) H. Mahler, 1973–88 (Denmark) H. Nakajima, 1988–98 (Japan) G. H. Brundtland, 1998–2003 (Norway) Lee Jong-wook, 2003–6 (S. Korea) A Nordström, 2006–7 (Norway) M. Chan, 2007–17 (HK, China)	E. W. White, 1948–69 (UK) O. Long, 1968–80 (Switzerland) A. Dunkel, 1980–93 (Switzerland) P. Sutherland, 1993–5 (Ireland) R. Ruggiero, 1995–9 (Italy) M. Moore, 1999–2002 (NZ) Supachai, 2002–5 (Thai)	G. B. Bodenhausen, 1970–3 (Netherlands) A. Bogsch, 1973–97 (USA) K. Idris, 1997–2008 (Sudan) F. Gurry 2008–14 (Australia) F. Gurry 2014– (Australia)

(*continued*)

Table 1.1. Continued

	FAO	IMF	World Bank	WHO	WTO	WIPO
	J. Graziano da Silva, 2012–15 (Brazil) J. Graziano da Silva 2015– (Brazil)	H. Kohler, 2000–4 (Germany) R. Rato, 2004–7 (Spain) D. Strauss-Kahn, 2007–12 (France) C. Lagarde, 2011–16 (France) C. Lagarde, 2016– (France)			P. Lamy 2005–13 (France) R. Azevêdo 2013–17 (Brazil) R. Azevêdo 2017– (Brazil)	
What do they do?	• Eliminate hunger, food insecurity, and malnutrition • Promote sustained agriculture, forestry, fisheries • Reduce rural poverty	• Ensure stability of international monetary system • Surveillance • Lending • Capacity development	• Reduce poverty • Support development	• Promote health normative standards • Provide technical advice and assistance on health matters • Advocate change in health policy, standards • Shape research, policies	• Trade negotiation • Monitoring • Dispute settlement • Build trade capacity • Outreach	• Provide IP services—filing patent, trademarks, etc. • Technical assistance • Encourage creativity • Promote protection of IP • Modernize IP implementation

Source: from the official website of each IO: http://www.fao.org; http://www.imf.org; http://www.worldbank.org; http://www.who.int; https://www.wto.org; http://www.wipo.int (accessed 15 March 2015).

In national governments, decision-making is shaped and often decided by the interactions among politicians and between politicians and civil servants. In IOs, political masters (member states and specifically their representatives in IOs), the heads of IOs (represented by directors general (DGs) and their senior management), and bureaucracy of international civil servants interact, negotiate, and bargain to produce policy results. It is axiomatic in public policy literature that (i) who decides often determines what is decided, and (ii) control over how a decision is made often determines what decision is made. By drawing insights from those studies on domestic decision-making, we can at least develop an understanding of the different interests, value systems, skills, and resources of these players, their interpretations of missions and choice of actions, and the environment and the incentive systems within which all players work. Thus, we are inclined to the view of Duncan Snidal that 'a good theory of institutions should explain both the similarities and differences between domestic and international politics'.[9]

To do so, we have followed the footsteps of Hugh Heclo, Aaron Wildavsky, and many others[10] and conducted extensive and intensive interviews of state representatives, several DGs, many international civil servants, and 'other' players in all six IOs. IOs are not only the world of powerful states but also a world of many 'puzzled' people[11] whose daily life is to assess options and make choices. To understand how they behave, we 'see the world through their eyes', and analyse the interaction along regular circuits among three groups of players from within IOs. We have observed and talked to them in order to provide rich *empirical* explanations of the dynamic internal politics of decision-making of an IO and shed light on the organizational designs of IOs that shape how players define their interests and make decisions. Our concern is how IOs work, who has what influence, what factors shape their decisions as well as those of the organizations, rather than assuming states dictate the actions of IOs. It is an approach that relies on understanding processes, formal and informal rules, expectations and norms. When we talked to those who worked in and around the IOs, their concern was that we provided an accurate account of the ways they actually work in IOs. A Scandinavian ambassador implored that we 'provide an account of what we do, not what we should do'. That indeed is our intent. This is an inductive study largely built on documents and interviews of practitioners. While we have analysed six IOs, our concern is always with their functioning as international organizations, as institutions. There are sufficient analyses that want

---

[9] Duncan Snidal, 'Political Economy and International Institutions', *International Review of Law and Economics*, 16/1 (1996), 121–37.

[10] Hugh Heclo and Aaron Wildavsky, *The Private Government of Public Money: Community and Policy inside British Politics* (London: Macmillan, 1974).

[11] Hugh Heclo, *Modern Social Politics in Britain and Sweden* (New Haven: Yale University Press, 1974), 305.

them to do something different. Unrealistic accounts or aspirations merely mislead. We argue that first we need to know what they do, in all its complexities, before we can provide normative prescriptions of what they ought to do.

THE STUDY OF INTERNATIONAL ORGANIZATIONS

Studies of formal IOs lost their attraction in the field of international relations during the cold-war period not only because of the bipolar superpower stand-off but also because the field was dominated by the realist view that states, and states alone, determined the game of international politics. IOs, they argue, are the creations of the dominant powers and instruments of power politics among sovereign states. They 'reflect state calculation of self-interest based primarily on concerns about relative power; as a result, institutional outcomes invariably reflect the balance of power'.[12] It was seen as naive to treat IOs as serious international players, because states would never cede sovereignty to supranational organizations with the strong enforcement capacities necessary to overcome international anarchy.[13] This view of state primacy in international politics is deeply rooted in studies of IOs. It has remained popular after IOs returned as a topic of study in international relations since the 1990s. That is, IOs do not have an independent role to play in international politics. IOs are no more than instruments of states or 'glorified permanent conferences' for states.[14] These studies do not treat IOs as a dependent variable that needs to be explained; nor do they take seriously internal operations of IOs. They see no need, for instance, to distinguish between those who serve IOs under oath as international staff to pursue and promote the collective interests and those who represent states in IOs in various capacities, or to examine the relationship between IO leaders and international civil servants. This view may be held by only a small group of scholars now, but it is strongly endorsed by many IO member states, at least rhetorically.

As states have been pursuing increasing cross-border cooperation to solve collective action problems, IOs have expanded in number, size, coverage, and capacities. Unable to explain the cooperation solely by focusing on states, their relative degrees of power, and short-term calculations of self-interest, scholars have expanded their studies on IOs in a much more sophisticated way. IOs are

---

[12] John Mearsheimer, 'The False Promise of International Relations', *International Security*, 19/3 (1994–5), 82.

[13] Charles L. Glaser, 'Realists as Optimists: Cooperation as Self Help', *International Security*, 19/3 (1994–5), 50–90.

[14] Barry Buzan and Richard Little, *International Systems in World History* (Oxford: Oxford University Press, 2000), 266–7.

no longer formal organizations, but also a set of formal and informal rules that shape the behaviour of all involved.[15] Rules, incentives, and procedures have become the centre of attention. IOs are valuable to facilitate information exchange, standardize communication, and reduce costs for states to get involved in cooperation.[16] These studies drew attention to those factors that make 'self-enforced' cooperation possible and attribute 'independent' roles to formal IOs. Their 'independence' may come from the initial delegation of power and authority by states that created them; it also evolves as IOs exercise the authority they were granted. A distinction is made between the formal agency, which is the amount of authority states have explicitly delegated to IOs, and informal agency, which is the autonomy these IOs have in practice.[17] Another study differentiates between the formal and the actual, arguing that the roles IOs fulfil give these organizations 'an influence well beyond their material power which is trivial on conventional measures'.[18] This distinction leads to a series of analyses of why states deliberately delegate authority to IOs in the first place;[19] and what specific authority is delegated and under what conditions. The focus still concentrates on the actions of states because, it is argued, 'IOs gain autonomy as a result of intentional state decisions, not through a careless process driven by staff'.[20] Their questions are what authority states delegate to IOs and why,[21] and how to make IOs accountable to their principals.[22]

While delegation of authority to IOs by member states is important, other scholars started asking how IOs exercise their delegated authority, and how principals (states) can control the behaviour of IOs as agents. The basic assumption is that, once authority has been delegated, principal and agent

---

[15] Stephen D. Krasner, 'Structural Changes and Regime Consequences: Regimes as Intervening Variables', in S. Krasner (ed.), *International Regimes* (Ithaca, NY: Cornell University Press, 1983).

[16] Kenneth Oye (ed.), *Cooperation under Anarchy* (Princeton: Princeton University Press, 1986); Joseph M. Grieco, *Cooperation among Nations* (Ithaca, NY: Cornell University Press, 1990); David Baldwin (ed.), *Neorealism and Neoliberalism* (New York: Columbia University Press, 1993); Oran R. Young, *International Governance* (Ithaca, NY: Cornell University Press, 1994).

[17] Darren G. Hawkins et al. (ed.), *Delegation and Agency in International Organizations* (New York: Cambridge University Press, 2006).

[18] Abbot and Snidal, 'Why States Act', 9.

[19] Helen Milner, 'The Assumption of Anarchy in International Relations Theory', *Review of International Studies*, 17/1 (1991), 67–85.

[20] Lisa Martin, 'Distribution, Information and Delegation to International Organizations', in Hawkins et al. (eds), *Delegation and Agency in International Organizations*, 141.

[21] Barbara Koremenos, Charles Lipson, and Duncan Snidal, 'The Rational Design of International Institutions', *International Organisation*, 55/4 (2001), 761–99; Daniel L. Nielson and Michael J. Tierney, 'Delegation to International Organizations', *International Organization*, 57/2 (2003), 241–76; Barbara Koremenos and Duncan Snidal, 'Moving Forward, One Step at a Time', *International Organization*, 57/2 (2003), 431–44.

[22] Ruth W. Grant and Robert O. Keohane, 'Accountability and Abuse of Power in World Politics', *American Political Science Review*, 99/1 (2005), 29–43.

will develop different interests, and agents, IOs, will 'carry out their functions independent of the influence of the member states'.[23] To understand how IOs as agents develop their 'independent' interests, scholars have contended that IOs need to be examined inside out. Barnett and Finnemore pioneered the study of IOs as bureaucracies by applying sociological and organizational insights to examining the pathology of IOs. They are particularly concerned to provide 'a more complete understanding of what bureaucracy is [and] explanations of how certain kinds of bureaucratic behaviour are possible'.[24] The importance of their studies is that IOs are institutions that should and can be analysed as complex bureaucracies. As bureaucracies, IOs have a life of their own, independent from interests of any single state, and they may not function the way they were initially designed.

Indeed, an increasing number of studies examine the decision-making process within IOs and conclude that permanent secretariats not only enjoy broad authority and autonomy in decision-making, but also have the expertise, access to information, and control of decision-making procedures, which together allow them to define problems in ways that meet their institutional objectives.[25] Member states have a hard time reining in and reforming IOs' bureaucracies despite control mechanisms put in place, such as 'detailed rules, screening and selection, monitoring and reporting requirements, institutional checks and sanctions',[26] because bureaucratic culture and standard operation procedures are resilient to external monitoring and demand.[27]

Once it has been acknowledged that IOs are not 'a black box that somehow transforms international ideals and national contributions into a better world',[28] we need to examine the complex interactions among players inside and outside IOs to understand actions or inactions of IOs: who has what capacity in shaping IO decisions and actions; why some IOs function

---

[23] Mark Pollack, 'Delegation, Agency, and Agenda Setting in the European Community', *International Organization*, 51/1 (1997), 101.

[24] Michael Barnett and Martha Finnemore, 'The Politics, Power and Pathologies of International Organizations', *International Organizations*, 54/4 (1999), 701. See also Michael Barnett and Martha Finnemore, *Rules for the World* (Ithaca, NY: Cornell University Press, 2004).

[25] Barnett and Finnemore, *Rules for the World*; Mark S. Copelovitch, 'Master or Servant? Common Agency and the Political Economy of Lending', *International Studies Quarterly*, 54/1 (2010), 49–77; Michael Barnett and Liv Coleman, 'Designing Police', *International Studies Quarterly*, 49/4 (2005), 593–619; Bob Reinalda and Bertjan Verbeek (eds), *Decision Making within International Organizations* (London: Routledge, 2004); Stephen Bauer, 'Does Bureaucracy Really Matter'?, *Global Environmental Politics*, 6/1 (2006), 23–49; van de Graaf and Lesage, 'The International Energy Agency'; Chwieroth, *Capital Ideas*.

[26] Hawkins et al. (eds), *Delegation and Agency in International Organizations*.

[27] Catherine Weaver, *Hypocrisy Trap: The World Bank and the Poverty of Reform* (Ithaca, NY: Cornell University Press, 2008).

[28] John W. Peabody, 'An Organizational Analysis of the World Health Organization: Narrowing the Gap between Promise and Performance', *Social Science & Medicine*, 40/6 (1995), 732.

effectively while others are dysfunctional; why some are more independent in acting on behalf of collective interests than others. It is the interaction among players that shapes the direction of IOs.

THE INFLUENCES ON PLAYERS AND THEIR INTERACTIONS

To explain how the collective decisions are reached within an IO, this study builds on a combination of public policy studies that emphasize the importance of the bureaucratic apparatus in decision-making processes of political organizations[29] and political institutionalism that highlights the impacts of formal and informal rules on individual and organizational behaviour.[30] We take as given that IOs are goal-oriented institutions that seek to maximize their influence.[31] Yet, we do not see them as unitary players and argue that their decisions, actions, or inactions can and should be analysed layer by layer. Four perspectives provide the theoretical background for a study: *rational choice, organizational structure and processes, organizational history and culture,* and *political persuasion.* These four are cumulative, not alternative, if we want to explain policies as options, as well as outcomes, in a dynamic process.

Rational choice is at the core of public policy and institutionalism (political, economic, and social). It argues that all players, as individuals and groups, make rational decisions in order to maximize their interests. Their rationality is shaped by their positions, their perspectives, individual value systems, commitment to the cause, and tangible interests. What rationality adds to individual choices is consistency: 'consistency among goals and objectives relative to a particular action'.[32]

Organizational structure and processes. Each IO has its distinct organizational logic that defines its objectives (mandates) and rules. Formal rules and initial

---

[29] Graham T. Allison and Philip Zelikow, *Essence of Decision* (New York: Longman, 1999).

[30] James G. March and Johan P. Olsen, 'The Institutional Dynamics of International Political Orders', *International Organization*, 5/4 (1998), 943–70; James G. March, 'Understanding how Decisions Happen in Organization', in J. G. March (ed.), *The Pursuit of Organizational Intelligence* (Boston: Basic Blackwell, 1999); Kathleen Thelen, 'Historical Institutionalism in Comparative Politics', *American Review of Political Science*, 2 (1999), 369–404; Paul Pierson and Theda Skocpol, 'Historical Institutionalism in Contemporary Political Science', in Ira Katznelson and Helen V. Milner (eds), *Political Science: The State of the Discipline* (New York: W.W. Norton, 2002), 693–721.

[31] Ernst B. Haas, *Beyond the Nation-State*, 2nd edn (Stanford: Stanford University Press, 1968); Barnett and Coleman, 'Designing Police'.

[32] Allison and Zelikow, *Essence of Decision*, 17.

delegated mandates are always subject to interpretation; they evolve. Institutional factors, such as the scope of issues, organizational design, the configuration of authority, rules of the game, or organizationally embodied routines, 'play a crucial role in allocating resources and structuring the incentives, options, and constraints faced by political participants'.[33]

To examine the formal organizational structures and rules, several issues are important: (*a*) the mission: the mandate that the IO has been given and the formal and informal ways it can be interpreted, (*b*) the salience of the organization to states: are its decisions binding or non-binding, soft or hard, direct or indirect, and to what extent do decisions affect the level of state involvement, (*c*) the formal organizational structure: centralized or decentralized, negotiation forum or decision-making body, location, the sites and forums in which the organization works, and (*d*) the authority delegated at each level. The bounded rationality of players needs to be understood in the context within which they, be they state representatives, heads of IOs, or the secretariat, interact.

Organizational history and culture. Institutions contain not only formal rules, but also sets of informal norms and organizational cultures. These informal factors may be intangible; they have the similar force as organizational forms and rules in shaping the incentives and choices for players.[34] They explain how people interpret their jobs, what motivates them, how they regard their superiors, and the priorities of the organization: all those factors that are of daily significance but almost never written down. All organizations have a history and are constantly remade over time.[35] Their traditions are often contested as the players seek to shape them for their own ends. In the process, sets of institutional expectations develop;[36] they can be powerful constraining factors on individual behaviour. So we can ask what their organizational culture is (hierarchical or consensual); what expectations are (passive or proactive) and how they are created; where the institutional memory resides; who has the experience in the daily operation of IOs; what their relationships are with each other; and how and why they change.

---

[33] Pierson and Skocpol, 'Historical Institutionalism', 706.

[34] Heclo and Wildavsky, *The Private Government*; Ronald L. Jepperson, 'Institutions, Institutional Effects, and Institutionalism', in Walter W. Powell and Paul J. DiMaggio (eds), *The New Institutionalism in Organizational Analysis* (Chicago: University of Chicago Press, 1991), 143–63.

[35] Thelen, 'Historical Institutionalism'; Kathleen Thelen, 'How Institutions Evolve', in James Mahoney and Dietrich Rueschemeyer (eds), *Comparative Historical Analysis in the Social Sciences* (New York: Cambridge University Press, 2003), 208–40.

[36] Douglass C. North, *Institutions, Institutional Change, and Economic Performance* (Cambridge: Cambridge University Press, 1990).

Political persuasion. Policies and decisions of organizations do not necessarily represent the intent of any one actor, and often they are the unintended and unanticipated results of bargaining, pulling, hauling, and convincing other participants. We should not assume that any group wins all the time, or that any conclusion reflects a single perspective. To understand this process of bargaining and political persuasion, we ask (*a*) what leverage each group of players has within an institutional context; (*b*) what access to information they have; (*c*) how committed players are to the mandate of the organization; (*d*) how much they care about specific issues; and (*e*) within what time frame decisions are made. Studies have argued that state representatives in IOs have four distinct roles to play: '(1) political counterweight, (2) performance police, (3) democratic forum, and (4) strategic thinker' and it is the *trade-offs* of these roles that allow IOs to build and expand their independence and autonomy.[37] How state representatives perform these functions then is an empirical question. Some observers show that a few heads of IOs set the direction for the organisation, while others end up as followers rather than leaders.[38] We need to explain the variations by examining the opportunity and capacity each has to shape the decision-making process and their differences across IOs.

The key to understanding the dynamics of IO operation is the interaction between the players in this process of *bargaining and political persuasion*. We do not expect players to be interested in exactly the same types of decisions; rather we expect each player to have a *range of interests*. Neither do all players have the same resources and capacity to pursue their interests. Meanwhile, neither their interests nor their capacity can be equated to their formal positions. That is, an executive director of the United States may or may not have the same impact on decision-making in the board room of the IMF or the World Bank despite the general assumption he or she does. A director on a third level of an IO bureaucracy may bring substantive issues to the agenda and change the direction of an IO. Scholars in domestic politics have argued we need to strip away the official veneer to identify who really does what, not where responsibility may be nominally allocated. It may be the network, may be the expertise, may be the right time, or may be a combination of them all, that brings serious changes to an IO's operation.[39] Graeme Allison illustrated that in his account of US foreign policy; process and position shape outlook.[40] The same can be said about IOs—the players bring different contributions to

---

[37] Leonardo Martinez-Diaz, 'Boards of Directors in International Organizations', *Review of International Organization*, 4/4 (2009), 385.

[38] Robert W. Cox, 'The Executive Head', *International Organization*, 23/2 (1969), 205–30; Robert W. Cox and Harold K. Jacobson (eds), *The Anatomy of Influence* (New Haven: Yale University Press, 1973); Sebastian Mallaby, *The World's Banker* (New York: Penguin Books, 2004).

[39] Heclo and Wildavsky, *The Private Government*.

[40] Allison and Zelikow, *Essence of Decision*.

the table; the crucial element may be expertise or proximity, not authority. Decisions may come through networks of the influential, some of whom may hold no formal position at all. Hierarchy may be more nominal than influential. It is critical to understand the variations of IOs along this line. These perspectives provide the insights within which we analyse our six IOs.

THE PLAYERS

In the following subsections, three groups of players of IOs are examined—state representatives (see Chapter 2), heads of IOs (see Chapter 3), and international civil servants (ICS) (see Chapter 4). All IOs are created to bring about a culture of mutually recognized values and rules, whether about development, global health, trade, or intellectual property rights, and to facilitate multilateral cooperation to short-circuit the dividing and disruptive effects of states' narrow and self-interested outlooks. Heterogeneous state interests and objectives can be more readily balanced through a process of negotiation coordinated by a group of impartial international civil servants led by the head of IOs. To assess the success and effectiveness of the process of multilateral cooperation, we need to understand the players.

State Representatives

States participate in IO decision-making through their representatives; they are part and parcel of the process. They are not 'states' per se; they represent member states in IOs. It is important to make the distinction, because, as state representatives, they are 'delegated' certain authority to act on behalf of the state in IO decision-making. The literature on principal–agent analysis repeatedly emphasizes the gap between the principal and the agent in terms of their perception of interest and the ways to manage the problem. The agent is always the IO. Seldom is the principal–agent relationship between the capitals and the state representatives in the field examined by scholars who focus on IOs. States are often regarded as a single entity that knows its mind and has the desire and capacity to determine what is implemented. Those who do dissect the principal (the state) do not examine the distinct role its representative plays in IOs' operations.[41] If the argument that

---

[41] See Mona M. Lyne, Daniel L. Nielson, and Michael J. Tierney, 'Who Delegates: Alternative Models of Principals in Development Aid', in Hawkins et al. (eds), *Delegation and Agency in International Organizations*, 41–76; Kathryn C. Levelle, *Legislating International Organizations* (New York: Oxford University Press, 2011).

officials of IOs may become 'socialized' through repeated interaction at the supranational level by adopting the norms and culture of supranational organizations is true,[42] we would expect those representing the states in IOs over long periods of time to share a similar pattern of socialization. We need to identify whether state representatives are socialized into the IO clubs and how they are then able actually to 'represent' state interests in the IO decision-making process with a 'Janus face'.[43]

In political reality, state representation varies significantly, not only across IOs, but also among member states. Who are the representatives (politician, diplomat, or technocrat) and how do they see themselves (representative of the state or also part of the club/community)? How do they reach the position (political appointees or career civil servants), with what qualities and conditions (experts or career representatives, the term of their service)? What is the expectation on state representatives from government? How do they interpret the national interests and pursue them in relation to other players? What is the organizational arrangement of state representatives within an IO? What networks are they able to build (long-serving versus frequent rotation), or how close is the relationship with their capitals (continually monitored or free range)? These are all important in shaping the 'rational decisions' of state representatives and their perceptions, expectations, and activities.

Instead of assuming member states always know what they want from IOs and present 'coherent' demands to their counterparts and the secretariats, we need to ask how they participate in IO activities and represent their 'national interests'; to what extent governments do pay attention to IOs; and how willing governments are to spend their political capital to pick a fight in IOs, whether with other states or within IOs. In so doing, we can truly understand the mottos of 'member-driven' IOs and the 'member-driven' processes in IOs.

Chapter 2 is thus organized around two issues: *representation* and *participation*. In all IOs, member states have their representation, either at annual assemblies, through local diplomats, or through individual or group representation at the various kinds of executive boards. Each arrangement provides opportunities and challenges for member states. Representation does not equal participation, which depends, as explained, on how state representatives see themselves, the networks they have built, and their relationship with the capitals.

---

[42] See the special issue on 'International Institutions and Socialization in Europe,' *International Organization*, 59/4 (2005), 801–1079.

[43] Jeffrey Lewis, 'The Janus Face of Brussels: Socialization and Everyday Decision Making in the European Union', *International Organization*, 59/4 (2005), 937–71.

Heads of IOs

Leaders matter. They make a difference to the operation of IOs and sometimes to world politics too. In domestic politics, individual leaders can shape political outcomes because of either their moral standing, their unique skills, their personal capacities, or the institutional support they have.[44] Leaders of IOs need these capacities and more, because of the ambivalence of their position. The position of secretary-general of the United Nations was described as 'the most impossible job on earth', in part because of its combination of political, diplomatic, and administrative responsibilities, and more importantly because its power and authority are delegated by states that do not have coherent and consistent views on what they would like the UN to do and how.

Member states care about who the leaders are, and, when they can, they vigorously contest the positions. We thus need to examine where they come from (geographical origin as well as profession); how they become heads of IOs (selected, elected, or appointed) and the enduring impact of these methods; their career paths, their 'ambition and ambition's limits',[45] and the qualities regarded as necessary for successful tenure, which include: expertise, legitimacy, and trust. More broadly, we need to determine what leverage (formal and informal) they have, and how effectively they are able to fulfil the obligations.

To do so, Chapter 3 focuses its discussion of the three roles all heads of IOs must play—managerial, diplomatic, and political. Leaders of IOs are international figures who represent the agency in public and whose pronouncements are given attention and weight because they are not responsible to a single person or state. They speak on behalf of the IO; it is also their responsibility to promote and advance the collective interests of the organization to the international community and its member states. This is the *diplomatic* role all heads of IOs are expected to undertake. Heads of IOs are also *politicians* in the sense that they must be able to manage the relationships of member states (whether large and powerful, or small), among member states themselves (working as individual states or in groups), and with the organization (as supporters or opponents of multilateral causes). Of course, if member states do not wish to act, the head of an IO has little independent authority. The ability to 'lead from behind', to nudge without being seen as pushing, to master while being a servant of member states, nonetheless may prove to be 'the most critical single determinant of the growth in scope and

---

[44] See, e.g., Michael Foley, *Political Leadership: Themes, Contexts and Critiques* (New York: Oxford University Press, 2013); R. A. W. Rhodes and Paul 't Hart (eds), *The Oxford Handbook of Political Leadership* (New York: Oxford University Press, 2013).
[45] Mallaby, *The World's Banker*, 10.

authority of international organization'.⁴⁶ The nature of IO leadership must be contingent, depending on agency and opportunity. Bureaucracies need to be led; they are not machines or instruments that work on cue. These international bureaucracies may be large or small, centralized or decentralized, well funded or resource poor. They all consist of people from diverse intellectual, cultural, and geographical backgrounds. To be able to *manage* such an international bureaucracy, according to some state representatives, is 'the most difficult challenge for DGs'. How heads of IOs balance these three roles often determines their capacity to shape the outcomes of their organization.

International Civil Servants

The international civil servants (ICS) of the permanent secretariat of IOs drew increasing attention from scholars once it had been accepted that IOs have an independent role to play. Building on our earlier studies of international civil servants,⁴⁷ we study the top echelon of international civil servants by asking who they are, how they got the position (national quota or professional skills; selected, appointed, or recruited on merit); what their qualities are (political or technical expertise); on what basis they serve the institution (permanent, contract, long or short); and their career trajectories. International civil servants share some distinct features with their domestic counterparts. As experts, career civil servants, boosted by professional standing and status as members of an elite cadre, with years of experience in the past and a critical position as adviser or manager to fulfil, can be effective and influential in IOs. These characteristics describe potential, not power. The impact of civil servants is in part institutional, in part personal. Their roles and influence are all well documented in studies of national civil services, to the extent that they would now be regarded as uncontested.

Chapter 4 thus examines the role and behaviour of IO secretariats by focusing on (*a*) formally delegated authority; (*b*) long-term practices and expectations; and (*c*) the relationship between staff and member states. This chapter provides a brief description of the staff (their recruitment, professions, and their background), their technical expertise, and access to information. It then examines how these international civil servants seize or create opportunities to influence outcomes and the means by which they interact with the representatives of member states.

---

⁴⁶ Cox, 'The Executive Head', 205.
⁴⁷ Xu and Weller, *The Governance of World Trade*; Xu and Weller, *Inside the World Bank*; Patrick Weller and Xu Yi-chong (eds), *The Politics of International Organizations: View from Insiders* (New York: Routledge, 2015).

INTERNATIONAL ORGANIZATIONS IN ACTION

Resources underpin capacity. Structures shape procedures. Information is a source of power. To demonstrate these specific points, in Chapters 5–7 we illustrate our argument by analysing the way that IOs work in practice by concentrating on three areas that provide common challenges: the setting of agendas, the allocation of resources, and the location of staff.

In Chapter 5, we examine how players interact in agenda setting in all six IOs: who shapes and determines the long-term strategies, the intermediate priorities and normal work programmes of IOs? What is the process of initiating, proposing, and deciding what IOs do? How do they differ from one IO to another? We know that (*a*) states jealously guard their prerogatives; (*b*) states often do not agree what they would like IOs to do or achieve; (*c*) their diverse interests and demands tend to lead to a rapid expansion of agendas for IOs; (*d*) those state representatives involved in agenda setting come with different backgrounds, expertise and capacities; and (*e*) some leaders of IOs have visions while others do not. All these elements matter in the process of agenda setting.

Chapter 6 examines the formal and informal sources of finance of the six IOs, the distribution of the resources, the political, diplomatic, and operational impacts of different financial systems on the operation of IOs, and, more importantly, the question of contribution and control. Who pays the piper? How are the IOs funded and by whom? Are the sources constant? What impact might the arrangements have on the options that are available for the different players? If the argument is that the financial dependence brings obedience and restricts discretion, is there an identifiable link between levels of self-funding and organizational influence? It will show that, as the traditional sources of financing are changing (for example, a declining share of assessed contributions from member states, the waning willingness of traditional members to increase their share, and increased preparedness of non-traditional contributors and non-state actors to participate), some IOs have managed to increase their range of financial partners and levels of funding to support their ever-expanding agendas, while others struggle with ever-declining financial resources. These differences will be examined by analysing the role played by the heads of IOs, the relationship between state representatives and the staff, and the dynamic process of budget and finance committees of all six IOs.

Chapter 7 examines the question of location—where the staff work, both geographically and functionally. Some IOs are structured around functional responsibilities; others organized by geography; some are matrix managed. Each structure shapes information, programmes, and staff in ways that will affect their contribution. Relations with local countries will be different if the IO's officers are on the spot. The chapter will examine how they balance demands for geographical representation and subject specialization, how they reconcile the contradictory expectation to be standard setter or local adviser, whether and how decentralization leads to greater discretion for the staff and more control of member states over the local decisions of IOs, and how some heads of IOs strive to ensure that they lead a single institution when some decentralized staff become as much the agents of the countries as of the IOs for whom they work.

We recognize that IOs constantly deal with players other than member states, large foundations, or for- or non-profit organizations. These non-state players have expanded rapidly in size and number. They have also become quite aggressive and assertive in pushing their interests, agendas, and causes to multilateral institutions. Some of them are formally integrated into the working of IOs while many come in and out on an ad hoc basis. Member states may not always be comfortable in dealing with all these non-state players and, occasionally, they prefer the secretariat to manage the relationship. Rather than discuss the dealings with non-state players in IOs in a separate chapter, we have chosen to integrate them in the analysis in appropriate places. The significant point is that, as IOs have cooperated and intersected with non-state organizations, the precise boundaries of their activities have become blurred.

The operation of IOs is much more complex than any single set of relationships, such as principal–agent linkages, can explain. It can, however, be explained by adopting analyses that highlight the importance of players, their capacities, and their interactions. The old adage 'where you stand depends on where you sit' is still in part a valid explanation of how state representatives, the heads of IOs, and the staff generate their ideas, assess their options, select their decisions, and thus influence the outcomes. Given that all international agreements that created IOs were ambitious and thereby inherently ambiguous, how political control is exercised by member states through their representatives and how influences are exerted by the head of IOs and the staff are questions that cannot be answered from first principles but need to be explored from one IO to another to identify the differences and the reasons for those differences. This study will provide a balanced analysis of this interaction that shapes the operation and development of the six IOs.

In this study, we pay attention to IOs as bureaucracies. We examine them from the perspective of players—those working in the IOs' world—in order to reach a conclusion on how IOs operate. These intricate dynamics are the IO politics in the real world. For this, we follow the plea of one senior IO official:

> So I always say—when you especially as academics examine the governance issue, do go behind the structures, the systems, the processes, and the procedures. They are meaningful only when you examine how *people* function in these organizations and what relationships they have built over the years that shape the operation of these IOs.

2

Representatives of Member States

States participate in multilateral institutions to take 'advantage of the centralization and independence of IOs' to achieve goals that they cannot accomplish on a decentralized basis.[1] Participating states delegate a wide range of authority and/or policies to *enforcing agents*—international organizations (IOs)—so that they can 'reap gains from specialization, as well as capture policy externalities, facilitate collective decision-making, resolve disputes, enhance credibility, and lock-in policy biases'.[2] In so doing, states confront inevitable collective-action problems that lead to 'agency slack' out of laziness and shirked responsibilities, because agents' interests differ from those of principals. To overcome collective-action problems before giving marching orders to IOs, states must put in place a series of 'control mechanisms' to ensure multilateral cooperation, whether through their organizational structure, their voting patterns, or their decision-making rules. The formal rules 'represent the broad interests of the membership, and reflect the preferences of weak states out of proportion in their resources', while informal rules 'provide exceptional access to decision-making for powerful states when their core interests are affected'.[3] Thus, much of the attention is paid to what 'authority' or 'policy' states delegate to IOs; why they do so in the first place; what alternative control mechanisms can be chosen, and how a monitoring system can be created to ensure IOs behave the way they as principals want them to.

Delegating authorities to IOs and setting up mechanisms to control IOs, however, cannot be equated to state representation or participation in the same way as electing politicians to run the country is. They are only one way to shape the outcomes. To understand how states are represented in IOs and how they participate in IO activities, we need to examine those principals 'closest to the agent in question', not only because these proximate principals have

---

[1] Kenneth W. Abbott and Duncan Snidal, 'Why States Act through Formal International Organizations', *Journal of Conflict Resolution*, 42/1 (1998), 29.
[2] Darren G. Hawkins et al. (eds), *Delegation and Agency in International Organizations* (New York: Cambridge University Press, 2006), 19, 23.
[3] Randall W. Stone, *Controlling Institutions: International Organizations and the Global Economy* (New York: Cambridge University Press, 2011), 31.

the responsibility and possess the ability to aggregate the demands of their constituents (government agencies, interest groups, and individuals at home) but also because they are in the position to weigh one against the other before making demands on and in IOs.[4] States are collective principals of IOs. However, while we accept the argument that state leaders cannot stray too far from the preferences of the 'selectorate' without risking their position of power,[5] we cannot assume state leaders always know what they want from IOs, pay sufficient attention to their agenda and activities, or are willing to use their political capital in managing counterparts in IOs. Thus, it is important to examine those who represent their states across IOs.

Recent studies have raised the issues of both accountability and legitimacy of decision-making at the global level. Grant and Keohane argue that new international and global players (non-governmental organizations (NGOs), multinational corporations, or transnational networks) operating in transnational decision-making arenas tend to escape the reach of territorially democratic representation. In comparison, however, multilateral organizations are more accountable because, with member states as the accountability holders, they are 'constantly subjected to delegated as well as participatory accountability'.[6] The argument assumes that states not only delegate authority to IOs, but participate in IO activities to ensure they are accountable to their political masters—participating states. How do states participate in IO activities? More specifically, how do those who are delegated to represent their states participate in IO activities?

A large body of literature in domestic politics has analysed two types of representation: trustee versus delegate.[7] It is equally important to ask whether those who are 'delegated' with the authority to represent their country in IOs see their role as representatives and how they actually do represent it. Do they act as trustees, actively participating in IO activities, or as delegates whose main role is to oversee the operation of IOs? How would these two types of representation affect their relationship with the heads of IOs and the secretariats? How do state representatives make the management of IOs

---

[4] Daniel L. Nielson and Michael J. Tierney, 'Delegation to International Organizations: Agency Theory and World Bank Environmental Reform', *International Organization*, 57/2 (2003), 241–76.

[5] David Mayhew, *Congress: The Electoral Connection* (New Haven: Yale University Press, 1974); Philip G. Roeder, *Red Sunset: The Failure of Soviet Politics* (Princeton: Princeton University Press, 1993).

[6] Ruth W. Grant and Robert O. Keohane, 'Accountability and Abuses of Power in World Politics', *American Political Science Review*, 99/1 (2005), 29–43.

[7] There is a large body of literature on the issue of representation. See, e.g., Hanna Fenichel Pitkin, *The Concept of Representation* (Berkeley and Los Angeles: University of California Press, 1967); Robert A. Dahl, *Democracy and its Critics* (New Haven: Yale University Press, 1989); David Runciman, 'The Paradox of Political Representation', *Journal of Political Philosophy*, 15/1 (2007), 93–114.

accountable? As an increasing number of issues are discussed within IOs, how do they actually advocate and promote the collective interest of their country in the bargaining process? To understand these big questions, we must first examine those who represent their countries in IOs.

The first question is *who* represents states. States' decisions on their representation across IOs are shaped not only by domestic politics—the so-called partisan politics, personal political networking, or bureaucratic politics—but more importantly by the missions of IOs and the priority the state gives them. Singapore, for instance, has always sent its most talented top civil servants with both expertise and diplomatic skill to the World Trade Organization (WTO) and World Health Organization (WHO), while other countries are satisfied with career trade or health officials. Canada from time to time sends retired or retiring ministers to represent it in all three Bretton Woods institutions; by contrast, the UK uses the International Monetary Fund (IMF) and the World Bank as training grounds for its promising young officials. Politicians (whether current or former ministers) and career civil servants, and those who are at the end and those who are at the beginning of their careers, not only have had different experiences, but also have different perspectives and networks in their capitals and in the international community as a whole.

The second question is what qualities these representatives of member states may possess. They include both individual and institutional capacities. On the individual level, some are willing to be active, while others are less dedicated in participating in IO activities. Some know how to mobilize domestic and international resources to pursue the national interests in IOs, while others are ill prepared for the job. Institutionally, some have well-coordinated domestic institutional support; some frequently receive conflicting demands from the capital; others are left to their own devices. High levels of participation in governing institutions are not only desirable but also serve as a direct accountability mechanism. Thus, the questions whether IOs are accountable to their member states, and whether a few powerful states or even non-government organizations dominate IOs must be examined by paying attention to participation, especially effective participation, of state representatives in IO activities.[8]

The third question is how state representatives act and interact with their governments, their counterparts, the heads of IOs, and international civil servants in 'pursuing and defending' national interests in the multilateral environment. Nothing can be taken for granted. There is a substantial gap between the view that inevitably IOs are 'dominated by a small group of

---

[8] See, e.g., Loren A. King, 'Deliberation, Legitimacy, and Multilateral Democracy', *Governance*, 16/1 (2003), 23–50; Kate O'Neill, Jörg Balsiger, and Stacy D. VanDeveer, 'Actors, Norms, and Impact', *Annual Review of Political Science*, 7 (2004), 149–75; Robert Keohane, 'Accountability in World Politics', *Scandinavian Political Studies*, 29/2 (2006), 75–87.

countries and there is a lack of even-handedness'[9] and a judgement that 'states deserve the IOs they own'.

These issues are examined here both in the context of formal or legal arrangements that define the 'institutional authority' of state representatives in IOs and their delegated authority from their government, and also in the context of cascading relationships—that is, state representatives are both principals and agents. In discussing representation in domestic politics, Hannah Pitkin made it clear that representation is a social relationship. Representation at IOs involves institutional and evolving relationships[10] among state representatives, and between them (here as principals) and international civil servants (agents); it will vary significantly regardless of formal and legal arrangements.

FORMAL AND LEGAL REPRESENTATION

The formal rules that govern IOs establish 'a stable (but not necessarily efficient) structure to human interactions'.[11] They are embedded in the Articles of Agreement or Treaties and are the products of negotiations among states, as 'rational designs' of power politics.[12] The rules tend to be broadly defined and are often loaded with ambiguities. Ambiguities can be political and technical. Political ambiguities are the result of states' willingness to create common rules, yet their reluctance to subject their 'sovereignty' to common rules. Technical ambiguities are in part 'because of insufficient information' at the time of negotiation.[13] Ambiguities meanwhile can be constructive as 'the process of defining and managing ambiguities is, by its nature, political'.[14] As formal rules are interpreted and reinterpreted by the players involved, changes in IOs do occur, but they tend to be slow and at the margin. The formal structures and rules are often set in stone, hard to change without a consensus that is difficult to manufacture. Rather than attempting the impossible, the actors learn to live within those rules and the structures, adopting and adapting informal processes and understandings to 'get around' the road

---

[9] Mike Callaghan, 'IMF Governance and Decision-Making Processes', in Patrick Weller and Xu Yi-chong (eds), *The Politics of International Organizations: Views from Insiders* (New York: Routledge, 2015), 121.

[10] Pitkin, *The Concept of Representation*.

[11] Douglass C. North, *Institutions, Institutional Change and Economic Performance* (New York: Cambridge University Press, 1990), 6.

[12] Barbara Koremenos, Charles Lipson, and Duncan Snidal (eds), *The Rational Design of International Institutions* (New York: Cambridge University Press, 2001).

[13] Jacqueline Best, *The Limits of Transparency* (Ithaca, NY: Cornell University Press, 2005), 3.

[14] Best, *The Limits of Transparency*, 6.

blocks so the constitutions written in the 1940s can still work seventy-five years later. Accepting that the rational design of IOs is not accidental and redesigning them is difficult, we need to understand the diverse institutional arrangements of the six IOs under review; appreciate how they structure the life of member states; and explain what incentive structures these arrangements provide for state participation in IO activities.

The six IOs in this study have different institutional arrangements for state participation. In principle, all members are represented by each IO's highest governing body: the Food and Agriculture Organization (FAO) Conference meets once every two years, the World Intellectual Property Organization (WIPO) General Assembly, the World Health Assembly meet once or twice a year, Boards of Governors at the IMF and the World Bank meet twice a year, and the ministerial conferences of the WTO, which are known as 'the topmost decision-making body', are held usually every two years. The frequency of the meetings of the highest governing body in IOs shows the importance members give to these organizations; so does the seniority of the participants in these governing bodies. Finance ministers or treasurers, along with heads of central banks, attend Board of Governors meetings at the IMF and the World Bank. Trade and health ministers, assisted by ambassadors to the WTO and health attachés, attend the WTO ministerial meetings and the World Health Assembly. Less than half the member states will be represented by ministers in the governing body's conferences at the FAO and WIPO; most countries are represented by a mixed delegation of local diplomats and specialists from the capital. Because the governing bodies of IOs meet only infrequently, these meetings tend to serve as formal occasions where ministers endorse decisions already determined and iron out the remaining differences over a few difficult issues. The highest governing bodies of IOs delegate most responsibilities to much smaller councils or boards of directors. Daily representation of members varies significantly from IO to IO and from country to country. This is what we are interested in.

The daily representation of member states at these IOs occurs in two forms. One is in a governing body that has been delegated authority from the Board of Governors or Assembly of these IOs—the Executive Board (EB) of directors or the council where issues are raised and debated, making recommendations for approval by the Assembly. The other level is the continuing contact through country diplomats in their missions to UN agencies in Geneva or Rome or through group representation in executive director (ED) offices at the IMF and the World Bank. The size of the board of directors and council varies across IOs; so do their operations. All member states of the WTO are represented on the General Council by 'non-residential', yet mostly full-time, ambassadors to the WTO or ambassadors to the UN in Geneva. The General Council meets six or seven times a year. The Coordination Committee (CoCo) of WIPO consists of eighty-three members, the FAO Council of forty-nine. The EB at the WHO had thirty-four members, who were initially 'individuals technically qualified in the field of health, each one designated by a member state' elected based on a regional rotation. They are recognized as state representatives. The WHO EB meets twice a year for a week each time.

The Board of Directors of the IMF has twenty-four members while its counterpart at the World Bank has twenty-five. The members of both EBs in Washington are residential, full-time, and paid by the two institutions, rather than directly by their own governments. They meet several times a week, and indeed their workload has been increasing.

Scholars seldom pay attention to these governing bodies, because it is assumed all decisions are made back in the capital and these governing bodies serve as no more than a forum where states bargain and trade under strict instructions from capitals. One or two articles have been written on the boards of directors of the IMF or the World Bank.[15] The boards or councils may serve as a forum where member states raise their concerns and oversee the management of IOs. We want to emphasize that state representatives in these governing bodies, however they represent their countries, are not states themselves. We need to explain how states are represented, how state representatives interact with their peers, and what relationships they have with the heads of IOs and the secretariat, not least because of the cascading delegated responsibilities and their inevitable gaps, between principals (governments in capitals) and agents (state representatives); and between state representatives (as principals) and IOs' leaders and staff (agents). The following section explains the formal arrangement of representation, followed by a discussion of the modes of representation.

Representatives of Member States in IOs

It is widely argued that 'states delegate certain tasks and responsibilities to IOs' and 'states control IOs once authority has been delegated'.[16] Most studies do not distinguish between states and the representatives they send to IOs. It is seldom asked *who* represents states in IOs and *how* they represent states. Yet, practitioners often say state representatives make a huge difference in the relationships and operations of IOs. Some can have a disproportionate impact on the decisions of IOs, while others may choose not to 'influence' the behaviour of IOs for a variety of reasons.

---

[15] Ervin P. Hexner, 'The Executive Board of the International Monetary Fund: A Decision-Making Instrument', *International Organization*, 18/1 (1964), 74–96; Leonardo Martinez-Diaz, 'Boards of Directors in International Organizations', *Review of International Organization*, 4/4 (2009), 383–406; Bessma Momani, 'Canada's IMF Executive Director', *Canadian Public Administration*, 53/2 (2010), 163–82.

[16] Hawkins et al. (eds), *Delegation and Agency in International Organizations*, 4.

In most UN agencies, representatives are diplomats, trained to represent, defend, and promote the national interest, however it is defined.[17] Diplomats are not the only people to represent member states in the six IOs of this study, as they are by and large technical institutions. In Washington, state representation at the IMF and the World Bank is based on 'subscription'. Each of the five largest 'subscribers' (the USA, Japan, Germany, France, and the UK) appoints its own ED and alternate to the EB at both the IMF and the World Bank; three countries (China, Russia, and Saudi Arabia) appoint their EDs too. The other 180 member states in the IMF and the World Bank are represented through 16/17 groupings; members choose to which grouping they wish to belong and then 'elect' or 'select' their EDs. In some groups, the country holding the largest share of subscription always holds the position of the group ED, while the alternate rotates. Canada, for instance, is always the group ED in both institutions, representing ten micro-states from the Caribbean and Ireland, which tends to serve as the alternate. In the group to which Australia belongs, however, Australia has rotated with South Korea or New Zealand as the group ED and the alternate. Voting power therefore does decide who is represented at the EB of these two institutions. How they represent, however, is a different issue.

For those countries that appoint their own EDs and alternates, the practice is never quite the same. In 2015–16, France remained the only country that still had the same person representing the country in the EB at both the IMF and the World Bank. Historically, Germany and the UK had the same practice, although both have split representation at the IMF and the World Bank, to the regret of some former EDs, who saw the value in the different perspectives and insights the joint appointment offered. It is often argued that the governments who appoint EDs and their alternates would expect their total loyalty to the country. To ensure such loyalty, EDs and their alternates from France, the UK, and the USA are paid by their governments, with the funds transferred from the IMF.[18] Even then, different practices exist: the EDs from China, France, and the UK and their alternates are 'seconded' to the IMF, as they will return to their departments. In the USA, however, because its EDs and the alternates are appointed by the President and confirmed by the Senate, they serve a defined term. They may or may not be government

---

[17] Studies on diplomats in general tend to emphasize three roles played by diplomats: knowledge producer (including information-gathering and analysis), representative of their country, and bureaucrat in a hierarchical institution. See, e.g., Iver B. Newmann, 'To be a Diplomat', *International Studies Perspectives*, 6/1 (2005), 72–93, and Jérémie Cornut, 'To Be a Diplomat Abroad', *Cooperation and Conflict*, 50/3 (2015), 385–401. All three functions are relevant when IOs are concerned. We in this chapter emphasize their role only as representatives of member states to IOs.

[18] Momani, 'Canada's IMF Executive Director', 180.

officials at the time of their appointment and they do not automatically go back to work for the government.

Former central bankers or senior officials from the treasury or finance ministry dominate the EB at the IMF. EDs at the World Bank tend to be officials from either the finance or the development agencies. As in each country there can be only one monetary policy, and the IMF is 'the only organization that has a mandate to examine on a regular basis the economic circumstance of virtually every country in the world',[19] the communication between the IMF and 'the government' is crucial. Thus, EDs of the IMF must have direct access to the Treasury or Finance and key decision-makers in government. A few EDs had served at regional development banks or other international financial institutions before being posted to the IMF or the World Bank. The rank of those serving on the EB at the IMF is often higher than those at the World Bank. 'Compared to the IMF's EDs, who are from central banks and are technical experts, our EDs', explained one vice president (VP) at the World Bank, 'tend to come from many different backgrounds and they can be political appointees too, such as in the US with no background at all in development. Some EDs from developing countries can be quite good and knowledgeable people, while others are less so.'

It is the priority governments give to these institutions that decides the level of officials they select. South Korea, for instance, has been an active participant in most IOs. In 2016, its government sent a deputy minister of foreign affairs to replace its alternate ED at the World Bank, who in turn became chairman of the Korean Investment Corporation (the country's sovereign wealth fund). In contrast, the position of US ED at the IMF was kept vacant, while its alternate came from the private sector and had no experience working in the Treasury.[20] China often sends mid-rank promising officials from the Ministry of Finance to serve as EDs and alternates at the IMF and the World Bank, so they can learn how multilateral financial institutions work and be prepared for senior positions in the ministry or other international organizations.[21] The UK government uses EBs at the IMF and the World Bank as a training ground for its promising officials from the Treasury. Other governments rotate their

---

[19] IMF, 'Report on the External Evaluation of Fund Surveillance', 30 June 1999.

[20] The vacancies at the EB of both the IMF and the World Bank are due to the fact that Obama's nominations were very much delayed and remained unconfirmed by the Senate eighteen months after the initial nomination. An argument could be made that the US government could afford to keep its ED position at the IMF and the World Bank vacant because both institutions are just across the street from the US Treasury.

[21] A number of former and current senior officials at the IMF, World Bank, and other multilateral financial institutions served first as alternate and then as EDs at either of these institutions. They include the MD of the World Bank under Jim Wolfensohn, Shengmen Zhang (1999–2005), one of the MDs under Jim Kim, Shaolin Yang, one of the VPs of the World Bank under Robert Zoellick and Jim Kim, Zhu Xian, the president of the Asian Infrastructure Investment Bank, Jin Liqun, and the DG of UNIDO 2016, Li Yong.

international finance or international development senior officials between domestic and international assignments. In a few cases, the EB at the IMF or the World Bank ended up with good EDs, not because of their choice, but by default. 'We got this really good ED from—, who had been the head of the Labour Party under attack domestically. He got the appointment because the government wanted to get him out of country so that he would be safe.' In general, however, as one former corporate secretary at the Bank explained:

> The quality of the board members at the Bank has declined. At one point, one of the suggestions was to develop a term of reference or a job description for the executive directors here at the Bank. Some key members of the EB opposed that strenuously on the ground that it was interfering with the sovereign right of the government. Yet their minister probably in many cases spent ½ hour a year, or ½ hour every six months focused on the World Bank. So the idea what an ED does was not something deeply embedded in their understanding.

The choice of EDs is made by governments, and the appointments rarely draw public attention at home or globally, even though the quality of EDs affects their representation and participation at these IOs. Despite comments on the relatively low quality of EDs at the World Bank in comparison with the IMF, they are often more knowledgeable than those representatives in other IOs. One senior official who has worked in the FAO and the World Bank compared the quality of state representation in these two institutions:

> Not only is the Executive Board at the World Bank much smaller than the Council at FAO; the board members are from ministries of finance or development; so people know what they are talking about. The quality of the Bank's Executive Board varies but within the reasonable range. Here [at the FAO] the quality of permanent representatives varies tremendously. Not all, but most of them, come from the ministry of foreign affairs. They are diplomats; they don't know much about either agriculture or economics or development. They know a lot about politics. When you go to meetings, it is very difficult to keep them focused on the substance. They then invariably end up in procedural issues and the result of the governing body meetings is much more about politics than those at the World Bank. Politics is important at the Bank, but it plays a role in the background. Whereas at FAO, I sometimes think politics is the only thing people care about for a specialized institution.

Who state representatives are, what their expertise is, and how they think of IOs vary from IO to IO and from one state to another, yet they have direct impact on the representation and participation in IOs.

Given the nature of the WTO, most member states (with the exception of very small island states, particularly from the Pacific) have their representatives dedicated to working on trade matters. Some twenty countries have two separate missions in Geneva: one representing the country to the WTO (and often WIPO) and another to a range of UN agencies in town. Ambassadors to the WTO can come from foreign affairs or foreign trade. Each of the other 100 plus countries has a single team representing the country in all UN agencies in Geneva, but with at least one person focusing on the WTO. The responsibilities of the ambassadors from many countries include representing the country not only to all UN agencies in town, but also to Switzerland and other neighbouring states, and occasionally to the EU in Brussels too. These ambassadors to UN agencies tend to be career diplomats with limited experience of economics, trade, health, or intellectual property (IP) rights. One ambassador to the WTO from a small European country is a typical example:

> I am a career diplomat. Yes, I studied economics and history, but I have always been with our foreign ministry. Ideally, you need to understand the substance to engage in interesting discussions with your colleagues here. Meanwhile, this is not brain surgery. Trade negotiations are not that more complicated than many other things. Of course, I need to do my homework, understand the background.

Another ambassador from a small rich European country added: 'our trade representative flies in from home only when there are negotiation meetings. I am a career diplomat and I attend governing meetings at WTO and WIPO, but we have to rely a lot on the decisions made in Brussels.'

In contrast, designated ambassadors to the WTO tend to be the veterans in multilateral and bilateral trade negotiations. The deputy of the US ambassador to the WTO in 2013, for instance, started working at multilateral negotiations during the Tokyo Round (1973–9) and moved to Geneva in the early days of the Uruguay Round (1986–94). The Chinese ambassador to the WTO in 2011–13 had been working on trade issues since the mid-1980s and was involved in choosing the current location of the Chinese mission to the WTO when China was an observer during the Uruguay Round. The longest-serving ambassador to the WTO in 2014 had been sent to Geneva in 1992. These ambassadors have accumulated institutional memories of trade negotiations and built extensive networks in town.

Some countries rotate their representatives to the WTO. For instance, a large developing country, known for rotating its ambassador to the WTO as part of the national civil service system, parachuted an ambassador to Geneva just before a major ministerial meeting. Not knowing too much of the continuing negotiation and just coming from a domestic politics background, the ambassador immediately took a stand that not only reversed the position the country had taken before, but also blocked a deal countries had spent months in negotiating. 'Do you know what Romans say about *pacta sunt servanda*, what you agree and you sign, you respect,' we were told by a furious senior official at the WTO after the event. 'This is the basis of any civilized relationship. What that country ambassador did was to break Richard Wagner's Ring Cycle and that left all of us in a state of jungle, can't you see?' Another ambassador reflected: 'It might not be a bad idea to throw people into the pool so they can start swimming right away; but this is not a low-level position of representing the country in an IO. For a state, once a decision is announced, you cannot retrieve it.' It then took some months before any equilibrium was achieved at the WTO and with that country. The different career expectations and expertise shape how they see trade issues and how they manage relationships with their peers at the WTO. The asymmetry of state representatives at the WTO in terms of knowledge, experience, and networking is so stark that it shapes the daily operation of the WTO and processes of trade negotiations in Geneva.

Tenure of representatives in other IOs makes a difference too: 'If you think about the outstanding EDs, some of them are the ones who have been here for a while and learn the ropes,' explained one long-serving VP at the World Bank.

> For instance, one ED representing African countries came from Guinea-Bissau of all places: he came as an assistant in the ED office, became the Alternate, then the adviser and the ED. There have been a number of EDs who have had the similar experience. When they have had enough time here, they can be quite effective in participating at the board activities and representing the group. They know how to ask right questions, such as 'How was it that we did not do XYZ or what should we be doing in the future?'

At the WHO, member states are represented by staff from their mission to UN agencies in Geneva. On important issues, such as the election of DGs or changing rules on financing, ambassadors would attend the meeting and participate. A growing number of countries now have their dedicated health attachés (over thirty of them) actively participating in WHO discussions on substance matters. These include many small and poor countries, as health is one of the key responsibilities of all governments, rich and poor. However, even though health, in nearly all countries, has a dedicated central government agency, it has diverse responsibilities and needs to cooperate with foreign affairs to engage in the WHO activities.

At WIPO, a few states are represented by their ambassadors to the WTO, while the majority are represented by their ambassadors to UN agencies. One ambassador from a large developing country explained:

> I am from foreign affairs, here for only three years covering several IOs, from human rights, ILO [International Labour Organization], IP, to health, etc. I am very interested in what is going on at WIPO, but I have to rely on the advice of experts. The government does not like to keep us in one position for more than four years. This makes it difficult.

Unlike the representation at the WTO, few countries have IP specialists in Geneva. Technical experts come to WIPO meetings from capitals only when necessary. Thus, getting the attention of member states is one of the challenges facing the DG and his senior managers. The FAO is somewhere in between the WHO and WIPO in the sense that member states are represented by the local missions in Rome, but, because there are several IOs covering similar issues—the FAO, the International Fund for Agricultural Development (IFAD), and the World Food Programme (WFP)—large missions tend to have one or two people who have specialized on agriculture or food. In all these cases, ambassadors are career diplomats with little knowledge on any specific issues. Yet, their individual interests can make a difference in terms of participating in IO activities and representing the country's interest.

At these so-called technical IOs, the choice of who participates in their activities, whether technical experts from capitals or diplomats, creates special challenges for both member states and the secretariat. There is an inherent tension between the two groups of representatives. One official explained:

> When it is informal discussion and mission briefings in Geneva, they are diplomats from local missions. When it comes to governing body meetings, they are from the department of health. We have this disconnection between those who speak on behalf of departments of health and those who are from ministry of foreign affairs, speaking on finance and other political issues. The diplomats in town, particularly the more engaged ones, often feel very frustrated. They say: 'we are following this process of reform or discussion, and we understand your organization and operation very well. Some of these jokers from the capital, from the department of health, really do not know which way up and they are not familiar with the development here, but insist that this is their jurisdiction while diplomats have no say over these issues'.

An opposite comment, expressed with similar frustration, was made by a senior official at WIPO.

> When we have to discuss and decide technical matters, which is our main business, member states tend to bring in a few officials from the IP office in capitals to attend meetings. Often they sit along with local diplomats in their missions. This triggered a lot of frustration: those from capitals have the technical expertise on the subject matters our meetings have to deal with. When ambassadors come in from time to time, or sit behind the technical people and give directions on what they should or should not say, and what position they should adopt, regardless of their ignorance of the technical matters, you can see the tension.

Another added:

> Diplomats from certain missions, particularly developing countries, are, frankly speaking, vastly superior in negotiating skills to the technical experts. They may not know much about the technical issues under the discussion, but that does not matter; they know the procedures and know how to make a political case; their default position is 'state sovereignty', regardless of issues under consideration. This is often the reason for a blockage.

Professionals participating at IOs emphasize the technical aspects of the issues, and their own professional differences can define their views and positions (for example, central banks versus treasury, epidemiologists versus specialists, physicians versus lawyers, or economists versus engineers).[22] In general, when technical debates trump ideological or diplomatic differences, it is easier to generate common views on issues. Yet, they may not always carry political weight when decisions are required back home.

There is no agreement among the secretariats whose participation, professionals or diplomats, would better facilitate multilateral cooperation. Some have argued that, even though development is a part and parcel of all IOs, the FAO, WIPO, WHO, and WTO remain by and large technical organizations, and thus technical professionals should be the primary representatives of member states. Some emphasize that multilateral cooperation would not be possible without political support in capitals, and diplomats are much better than technical experts in working out political compromises. Some senior officials at IOs believed that 'it may not be a bad idea for diplomats to participate in our discussions on technical issues, because, whatever decisions are made, we would like to have the endorsement from governments'. Another added: 'technical experts from domestic bureaucracies bring their understanding of the complexity of the issues, but are not as aware of the political implications as diplomats or former politicians, who tend to see the world through the kaleidoscope of politics, which is the essence of multilateral cooperation'.

An alternative perspective insists the issue is not diplomats versus technical professionals in representing member states. Rather, it is the quality of state representatives. 'Some diplomats lack both technical expertise and political skills and they are even unable to engage in discussion or debate. They simply read their prepared statements.' With these state representatives, it is very difficult to engage in substantive discussions and reach decisions on issues. The process is further complicated by what an ambassador called 'herd mentality':

> If a few ambassadors attend a meeting, others also have to go because their delegates attending the meeting start feeling uncomfortable. They call up their ambassadors and say, 'so many ambassadors are over here, can you please come?' Delegates often have some hesitation in taking on ambassadors if there is an issue coming up. As I said, normally I do not go to WHO meetings because they often

---

[22] An ED at the IMF gave a very good analogy: 'the difference between being minister for finance and being a governor of a central bank is that being the finance minister is like being a fighter pilot: you have a big battle every day, a very public battle, while being the governor of the central bank is like flying a 747 and it is very quiet up there but you have a lot of passengers. We are kind of a mixture. In a crisis we are a fighter pilot but with a lot of analytical support. During the crisis, we are a combination of fighter pilot and flying a 747.'

discuss technical issues which I have no knowledge of. But I can be called to some of them because we are both a donor and a recipient country and we fund a lot of our health programmes. Our technical experts feel political weight is needed.

Representation means more than just being present; it requires voicing views, advocating positions, and promoting interests. Representation requires a delicate balancing when member states send both diplomats and technical experts to attend and participate in IO activities and need to align their views.

Quality of Representation

The quality of state representation has two dimensions—individual and institutional—and it depends on at least two factors: *access* to key decision-makers in capitals and the availability of *support* on which state representatives can draw. Both are shaped by the importance of the IO to member states.

Access has two dimensions: individual and institutional. On the individual level, it concerns the ability of representatives to connect with decision-makers in their capitals. Those who represent their country at the IMF as EDs, as alternates, or through groupings often have ready access to the core decision-making machinery in capitals, at least in Treasury or Finance departments. Some owe their access to their long service in the central bank or the Ministry of Finance before going to Washington. Most maintain access because governments take the IMF seriously, not necessarily because they have to borrow from IMF to deal with temporary problems of current account imbalance but because what the IMF says on their economy can have an impact on markets, and because monetary policy and the stability of exchange system are important to the national economy and often to the survival of the government. This is true both for the fifty states that have presence in the IMF either as EDs, or their alternates, or with staff in ED offices, and for the other member states when they have to deal with the IMF on monetary matters.

One ED at the IMF explains: 'we participate in the discussions on "strategic decisions" at the board meetings, rather than on building schools, bridges or hospitals in Africa or around the world, as our colleagues across the street do. We therefore need to deal with the central bank governors, the Minister of Finance and the Prime Minister directly.' Another ED agreed:

> When important decisions have to be made at board meetings, I ask the Prime Minister; I inform the Finance Minister and the Deputy Minister and the governor of the central bank, in this order. Sometimes, the Prime Minister does not want to make a decision and prefers to defer the decision to either the Finance Minister or the governor of the central bank.

This access extends to core decision-makers in countries that EDs are designated to represent: 'I am off to visit—' (the second largest stakeholder in the group), explained one ED. 'Who am I going to see? The governor of the central bank and the Prime Minister as the two Finance Ministers will discuss some issues here. These are the strategic leaders; EDs at the Bank tend to meet the Minister of International Aid, if ever they meet any ministers.' The EDs at the IMF are often 'amazed' at what they hear or see of their counterparts across the street at the World Bank.

From time to time, senior officials at the IMF in particular would remind EDs and those who deal with the IMF that direct access to core decision-makers in capitals is critical for its operation: 'I love your views,' a former corporate secretary at the IMF told the board members, 'but I want your capital's view. This is not a seminar to exchange views; this is to engage you as stakeholders. We need to know the position of your government.' A long-serving corporate secretary, Leo Van Houtven, echoed the view: 'They [member states] should take the lead in ensuring that senior, highly qualified officials are appointed to the Board.'[23] For the management, it is crucial that EDs at the IMF and the World Bank have the ear of core decision-makers in capitals and they can represent the position their government is willing to take.

Access to core policy-makers in capitals is an institutional matter. Sometimes the position of representatives is ambivalent. Trade ambassadors to the WTO find themselves in such a position. Unlike monetary policy, not all trade issues are important to all countries all the time, and domestic politics over trade issues can be divisive. Yet countries take what is going on at the WTO seriously, in part because trade plays an increasingly important role in the economy, but, most importantly, because decisions made at the negotiation table at the WTO are binding on its members. Most countries have a dedicated trade department from which country ambassadors to the WTO draw their support and instructions, even if final decisions may not be in the hand of the trade department.

As ambassadors, they are the representatives of their country and conscious of their standing. When DGs choose to bypass them and contact their trade ministers or Prime Ministers directly and sometimes secure a promise from the Prime Minister or trade minister that they would support certain issues or positions at the negotiation table in Geneva, ambassadors are offended and feel squeezed. 'Look, I get instructions from the same minister, the one the DG talked to, the one who is sending me the instructions,' complained one ambassador to the WTO. 'It is ineffective for him [the DG] to do so because eventually we, not the ministers, will need to settle the details of negotiations.' Behind this whinge, what the ambassador said has some truth in it—prime

---

[23] Leo Van Houtven, 'Rethinking IMF Governance', *Finance & Development*, 41/3 (2004), 19.

ministers make promises at occasions, such as G20 or other summits, with a much broader agenda in mind; the intricate negotiations in Geneva are the territory of those designated ambassadors. However, sometimes they welcome the same DG's efforts to talk to the key policymakers back in capitals because it helps them keep their policymakers focused.

For many other IOs, the management knows that the request to have the ear of core policymakers may not be attainable. States representatives at the FAO, WIPO, and WHO suffer from a lack of direct access to core decision-making in capitals for two main reasons: one is that they are primarily represented by the local missions to UN agencies where diplomats represent a range of IOs and need to balance the interests across various issues. Take the USA as an example; as one of the best-resourced missions in Rome, the US Mission to the UN Agencies may have at most one or two agriculture attachés from the US Department of Agriculture (USDA). They work with a team of diplomats, humanitarian assistance, and development staff. It is not easy to get attention and support from USDA, which has a mandate ranging from expanding 'economic opportunity through innovation, helping rural America to thrive; promoting agriculture production sustainability that better nourishes Americans, helping feed others throughout the world; and preserving and conserving natural resources through restored forests, improved watersheds, and healthy private working lands'. Its representatives to the FAO seldom get their voice heard at the USDA or any part of the government machinery in Washington unless the administration has a particular agenda to push, which does not happen often in institutions such as the FAO or even the WFP. Consequently, 'government representatives to FAO often act virtually on their own, without political input from capitals, interacting mainly with their own counterparts and often at a low level in order not to risk raising awkward issues'.[24]

The frustration of some state representatives at the FAO was clear: 'We are the representatives of our country at this IO, but our minister does not have time for us, nor does he have direct access to the cabinet members, not to mention the Prime Minister. We struggle to get attention of our minister, who then really struggles to get cross-department support and the attention of the core executive.' Lack of access to and attention of key decision-makers on a whole range of issues of IOs is a common phenomenon. Even on important decisions, such as electing the DGs, the functional ministries have little say. That decision is made among foreign affairs officials, whose priority differs significantly from that of the functional ministry. This was seen as one of the main reasons the FAO was dysfunctional for a long time: 'the low status of agriculture in domestic political hierarchies results in agricultural authorities having little influence over the appointment of Directors General, indecisiveness

---

[24] Charles H. Weitz, *Who Speaks for the Hungry? How FAO Elects its Leader* (Uppsala, Sweden: DAG Hammarskjöld Foundation, 1997), 11.

over the length of term for Directors General, and deficiencies in election procedures'.[25]

WIPO shares the similar problem: the IP office in most countries is a government agency accountable to a minister who supervises a wide range of activities, and who may or may not be a part of the core executive. The share of health spending in GDP around the world has been steadily rising, and health departments have increasingly been included into the core decision-making in government. This trend has not been translated into government's attention to the WHO, and most state representatives to the WHO remain diplomats from foreign affairs. Health attachés, like their counterparts at the FAO or WIPO, tend to be the third or fourth rank down the bureaucratic hierarchy in their own ministry. These specialists have serious problems in getting the attention of their own line departments.

We were repeatedly told by all three groups of players under this study—state representatives, heads of IOs, and the secretariat—that 'member states deserve the IOs they have got'. If IOs are inefficient in doing what member states want, that may be simply because member states do not know what they want or, more insidiously, care what IOs do. Seldom does what IOs do loom large in domestic politics. Seldom is there a common united position taken across government agencies. This indifference frustrates IO leaders, international civil servants, and state representatives, whether referring to substance or to process. 'This really raises the "ownership" issue of IOs,' commented a former ED to the IMF. 'Do states care enough about these IOs? Do they really take IOs seriously? I seriously wonder whether governments are held accountable for the positions that they take in international organizations and the outcomes of international organizations, which could positively or negatively affect the interest of people.' The international civil servants feel frustrated too with the lack of attention of governments: 'It sounds a bit of romantic to say it, but I think a lot of the more serious technical staff do feel that they have been let down by the member states and abandoned when they took no action at all facing the autocratic management.' Another added: 'members elected the DG, so you would think they at least would care about his way forward by agreeing or disagreeing with the DG, but they do not always do that'. One example given to us repeatedly is that of the FAO, whose two DGs were in power for over thirty-five years (1976–2011): 'Many member states complained about this DG, but they kept electing him. Can you tell me whether member states really care?'

Lack of access to core decision-making in capitals cannot be equated to non-participation of state representatives. Some are very active; some are even capable of mobilizing domestic support; and those active ones can have direct

---

[25] Weitz, *Who Speaks for the Hungry?*, 7.

impact on IO operations. One senior official at the WHO commented: 'For example, Monaco has quite some influence here because it has an active ambassador. Sometimes, you can have huge power-situated members who have bad [inactive] representatives; they have hardly any influence. It is up to a member state to decide when they raise their flag and make a case. When they do speak out, we as the secretariat cannot ignore them.' At the FAO, a representative from one agriculture department was not only active in participating in governing bodies but also

> has played a critical role not only in representing his country, [but also in]…in shaping the policies at FAO. By the time he was about to be rotated back to capital, his colleagues in the line ministry said, 'we wish we could clone him to keep the same impact on FAO's work'. People like him 'have excellent knowledge' and 'communication skill' to push ahead the ideas and programmes in a clear and concise way.

Support. Some countries supplement relatively low-ranking representation and the absence of direct involvement in core decision-making in the capital with more cooperative support across agencies in the capitals and support from regional groupings. This is especially the case with the FAO, WHO, and WIPO. Countries in the Organization for Economic Cooperation and Development (OECD) may have a single person representing the country at the FAO or WIPO, but domestic support is available. 'I have been here [FAO] representing my country for three years. I am here by myself in the mission, sharing a secretary with the Defence Attaché (laughs). So I have to draw knowledge and support from the capital where we have a team, which may be small but dedicated for FAO,' one representative explained.

> We can also tag support from other experts if necessary. When the Programme and Budget Committee meets here in Rome, all those documents are available on the internet. Our team in the capital are experts in the fields. They read documents and they give advice on this or that. I do get a lot of good information and advice from people back home. I also get instructions for every meeting.

The Nordic and Baltic countries have a joint representative on the IMF EB for the Nordic–Baltic constituency. The group has an institutionalized support of the Nordic–Baltic Monetary and Financial Committee consisting of senior officials from both the central banks and finance ministries of eight countries.

> The Committee meets at least twice a year before the spring and fall IMF–World Bank meetings. People in this Committee also meet between the two major meetings in DC, preparing for the discussion, working out strategic positions on major issues, discussing the draft of statements and taking the policy decisions on the most important issues. Consequently, as an ED at IMF, I provide input through the ED's office and I am also on the receiving line too.

This practice of pooling resources and providing support to representation is exercised most effectively among small developed countries.

In comparison, support offered through a grouping of developing countries is not always as concrete or effective. Regional groups at IOs serve more as a forum for exchanging information. When the member states do get some support, their assistance is often treated with suspicion by the secretariat, which prefers to offer whatever assistance member states want themselves. This is primarily because assistance offered to developing countries sometimes comes from 'non-representative NGOs', especially those from developed countries, which know how to 'manipulate resource-poor developing countries':

> A group of African countries were told to oppose this negotiation on the topic, saying it would hurt them all before we even decided terms of negotiation, explained one senior official. Indeed, these NGOs were against the position of their own government, which was the most active advocate for the negotiation on the issue. They did not like it; could not convince their own government to change the position; so they turned around and sold the idea to African countries before they had had time to study the whole issue at all.

From time to time, developing countries can get assistance from individual or groups of developed countries.

Representation at IOs often suffers when the capital does not show much interest. One representative in Geneva at the permanent mission of a medium-sized country with a population of over forty million explained:

> I cover the WHO and all humanitarian affairs. So I can only spend 20 per cent of my time there [WHO] and I really should spend more, as there are so many important things going on there. I am not an expert on health, while the topics discussed at WHO are often very specific and technical. I will have to focus on political consequences of things being discussed. I depend a lot on the feedback from our Health Ministry back home, but I have scarce and little feedback from our Health Ministry because basically our Ministry of Health prefers to focus its resources to battle at the Pan American Health Organization and it tends to neglect WHO—which is obviously a great mistake. To be honest with you, at the beginning, I was rather miserable at WHO, because I wanted to cover as much as possible, but I had no feedback from the capital and, of course, I had no instructions either.

For many state representatives, lack of access and lack of support are just part of their life. An ambassador of a large European country confirmed:

> we do not have a large team here in Geneva and each individual was in charge of two and sometimes three international organizations in town. It is important to have good councillors who are able to understand and determine what is important and what is not. When they see important issues in one organization, they would come and report to me, suggesting the responses. So I was jumping from one organization to the other, which is intellectually stimulating and extremely

interesting, from health to trades to labour relations, to immigration to human rights.

A representative from one G20 country in Geneva complained: 'We are really stretched. I rush to WIPO for a meeting and have to leave to rush back to WHO, where we have to decide on budget matters, but our health attaché is in Brussels now. I can only listen and report back to our health people. If they think it is important, they will come and participate and I will brief them.'

For developing countries, they get whatever help is available.

> After I retired from FAO, the government of my country asked me to become a representative here at FAO. It could not, and still cannot, pay me. I work free. It does not matter to me and I have got my pension. It would be very expensive for the government to retain me. I make all the decisions except the decision on electing the DG. That is a political one and I got an instruction for it.

Quality of state representation at IOs differs significantly depending in part on the priority government gives to the organization, in part on the access state representatives and their line ministers have to core decision-makers in the capital, and in part on the support system available to state representatives in capitals or through various groupings. In general, when decisions are on hard rules, as in the case of WTO most of the time, or when countries are negotiating treaties in other IOs, there tends to be more support from the capital than when routine work of the IO is under way. Governments are busy, and IOs do not occupy the top of their agendas.

TWO HATS

Representatives at IOs often wear two hats—both representing states, pursuing collective goods on behalf of the international community, and promoting and protecting the interests of IOs as institutions. This not only applies to resident representatives, as seen at the EBs at the IMF and the World Bank (not least because they are literally paid out of the IO budgets), but also to those state representatives who decide to serve IOs in various capacities, such as chairmen of committees.

'The accountability of executive directors must be assessed in terms of both their individual accountability and that of the EB as a body,' asserted an independent evaluation study of IMF.

> Executive directors *individually* are accountable to the governors who appoint or elect them. There do not appear to be any formal mechanisms for holding the individual directors accountable. If this is considered as a weakness, it would be for the governors to decide on a suitable mechanism. Executive directors *as a*

group are in principle accountable to the Board of Governors as a body. Governors at the present have no formal mechanism with which to assess this accountability.[26]

EDs at the IMF and the World Bank vary significantly in terms of representation of both country and the IO. Nearly all admit that they 'have a double hat to wear'. This includes those representing a single country. As one ED put it emphatically: 'I am an ED, not an ambassador. I do not take instructions from the capital, but I do take seriously any advice they may give me.' Some others, however, are honest with where their loyalty ultimately goes: 'Of course, we have a double responsibility but the one that prevails is the one of whoever appoints you into this office, whether being the Minister of Finance, or the minister of international development.' Some EDs may be on a short leash, as the 'finance minister expected continuing briefings on internal operation of IMF affairs',[27] and they occasionally get specific instructions when issues concern their own country. All EDs must balance these two sets of interests in activities at the EB. This turns out not to be very difficult because, in a residential board, EDs often get too involved in details rather than focusing on strategic issues. On details, staff have the advantage of both knowledge and information. The balance tilts towards them, rather than EDs.

Another ED explains:

> To a certain extent, of course, I am representing [my country's] interest in development policies; so I would like to see the Bank, as an institution, moving into a specific direction. Meanwhile, I consider myself as an ambassador for this institution in my own administration, my own country. So I try to promote and to make the Bank better understood among our parliamentarians. I consider it my responsibility to promote multilateral organizations and the comparative advantages of multilateralism.

This is also the expectation of the secretariat. 'Their main role is to facilitate the process, explain things to capitals,' explained one senior official at the IMF, 'as people in the capital are not focused; they focus on something briefly and move on to something else. We explain the issues to the EDs here and then they can help us explain it to capitals.' To ensure the multilateral spirit, the staff working with these EDs have also developed procedures that help EDs wear the two hats, and think and act as the defenders of the multilateral interests of IOs.

One former Corporate Secretary at the IMF showed us the board meeting room and explained:

---

[26] Alexander Mountford, 'The Historical Development of IMF Governance', Independent Evaluation Office, IMF (BP/08/02) (May 2008), 21; emphasis in original.

[27] Momani, 'Canada's IMF Executive Director', 169.

This is the room where we have our board meetings. There are 24 people around the table and they are representing 187 countries. The kind of battles you see outside does not happen in here. Seating is alphabetically arranged, according to their surnames. It is not uncommon that the representative from the United States is sitting right next to the representative from Iran. They are arranged clockwise one year and anti-clockwise the following year. These 24 people are officials of this institution who have got to leave their national hats at the door when they enter this room. Of course, we know they are voting in their country's interests with their shares of votes in mind. But they are also officials of this institution, and their loyalty lies to this institution and to the Articles of Agreement, which they have come here to defend and enforce, even though they are representing their country or countries. They need to know how to manage the balance, and we can see sometimes they are struggling.

A former corporate secretary at the World Bank commented: 'I think the very best of the EDs are those who could really wear that institutional hat; they could see it was in the interests of the institution to have a good working relationship with the President, even if occasionally these EDs might find it fun to set Wolfensohn up.' Representing the interest of the country or a group of countries when talking to their peers at the IMF or the World Bank thus exists side-by-side with representing and promoting the interests of these institutions and multilateral cooperation at the home front.

For those representing a multiple-member constituency, they are often surprised when they are asked how they represent the interests of the states: 'I am struck that you said that I am representing the interests of my country,' said one ED. 'I am here to represent the interests of my group of countries and promote the interest of this institution.' Another ED explained how the office represents the interests of all members in the group:

> We have all countries represented in this office, regardless of their size. The ED country would lead coordination; I would draft views, send them to all members; provide them with information; collect their views and formulate one position. We discuss all issues and they would tell me what they want and prefer. I do not say this is an instruction from our members, as I may end up saying something very different at the board meetings but I am accountable. They would expect me to do what I think is the right thing to do.

Indeed, not one ED at the IMF and the World Bank we talked to saw him or herself as an ambassador of his or her own country alone. The role of EDs was similar to that of board members of many institutions in the world; they would have to have the interests of the institution in mind. They were expected 'first and foremost to serve the interests of the institution' by the senior managers and among their peers too at these two institutions. None we talked to thought otherwise. Yet, they are different from board members of private companies. They represent quite unique independent interests—not their own national interests, not the interests of constituency countries, not the interests of the IO, but a bundle of all three. How to balance this bundle of interests is decided by the EDs based on their judgement, their valuation of multilateralism, and their understanding of the technical matters, but 'balance' is what is expected.

Some state representatives take these two hats—promoting national interests and defending multilateral cooperation—because they have become 'institutionalized' after serving in Rome, Geneva, or wherever IOs are for a long period of time. One ambassador to the WTO started working there even before the WTO became a formal international organization and has had non-interrupted service at the WTO for over twenty years. 'We are here because we believe in the system not because we want to destroy it. That is the reason we are willing to make compromises to preserve the system.' Another ambassador added: 'we care about the system. Now, all our energy is devoted to keep the system alive. To do that—I'm very frank and very pragmatic—we have to concede, even against our own interest, for the sake of the system.' Their long experience at, and deep knowledge of, an IO undoubtedly helped them represent the country interests. They also helped establish a special relationship among all those working for the system, from DGs, secretariats to their counterparts. Arthur Dunkel, DG of the General Agreement on Tariffs and Trade (GATT), provided a good example: 'sometimes I would get a phone call from an ambassador, "you will be horrified, but do not panic after you heard the instruction from our capital"'. This special relationship allows the secretariat to play a vitally important role in making multilateral cooperation work. The special relationship is not limited to DGs and some long-serving international civil servants, but also found among state representatives. As one representative explains, 'once you serve in one IO for a couple of years, you end up knowing everybody; it almost becomes a classroom; you call everybody by their first name and there is a certain level of informality within all that formality that is allowed.' This allows representatives to work together, trying to achieve common goals.

Socialization into the IO leads EDs to become the defender of the system at the IMF and the World Bank too.[28] At one time the Russian ED at the IMF was there for over a decade, so was the Brazilian ED. The Russian one was then appointed as the ED across the street at the World Bank. It is not a surprise to hear one ED of single-country representation say: 'I think in general, EDs, particularly those who serve more than the minimum two years, tend to identify quite strongly with the institution and the values of the institution.' It is noted that some of the representatives to the FAO 'have not even visited their own country for briefing in over a decade'.[29] The concern is that, when state representatives have served in one IO for a long period of time, they have,

---

[28] For the discussion, see the special issue, 'International Institutions and Socialization in Europe', *International Organization*, 59/4 (2005), 801–1079.
[29] Weitz, *Who Speaks for the Hungry?*, 11.

over the years, started identifying themselves far more with their peers at the IO than they do with the policies and even the interests of the government they are supposed to serve. They become 'a predicable force in favour of the status quo and of Agency power'.[30]

In all multilateral environments, when state representatives take on the responsibility to chair a committee, they put on the institutional hat, suspending their role of representing the interests of their country for the duration.[31] Even though most delegates to UN agencies in Geneva, including developed countries, constantly complain that they are overstretched in participating in IO activities in the town, many, from large and small countries, try to get elected to chair committees. When they chair a committee, these state representatives start working for multilateral institutions, rather than as state representatives. They are authorized by members to resolve and mitigate collective-action problems and to create a demand for an institutional response to the common problems. They can act as policy entrepreneurs, but more often than not, they can only nudge and persuade rather than impose. They need to play the role discreetly: 'I come back to my bottom line,' explained one chairman of the WTO General Council. 'You need to be a good listener and to try and extract from that conversation a sense of direction and to volunteer what you hear as possibly showing an emerging direction of consensus. Testing that on a different group, or a broader group and you build up and out.'

One example of a chairman acting as a neutral defender of the system is not an individual but a country. New Zealand, known for having more dairy cows (6.7 million) and sheep (29.8 million) than people (4.4 million), has been holding the chair of the special negotiation group on agriculture and that on cotton since 2004, not because of its agricultural interests, but because those committee chairmen from New Zealand managed to be fair and effective in facilitating negotiations. Despite the rotations, all its five ambassadors to the WTO had worked on trade issues before being sent to Geneva and all were elected to serve the position as 'trusted' defenders of the system.

> You do not normally have a country serving as a chairman of a committee if that country has great interest in the issue or several terms in a row. I am the fourth chairman of this committee from my country. I started working on trade issues back in the early 1990s and when I came, the chairman of the General Council asked me to put my hand up to replace my predecessor as the chairman of this committee. Just because we have interests over this issue, we believe it is critical to be fair and balanced in bringing members to the table. We have been a strong defender of the system.

---

[30] Douglass Williams, *The Specialized Agencies and the United Nations* (London: C. Hurst & Company, 1987), 120.

[31] See, e.g., Spyros Blavoukos and Dimitris Bourantonis, 'Chairs as Policy Entrepreneurs in Multilateral Negotiations', *Review of International Studies*, 37/2 (2011), 653–72.

Another chair of the General Council stated as a matter of fact:

> as a chair, you work for the system. To do it right, you need to give it time to gain consensus, and to spend hours talking to other ambassadors. To get a feel on a given issue, you do lunches, go social drinking, and meet ambassadors, sometimes one on one and sometimes fifteen or twenty people to see how ideas fly. If a large group agrees, I can take the issue to the Council.

Another ambassador agreed: 'being a chair is to contribute to the public good. Fortunately, I have got a large team here in Geneva and another one back in the capital working on our national issues. My job as a chair is to work for the institution and the system.' The two hats are shared between the ambassador and the delegate.

When one ambassador served as the chairman of the Trade-Related Aspects of Intellectual Property Rights (TRIPS) Council at the WTO, he spent nearly all his time serving the collective interest there. The demands of the task simply added to the pressures on the already stretched state representation.

> I know intellectual property rights is a huge subject matter and very, very interesting, and potentially there is a great opportunity for us to have an influence. I just do not have the time to attend to the matters there. I have asked the person who is looking after WTO to cover WIPO. The person is from the Ministry of Trade; he cannot be at two places when meetings are held at WTO and WIPO at the same time. He might have to sacrifice WIPO because his minister demands he work on WTO, even if what is going on at WTO was not as important as that at WIPO to our interests. I have asked the Ministry of Health to place at least one officer here, covering the WHO, UNAIDS [Joint United Nations Programme on HIV/AIDS], GAVI [Global Alliance for Vaccines and Immunizations], etc. and following possible funding issues and opportunities that could be arising.

As chairs of a governing body in IOs, state representatives have to act on behalf of collective interests. This is the reason that, in many IOs, state representatives from the five major powers do not normally chair committees, not necessarily because they are unable to balance the two sets of interests—national and multilateral—but because of the perception. IOs need system defenders; so does multilateral cooperation.

REPRESENTATION

When scholars discuss IOs from the principal–agent perspective, the attention to principals—member states—goes predominately to a very few large players. IOs have membership of over 180 states. Many of them have representation in IOs, but seldom participate in IO activities. Full representation can often mean little participation in IOs. Meaningful representation requires substantial resources (financial, human, and time) for participation that most member states do not have. This imbalance of representation and participation has created serious challenges for the heads of IOs and the secretariat, who are constantly reminded that they are obligated to pursue collective goods of member states.

When countries are represented by UN ambassadors who are responsible for a range of agencies in Geneva or Rome, officials in capitals potentially shape the representation either by providing substantial support to the delegates or by flying in to have direct participation. These tend to be relatively rich countries, especially those in Europe within a short distance. If senior officials happen to be interested in the international dimensions of an issue, whether health, intellectual property, or labour standards, they can carefully choose the colleagues and send them to IOs to represent national interests and make domestic support available. There is no one consistent pattern among countries that are active in IOs, yet a combination of factors can make a difference—personal interests of representatives, their access to political and technical support at home, and the resources they may be able to pool. Thus, such active representation often takes place among no more than a dozen or so of 180 or 190 member states. For many developing countries, it is a matter of lack of capacity (financial, human, and material) and often a lack of interest in what IOs do most of the time too.

The shared comment of senior officials across IOs and many state representatives themselves is: 'since states have created IOs, one would imagine they would care what IOs do and how they do what states want them to do. This is not always the case.' All member states are represented in IOs in one way or another, but only a very few actively get involved in shaping the activities of IOs, especially in Geneva, where a permanent mission of between three and six people represents the country in all IOs in town and sometimes even including the EU in Brussels. Even for those countries that can afford a separate mission to the WTO/WIPO, their attention tends to go to the WTO rather than WIPO. An ambassador simply said, 'I do cover WIPO, but I must say I have very little practical involvement with it. We have always been a very, very, strong supporter of the multilateral system generally. This is the line I will hold.' A former ambassador to the WTO and then the deputy director general (DDG) of another IO explained: 'Even for those representing only three IOs in Geneva, WTO, WIPO, and UNCTAD, most of their time and energy focus on WTO, as I did when I was the ambassador to WTO. I spent 95 per cent of my time on WTO and the rest on WIPO and UNCTAD [United Nations Conference on Trade and Development]. Now I am the DDG here, I am constantly amazed at the limited engagement of ambassadors in these technical organizations.' As most countries have a single mission to all UN agencies in town, their state representatives come to WIPO meetings only when an election of DG is under way or major decisions are to be made.

Many spend most time at the Human Rights Council. A former diplomat explained:

> The Human Rights Council was established in 2005. You can describe it either as a market or as a circus. Essentially everybody congregates in there; all the ambassadors are there. This body meets virtually all the time, and everybody hangs out there. WIPO is not a priority to many of the missions in Geneva. Many ambassadors spend vast amounts of time in the Human Rights Council also because it deals with political issues many ambassadors feel comfortable with. There they can understand 'the language' of diplomacy. The DG here gets irritated as he thinks issues in this IO are important to its members. Once I got a phone call from the DG. He said, 'I need to talk to these ambassadors and the meeting downstairs was not going well.' He asked me whether I knew where all the ambassadors were. I happened to be at the Human Rights Council. I said: 'there were thirty of them sitting there talking about I do not know what'. These ambassadors always stick there; it is a circus.

An ambassador from a developing country explained why he spent so much time at the Human Rights Council:

> We have a relatively large mission here in Geneva compared with other African countries. We have a team of eight professionals, covering WTO, WHO, WIPO, ITU [International Telecommunications Union], ILO, Human Rights Council, and the other IOs in town. I am the ambassador here, but I am also the ambassador to Switzerland, Austria, Greece, and Turkey. Among the seven professionals, there are three attachés: one covering health at the WHO and two covering trade issues at WTO, UNCTAD, and WIPO. Of these three, one is from Ministry of Agriculture, one from Ministry of Trade, and one from Foreign Affairs. Among the other four professionals from the Ministry of Foreign Affairs, two were devoted to human rights, one covered WHO, and one covered the rest. I have to spend a lot of time at the Human Rights Council, not only because my country has a very good record on human rights and we can set an example for others, but also because I can exchange information with other ambassadors on all other IOs in town.

For most member state representatives, participation in IOs is challenging: there are competing issues and competing schedules. As one ambassador said bluntly: 'we suffer from marginalization just on account of being absent at WHO, WIPO or other IOs.'

Meanwhile, engaging state representatives at many IOs, though difficult, is critical for DGs or the secretariat, as both their operation and legitimacy depend on participation of large numbers of member states. Thus, senior members of the management in all IOs often have to develop creative ways of getting the attention of member states: holding formal and informal meetings and consultations, or hosting breakfasts or lunches with a small group of ambassadors. Even then, DGs have only limited time slots to get these ambassadors together. 'I don't like to do breakfasts,' one DG said plainly.

But I need to if I try to talk about an issue with ambassadors. After 10 o'clock, they will be all gone; you won't be able to get them; you won't get twenty ambassadors together in one spot because they'll be dissipated around. I need to get ambassadors not because I want to inflate things, but because I need their attention and get their engagement first before I take the matter to the committee.

'Dragging' states representatives into the loop by inviting them to breakfast or lunch so that their input can be heard is necessary for IO operations. This description is quite different from what state representatives like the public to think about their role in IOs—they are the masters and drivers of IOs. This political reality also differs fundamentally from that described by many scholars—capacities or incapacities of IOs are 'a consequence of deliberate design of member states' or 'states initial IGO [intergovernmental organization] orchestration even when they themselves are its ultimate targets'.[32]

In theory, ambassadors represent their national interests. National interests are never a bundle of single and coherent interests. Ambassadors shoulder the responsibility of assembling, balancing, and deciding what the national interests are. From time to time, this particular role gives them the advantage in bargaining with their counterparts and at others it can create difficulties for their relationships with DGs and the secretariat. The internal political dynamics of member states often amaze even veteran staff at the secretariat. 'You need to understand IP [intellectual property] is a technical issue. So there you have people from the capitals who are technical experts, and of course you also have diplomats from the missions too. Often they are in a room together, but they do not seem to align with their ideas in any way.' When a team of experts from the capital and diplomats in the Geneva mission attend the General Assembly conference at both the WHO and WIPO, a senior official at the WHO added: 'we are often told by health attachés, "these people are from the Foreign Affairs, and you do not want to take too much notice of them"'. At WIPO, technical experts want to discuss the issues on the technical terms, while their counterparts from foreign affairs would often caution them about potential political and diplomatic consequences.

Some countries are better at aligning their internal interests than others. 'When we have a donor meeting once a year, the major top fifteen donors will be represented by several departments across government. It is getting better but this is only among less than 10 per cent of our member states.'

A few countries have been able to ensure their diplomats in Geneva are well informed, particularly on issues across several IOs where there are major differences across government agencies.

---

[32] Kenneth W. Abbott et al., 'Orchestrating Global Governance', in Kenneth W. Abbott et al. (eds), *International Organizations as Orchestrators* (Cambridge, Cambridge University Press, 2015), 366, 350.

For instance, at WHO, we have been working on a Foreign Policy and Global Health Initiative which was started by seven foreign ministers from Brazil, France, Indonesia, Norway, Senegal, South Africa, and Thailand. Initially, there was a clear split between those who worked on health and those on foreign policy. Foreign affairs ministers of these countries then took the lead at the UN General Assembly, proposing a resolution on foreign policy and public health, which turned out to be quite a useful way of getting subjects slightly through the backdoor to the international debates.

More often than not, however, 'diplomats can dominate the discussion and completely marginalize a few from the technical department from the capital'.

For meetings of WIPO's Standing Committees and its Permanent Committees, the relationship between the secretariat and technical people from capitals differs significantly from that between the secretariat and diplomats from permanent missions. The secretariat staff see mutual benefits in cooperation.

A lot of us have been working in this institution for ten, fifteen, or more years. We have been working with these technical people of country IP offices for all these years. They are civil servants, and a number of heads of IP offices have been the heads of their IP offices forever. They tend to stay around for a long time, and they know this organization inside out; they know a lot of their counterparts too; and we also know each other well. They understand what is available and what is not; what is achievable and what not. Sometimes, they may want us to help them get the message across to their peers here and pass it on to their policymakers at home too. They sometimes want us to have a meeting in their capital to grab the attention of politicians, and they would have an opportunity to have more interaction with their ministers or even prime ministers or presidents. DG or DDG would go to these meetings to lend a hand.

Participation of technical people nonetheless needs the support of their diplomats to be translated into real actions, and this is increasingly the case, as many issues at IOs can be politicized by states as well as by non-state players. Getting participation of both experts and diplomats and managing their tensions are part of the daily routine of the secretariat.

Sometimes, the division among those representing a country is not between experts and diplomats, but rather among people from different agencies. A small team of a country mission explained to us:

We have a very big dilemma as a mission: because we are a member of WHO and a member of WTO. Now which one should we defend when issues on tobacco are discussed? When you talk to our health attaché, she would say without any doubt: '"tobacco is bad and that should be our position'. When you ask us, representing our country at WTO, we would say 'tobacco export is an important source of our economy'. Which position should we take, and which statement are we supposed to be giving, particularly in WTO, where we negotiate this issue, and the decision will be binding? Initially, the farmers who are producing tobacco in my country were growing groundnuts. It was the government that urged them to shift the production to tobacco. 'Groundnut is not enough to earn you some money. Switch to tobacco,' farmers were told. Now, the same government is going to tell them: 'don't because tobacco is bad for health.' Can you see the political implications? So, now we do not say not to grow tobacco. But we are saying that changes have to be made; tobacco has to be replaced gradually and there has to be diversification, which may take a longer time than what has been discussed under the framework at WHO.

It is hard for diplomats to find a solution that evades the departments at home. State representation is indeed a strong concept—states insist on their ownership and control of IOs—but participation at IOs involves making difficult decisions that require political capital that governments may or may not want to spare. This includes large and small, rich and poor countries. One extreme example of this problem is the presidency of Paul Wolfowitz. Not long into his tenure problems emerged. One single-country ED explained:

Clearly, things did not work, not only because of disagreement on policies, but also because corporate governance was not working—staff papers which had been approved all the way up the line and were pulled out at the last minute. That was not supposed to happen. Even a number of governors started saying things that they were unhappy with the way the World Bank was working. We spend a lot of time saying we need to improve governance and need to run this bank better. But this is not the same thing as saying my government was about to oppose George W. Bush and tell him to get rid of the person he had just appointed. The bilateral relations tend to be more important than what happens in an international organisation.

IOs are just part of the calculation made by political and bureaucratic leaders in capitals. They cannot be isolated from domestic pressures.

The former Secretary of Treasury Hank Paulson told a good story about the unwillingness of both the IMF and the US government to risk its political capital in a direct confrontation with China at the IMF when both sides were under domestic pressures:

Currency issues [with China] continued to give me grief. In September 2007 Dominique Strauss-Kahn...sought our backing to make some much-needed changes, including a plan to sell some of the Fund's gold reserves. I made clear that our support was contingent upon the IMF's citing China for currency manipulation. The undervalued renminbi was a global concern, and the IMF was the proper forum to address it. Frankly, I was also tired of the US's always having to lead on this issue. DSK agreed that the IMF would cite China, but afterward he indulged in some backdoor manœuvring that sparked the protestations of my friend Zhou Xiaochuan, China's central bank chief. Zhou came up to me...and said, 'Hank, Strauss-Kahn says he does not want to cite us. He wants to give us some time to make progress, but you are insisting that he act now. If the IMF acts now, it will make it harder for us to move the currency because our people will think we're bowing to outside pressure.'...I was a bit irritated that

DSK had used me, albeit accurately, as his excuse for getting tough with China, but I didn't let on to my friend.

In the end, the IMF did not cite China, which promised to change as soon as reasonably possible. 'As it happened, our world was about to change dramatically, and China's currency would soon become the least of our worries.'[33]

With the US Treasury just 150 metres away, IMF management has a direct access if it needs to. The managing director (MD) of the IMF also discusses important global matters with the Secretary of Treasury prior to decision-making. IMF senior officials maintain frequent contact with senior officials at the US Treasury too. The issue of representation therefore does not work in the same way as for other countries. This nonetheless cannot be interpreted as direct control of the USA over IMF decisions because unilateral decisions in a multilateral environment always incur political costs beyond one organization that government may not be prepared to risk. However important an IO may be, it is only one of the many pieces in government decision-making. There is no exception for the USA.

GROUP REPRESENTATION

In all IOs, there are formal and informal, relatively permanent and ad hoc, arrangements among 'like-minded' countries as well as among 'unlike-minded' countries within broad coalitions. Groupings of member states serve several purposes in IOs. One is that, because it is difficult to get things done in a meeting with 180–200 member states, formal and informal groupings can work out shared positions beforehand. The most ubiquitous grouping is the EU, which develops common positions; it even has separate representation at the WTO, in addition to all the national ambassadors. EU members have elaborate consultation processes. As an EU official in Geneva explained:

> In all negotiation committees and in all negotiation sessions, the EU speaks with one voice; it coordinates with member states constantly, both here in Geneva and in Brussels. Here in Geneva, we have weekly, sometimes even daily, meetings with country ambassadors to WTO. We get information about what countries think about an issue. There are many more discussions, questions, and answers. We are very good at handling our divisions in terms of trade policy and building a common position. We then negotiate on behalf of all EU countries in trade negotiations. There is a single position. On other matters, member states may speak out with their positions, but not in trade negotiations.

---

[33] Henry M. Paulson, Jr, *Dealing with China* (New York: Twelve Hachette Book Group, 2015), 245.

In addition to formal representation of the EU at the WTO, multiple groupings participate in informal consultation and negotiation. According to Stuart Harbinson, who chaired the Negotiation Group on Agriculture when it was established in 2004, G10, G27 (EU), G33, G99, Africa, Caribbean and Pacific (ACP), least-developed countries (LDCs), the Tropical Products Group, and the Cairns Group were all involved in the agriculture negotiations. In addition, there were active bodies like the Small and Vulnerable Economies and Recently Acceded Members.[34] All these groupings remain active. Some, such as the African Union (AU) and ACP, have a long history and are present in most IOs. Members of these groupings normally appoint a country as a coordinator and focal point on various issues. For example, the AU, ACP, and LDCs are active at the WHO, WIPO, and WTO. 'From these groupings, we get information,' explained one representative from an African country.

> We have all these different issues under negotiation that are our concerns, but we cannot spare people to attend them all. On each issue in all these groupings, such as AU, ACP, and LDCs, there is a focal point. We can always get information from focal points—focal point in services, focal point in trade facilitation, focal point in agriculture, etc. We are at the moment the focal point in trade facilitation in the LDCs group. We feed back to the group where we are on each issue so that member states can take advantage of the information we provide. Before we go out and negotiate on behalf of the group on trade facilitation, we convene a meeting of members so that we can discuss what position we should take as a group. Members then leave to the focal point to advance the common position in the negotiation.

Groupings help small and developing countries in representing themselves in IO activities, but do not solve all the problems they are facing because of the shortage of resources. They still need to choose and select carefully where they commit their time and resources:

> Say there's a meeting at WIPO; there's a meeting at WTO; there's a meeting in Africa group; there's a meeting of ACP. We need to look at the issue that is being discussed. If the issue at LDCs is of interest to our country, we then go to that one. That will be our number one priority. If we do not go or if the same issue is discussed in the three different groupings, then somehow, somewhere we should be represented by the focal point of that particular issue. Thereafter this focal point will convene the LDC's group meeting to brief the group for those who couldn't attend that particular meeting.

One state represented explained, 'most developed countries have got a lot of support from their capital. So we form groupings, telling the rest of the world that, if they want to deal with us, they need to deal with us as a group.' The

---

[34] Stuart Harbinson, 'The World Trade Organization as an Institution', in Weller and Xu (eds), *The Politics of International Organizations*, 30–1.

common positions worked out in these groupings are not binding, and often the divisions among members can be greater than those between developed and developing countries. When the ACP group was coordinated by an African country and worked out a position for its members to negotiate on certain trade issues at the WTO, a long-serving ambassador to the WTO from the Caribbean region disagreed strongly with the common position of the group. 'What is this,' he said angrily. 'We are here to negotiate free trade, not how to strengthen protectionist policies.' The country he represented and the country that coordinator represented appear so similar: the same level of GDP per capita, resource-less economies, and close ties to their regional economies. Yet they had achieved the similar level of development by having adopted very different trade policies. One is a successful story, according to the World Bank, 'a strategy of outward-oriented growth, based on openness to foreign investment, and gradual trade liberalization'. The other seems to be an example of protectionism by restricting trade in key sectors. The former believes that trade liberation would help the country diversify its economy and build on its niche while the other believes that 'we have nothing in the ground or above the ground; we depend on trade for our export earnings in order to feed ourselves. Yet, we are such a small country. We need to be proactive to protect our sectors; and we have to drive a hard bargain.' For these two countries, their active participation in IO activities can make a difference to their interests. Consequently, group representation can place those small, less powerful, and resource-poor countries in a position where they may or may not want to be.

The division among developing countries and sometimes among groupings can create headache for IOs too. In 2011, for instance,

> South Africa chairs the African group in WIPO while Nigeria chairs the African group at the Human Rights Council. There was this internecine nasty fight because of the resolution of sexual orientation at the Human Rights Council with South Africa against everyone else. This significantly affects South Africa's relationship with other countries and, more importantly, the conflicts spread to WIPO where the leadership of South Africa in coordinating the African Group was just not attainable.

Groupings are not the phenomena of developing countries only. Small and often informal groupings of large players in IOs serve a similar function of coordinating actions among member states. An ambassador to the WTO from a North European country told us:

> We have had this underground movement every now and then, but you cannot do it in the open. Now we have this breakfast group where we discuss everything. It includes sixteen key players—well, the big guys and some chairs too—the US, the EU, China, India, Brazil, South Africa, Canada, Australia, Japan, Switzerland, Norway, and Chile; Jamaica for the ACP group, and Norway, Nigeria and Mexico—three chairs of the General Council, Trade in Services, and TRIPs.

Meetings are literally over breakfast. Everyone (ambassadors only, no replacement) is there at 8:45 a.m. The breakfast normally ends at 10:00 but sometimes, like this week, lasted until 11:00. Last year, we even went to Corfu. We had a great time and we also worked out MC9 and then handed it to the DG. Now we try to take stock and settle issues one by one.

Groupings make IOs more manageable. If member states in these groupings think they need help, they might approach the secretariat to provide data, information, and logistic support, but they are always careful, at least in respect of the WTO Secretariat, not to ask for opinions. 'When we ask the secretariat for help,' one ambassador explained, 'they provide us with information. The choice of position is ours.' Most IOs nowadays also help finance some of the groupings. DGs and the secretariat may also use chairs of these groupings to facilitate participation in IO activities and strengthen its legitimacy, as explained by the chief of staff at WIPO.

> While the existence of these groups is not mentioned anywhere in the WIPO convention, they can perform important roles. From the perspective of the secretariat, they provide a ready and accessible conduit for communication with member states... They [also] provide a very practical administrative device to facilitate complex multilateral discussion within WIPO.[35]

The growth in the number of member states who have chosen to be more active in IOs has increased the difficulty in building consensus. If on every issue ninety member states had to be consulted, rather than using the G90 or the ACP as their voice, the consequence would, as a state representative put it, be 'chaotic and messy'. The prior digestion of issues within groupings thus advantages state representatives under pressure and organizes demands in a way that makes them manageable for the IOs as a whole.

CONCLUSION

The evidence in this chapter challenges two of the traditional systemic explanations of the workings of IOs. The first asserts that all important decisions are made by the big powers, particularly the United States. We obviously accept that the United States is the most powerful participant in IOs' activities. If the USA is strongly opposed to an initiative, it is unlikely to proceed, at least at the time, until sufficient background work of persuasion has been undertaken. If the big powers are divided, as they often are over a range of issues and across IOs, nothing will happen. In no IO is there a

---

[35] Naresh Prasad, 'The World Intellectual Property Organization', in Weller and Xu (eds), *The Politics of International Organizations*, 143.

negotiation among equals; state representatives will always want to know where the big members stand.

This is, however, not to assert that the United States can, or wants to, dictate what IOs should do or that it can readily get its own way. To propose that would be to imply that everything that happens in Geneva, Rome, or Washington, where state representatives negotiate, is no more than a charade, awaiting US decision. It would not matter who the state representatives are, what they do, how effective they are seen to be, what resources they commit to multilateral cooperation, what the divisions of opinion are. Our evidence does not sustain such a proposition. There are times when the USA has dropped its initiatives because of the lack of support from other member states; there are times when US representatives have worked closely with the IO leader and the secretariat despite domestic opposition. The United States has not always managed to secure the election of its preferred candidates. It may often win by persuasion, coupled with its capacity to use other channels to supplement its arguments. But it is not the only actor.

Second is the proposition that the member states dictate what IOs do or do not do and that, therefore, the process is unidirectional: from states to IO leaders and the secretariat. The evidence shows how difficult it is for member states to develop clear instructions to IOs. It is also impossible to argue that the decisions of IOs are the calculated outcome of purposive policy developed in the capitals of member states. We have shown that the pace of activity across IOs is massive; resources, even for large states, are often stretched, as many ambassadors or representatives rush from one meeting to another and from one organization to another. State representatives particularly struggle when the government in the capitals does not give IOs a high priority or/and when line ministries focus on domestic demands and immediate crises at home. The accountability of politicians in the capital after all is through local politics and not international forums.

Some member states care about the issues in one IO but not in others: Singapore is a potent participant in the WTO; it depends on trade, but is less concerned with the FAO, as its immediate interests are less involved. The same is true across the board; participation of member states in IO activities depends on a variety of national political, economic, and financial interests as well as the commitment and competence of those representing the country in IOs. Sometimes levels of interest in the capitals are very low; one representative admitted that he received no instructions other than for a leadership election. The theoretical model that sees member states providing direction to an IO cannot be sustained in practice; the interplay among state representatives, between state representatives and the IO leaders and the secretariat, and between capitals and representatives, must be taken into account.

Further, in all IOs, a number of groupings, whether economic or geographical, have developed, so that some smaller countries can use the benefits of pooled resources and the power of multiple members to make their voice heard. Where capitals do not care or cannot maintain support across multiple IOs, these forums become important to underpin 'the strength of the weak'. Individuals, processes of negotiation, all provide variations that will shift outcomes.

In sum, it is important to note that, while all member states have their representatives in IOs, their representation varies significantly. They differ in the resources, capacities, and assistance that may or may not be available to them. Representation also differs because of who represents the country—diplomats or professionals; those who see themselves as messengers of their government in IOs or those who see themselves as intermediaries between IOs and their governments or those who believe they have commitments to both the country they represent and the IOs they serve; those who have served a relatively long period of time and have already built up their commitment to IOs and networks of relationships with their peers in IOs or those who have just come to Geneva, Rome, or Washington, with little knowledge of the working of IOs. When state representatives take on responsibilities as heads of committees, their loyalty and commitment are towards the organization and its activities rather their own national concerns. These complications are seldom included in analyses of IOs.

Rather than adopt those systemic arguments that are derived from theories of power, we have suggested a more nuanced role for state representatives that takes as a starting point the idea that state representatives are not in themselves member states. We can see the development of new patterns of behaviour: the growing involvement of often small states, the decline in the dominance of big power interest, the interdependence of IOs and the emergence of groupings are all evidence of changing ways. It is a story that does not deny the influence of big states but rather stresses (as participants do) the development of complex varied processes that differ from one IO to another but that are a necessary component of any explanation of how state representatives can shape the IO world.

3

Heads of International Organizations

Politicians, Diplomats, Managers

Heads of international organizations (IOs) personify their organization. Presidents of the World Bank, managing directors (MDs) of the International Monetary Fund (IMF), directors general (DGs) of the Food and Agriculture Organization (FAO), the World Health Organization (WHO), the World Intellectual Property Organization (WIPO), and the World Trade Organization (WTO) are often the only public figures from their organizations who are widely recognized. Some leaders have been public figures before they get to the position, while others emerge from within the organization, often known only to the epistemic community. Some are elected by member states based on the principle of one state, one vote; some through an elaborated process; others are chosen by a closed group or even by an individual. Some take on the job with visions for the organization to change; others prefer to continue doing what the organization has always been doing.

The position of the heads of IOs gives them an international standing. They mingle with heads of state at international gatherings. When they visit capitals, they often meet national leaders, whether presidents, prime ministers, or ministers in specific sectors. Their position, however, differs significantly from that of national leaders. IO leaders share with national leaders the need to work within structural constraints and to manage expectations. They too have to develop the capacity to persuade, the ability to present visions or at least strategies, for the future.

What they are lacking is clout. They are not provided with the authority to impose decisions on the member states, or to announce unilaterally what they will do, in the way domestic leaders can.[1] Once (s)elected, they are never granted the prerogatives of leadership or the scope for decisive action that

---

[1] Richard Neustadt, *Presidential Power and the Modern Presidents* (New York: Free Press, 1999); Archie Brown, *The Myth of the Strong Leader* (New York: Basic Books, 2013); James MacGregor Burns, *Leadership* (New York: HarperCollins, 1978).

national leaders have. Their political bosses are member states, so the heads of IOs must constantly negotiate their position with multiple masters. They have to respond to state representatives who oversee their every action, and listen to the demands and complaints of often middle-ranking bureaucrats who serve as state representatives and are jealous of their standing in 'member-driven' organizations. Even in those areas where their authority is explicit, over the secretariats that they appoint and direct, their authority may be limited. IO leaders are (s)elected for specific terms; their staff are mostly tenured, career professionals who can wait out the years until a new leader arrives.

It is a different form of leadership, too often ignored in international relations literature, that depends on the application of negotiating skills, the utilization of independent international standing, the powers of persuasion, and the strategic positioning to advance the agenda of the IO to which they are committed. We seek to intertwine three themes:

- how the heads of IOs can maintain support and legitimacy in the eyes of both member states and the secretariat;
- how the heads of IOs can respond to the demands of accountability to their state masters while retaining the ability to lead;
- how the heads of IOs can muster the necessary capacity, both politically and technically, to influence the agenda, understand the problems, and develop ways ahead for their institution.

The heads of IOs (we use 'director general' (DG) as a generic term to refer to the president of the World Bank, the MD of the IMF, and the DGs in the other four IOs under examination) walk a tightrope: to lead but not to command, to consult but not to hector, to inform but not to lecture, to encourage but not to nag. Skilful leaders are able to shape the organization. It was certainly easier in former days when the number of interested member states was fewer and leaders' tenure was not term limited, the more so in the peripheral IOs where national interest was still more marginal and where repeated re-election entrenched leaders. Yet, even now leadership is possible; to be the head of an IO provides opportunities to shape the course of actions, influence the agenda, direct the discussion, and alter the environment. Some manage to succeed while others fail.

This chapter will be organized in three sections. It will explore:

1. The qualities the DGs need to steer and shape their organizations; we consider their international standing, their expertise and their vision for the organization they hope to head.
2. The formal rules regulating the selection of the heads of IOs, and the actual way that they reach their positions; we ask what implications those procedures have and how they may constrain and enable the successful candidates, whether they were elected or selected.

3. The principal responsibilities the heads of the IOs must undertake and the forums where they must work. Leaders must work as *diplomats*, representing their organizations in international arenas, and 'selling' their agendas to the international community and heads of governments: *as politicians*, working with the member states, within their organization; and as *managers* of diverse multilateral organizations that are sometimes scattered around the globe. These three roles are distinct; they are also re-enforcing.

Rarely are IO leaders good at everything. In 1969 it was asserted that the 'quality of leadership may prove to be the most critical single determinant of the growth in the scope and authority of international organizations'.[2] We want to understand whether and how that may be true.

THE QUALITIES NEEDED TO LEAD IOs

Leaders of IOs need different qualities from those of national leaders; they work within structural and resource constraints, balancing political and technical demands, and often starting their terms with high expectations. What then might be the qualities required?

International Standing

The heads of IOs must be seen as international. The rules establishing the organizations demand it.

> The World Bank. 'The President, officers, and staff of the Bank, in the discharge of their offices, owe their duty entirely to the Bank and to no other authority. Each member of the Bank shall respect the international character of this duty and shall refrain from all attempts to influence any of them in the discharge of their duties.' (World Bank Articles of Agreement, Article V, section 5, paragraph (*a*))

> The WTO. 'The responsibilities of the Director General and of the staff of the Secretariat shall be *exclusively international in character*... The Members of the WTO shall respect the international character of the responsibilities of the Director General and of the staff of the Secretariat and shall not seek to influence them in the discharge of their duties.' (World Trade Organization, Article VI, section 2)

---

[2] Robert Cox, 'The Executive Head', *International Organization*, 23/2 (1969), 205.

DGs must lead the organizations in pursuing collective interests rather than those of the countries they are from. They are watched by member states that jealously guard their sovereignty and autonomy. Their legitimacy and reputation consequently lie very much on how 'international' they can be, whether they can be seen to be as supranational, as committed to the mission of the organization and as representing the interests of all. Some IO leaders have had no difficulties in assuming the international identity whether dealing with member states or international civil servants—whatever criticism the member states or civil servants might have had about James Wolfensohn, Pascal Lamy, Francis Gurry, or Margaret Chan, no one ever questioned their loyalty to the organization and multilateralism. In contrast, some brought their national identity or even their domestic partisan ties right into the organization. Paul Wolfowitz was widely regarded as an extension of the State Department after he took over as the president at the World Bank. By bringing compatriots into key positions, he immediately generated suspicion and indeed undermined his own credibility in dealing with the board and in managing the staff. Some never seem to make the transition, certainly not to everyone's satisfaction. In the FAO and WIPO Jacques Diouf and Kamil Idris respectively were seen as more interested in the concerns of developing countries than in the broader interests of their organizations, and thus lost the confidence of developed member states.

IO leaders have to balance trust, charisma, and leadership, an official noted, and to know when to play which personal card. They have to avoid offending members. There is one cautionary tale. Gro Brundtland 'burnt her political capital in the World Health Report 2000', an official recalled. 'The only thing people remember is the last column of annex two on page 148 which was an overall rating of the member states.' Telling some members they were the best states and others that they were the worst 'doesn't go down with your "political masters"'. Their personal integrity, which is constantly examined by states, NGOs, and their own staff, must be maintained if they are to enjoy a successful tenure.

Expertise

Expertise may be seen as essential but is not by itself enough. It can empower DGs. Francis Gurry, elected to lead WIPO in 2008, was a trained expert on intellectual property with twenty years of experience in the agency before he was elected; Margaret Chan became known worldwide because she effectively managed outbreaks of avian influenza and the SARS epidemic and had been appointed as the WHO assistant director general (ADG) in 2005 before winning the DG election in September 2006. So had her predecessor, Dr Lee (DG 2003–6). At the FAO, those who held office as DGs in 1968–2011 had been internal candidates; they had all worked for the FAO secretariat before their promotion. In the FAO's 2011 contest, all the candidates had direct experience of the organization, whether within the secretariat, as state representatives serving at the governing bodies, or as ministers who had dealt with FAO. In Rome, the Iranian candidate, a former Council chair and the chairman of the independent external evaluation, was regarded as the most suitable but for reasons of nationality as having no chance of election.

By contrast, in the cases of the World Bank and the IMF, where the selections are made from outside, none of the World Bank presidents (with the exception of Eugene Black) had worked within the organizations, and in some cases they had had little or nothing to do with the organizations they were chosen to lead. They were bankers, managing large financial institutions; there were also former politicians; Robert McNamara was a former Secretary of Defence, Paul Wolfowitz from the State Department and Robert Zoellick a former US Trade Representative. When the government contacted Jim Kim about becoming president of the World Bank, he confessed 'he had only the foggiest notion of how development finance works'.[3] None came in with experience in development. In the IMF, European finance ministers and central bankers were often selected; they had experience and connections across the key countries there, but not of the world of IOs. Detailed knowledge of the organization was not an apparent criterion for the top job of either the World Bank or IMF.

Ironically, while those IO leaders who were successful through an election had to have expertise in the precise field, the very process of their election militated against too open a use of that expertise, because the member states are conscious of their electoral power, appeal to their sovereign rights, and are less likely to give heads of IOs the authority to speak out.

The WTO reflects the ambiguities of leadership in IOs. Renato Ruggiero had been Italian Foreign Minister; he understood the processes of international negotiation. His successor, Pascal Lamy, had been the trade commissioner at the EU, where he made the policy decisions. When Lamy spoke as a trade expert, everyone acknowledged his deep knowledge of the subject. When he proposed particular solutions, he became suspect. Both found the experience frustrating. The member states want (so far at least) a respectable and expert leader; they baulk at most attempts to lead.

Visions and Strategies for IOs

At the heart of the process of selecting leaders of IOs there is a basic anomaly. On the one hand, member states insist that they, and they alone, determine the

---

[3] Andrew Rice, 'Is Jim Kim Destroying the World Bank: Or Saving it from Itself,' *Foreign Policy*, 27 April 2016.

agenda of the organizations. The IO leaders are, they repeat constantly, their servants. Yet, at the same time, they ask candidates who seek to lead the IOs what their vision is for the future of the organizations. They declare that they want to appoint on merit, to have substantive leaders with capacity to shape the agenda, because they assume that those futures will be tailored to the aspirations of members.

Leaders of IOs have the opportunity to interpret the missions of their organizations. Often those missions are expressed in general terms because they were of necessity compromises. Leaders could seek to stretch the interpretations of those agreements, perhaps by identifying implied powers or appealing to new developments. They needed to respond to the circumstances in which they found themselves. James Wolfensohn had an established commitment to development but took over an institution under siege, with the need to reshape its image and redirect its priorities. Gro Harlem Brundtland wanted to revitalize a demoralized WHO and put health on the international agenda; her programme priorities were to tackle problems of tobacco and malaria. Dominique Strauss-Kahn wanted to renew the organization; he commented: 'It would be interesting to try to "revamp" the IMF.'[4]

In contrast, others were more careful and specific. At the WHO, Dr Lee wanted a 'big' initiative and proposed his 'Three by Five': getting three million AIDS sufferers on treatment by 2005. He, an adviser noted, 'said he wanted to build on the success of the past' and identified 'decentralization of resources to countries, MDGs and particularly HIV, and a better human resource strategy for mobility and rotation'. Dr Chan had a six-point agenda, nothing very new, all focused on the organization; her own priorities were health in Africa and for women. There was always a need to reconcile their own initiatives with what the member states had agreed to in the five-year plan. Lee and Chan generally came in with an agenda for continuity. At the GATT/WTO, Peter Sutherland and Pascal Lamy wanted to conclude the Uruguay and Doha Rounds respectively. At WIPO, Francis Gurry had some precise plans, such as the conclusion of a treaty on published works for visually impaired people and audio-visual performances and a more general desire to incorporate developing countries into the IP regimes through a development agenda.

Sometimes, after their appointment, DGs were able to develop plans in relation to what they wanted to do and how they wanted to do it. With assistance from a Norwegian government grant, Dr Brundtland had collected her leadership team in Oslo and planned her first term as DG. She asserted she wanted to 'promote sustainable and equitable health systems in all countries'. More explicitly, on her first day on the job, she gave a speech identifying her approach:

---

[4] George Parker, 'Man in the News: Dominique Strauss-Kahn', *Financial Times*, 14 July 2007.

> Yes, there will be change. A change in focus. A change in the way we organize our work. A change in the way we do things. A change in the way we work as a team...we must pull WHO together by focusing our efforts around our core businesses...Our role is to give the best advice—support and develop the best policies—trigger and stimulate the best research.[5]

James Wolfensohn developed his Strategic Compact to redirect the World Bank's focus after he took up the post.[6] Jim Kim stressed the need for global initiatives and greater commitment to health as a key area of activity.

The broad visions were often from those appointed from outside; the more careful comments came from those with insider experience who appreciated the difficulties they would meet. The former could soon be blunted by uncomfortable realities. For those without experience of IOs, their sometimes byzantine workings can be a shock. Dr Brundtland came to the WHO after serving as prime minister of Norway. She was 'Norway's own "iron" lady, an energetic blend of doctor, manager, politician and international activist'.[7] The circumstances were different at the WHO.

> As head of government, you can exert discipline among your cabinet colleagues and your ministries and you can provide reasonably consistent political messages through the organization of government. You suddenly realize this place is a loose coalition of NGOs and national interests.

Wolfensohn was frustrated by the campaigns of NGOs, declaring 'fifty years is enough', and of the executive directors who would not readily accept his grand plans; he roared at his deputy: 'I know what the board is like; I have spent my life dealing with them; they always do what I tell them to do, just not here.'[8] A more realistic DG commented on the need to balance ambition with feasibility: 'If we want, for instance, to have an agreement on climate change that was too large to be realistic. It's just too large and unmanageable.'

A vision means that leaders understand the mission of an IO, know what they want and will be able to achieve during their tenure, and are willing and able to mobilize the resources to materialize their plans. The failure of a leader to have or develop a vision often leaves an IO without purpose, reacting to the currents of international affairs and threatening crises.

The qualities needed are highly contingent: a need to balance expertise with political sensitivity, an ability to chart a direction, one that is consistent with the inchoate aspirations of the membership, while always maintaining the trust of the different participants inside and outside the organization. Juggling

---

[5] Anthony Robbins, 'Brundtland's World Health Organization: A Test Case for United Nations Reform', *Public Health Reports*, 114/1 (1999), 30–9.

[6] Sebastian Mallaby, *The World's Banker* (New York: Penguin, 2004).

[7] Steinar Andresen, *Leadership Change in the World Health Organization: Potential for Increased Effectiveness?* (Lysaker, Norway: Fridtjof Nansen Institute, 2002), 15.

[8] Shengman Zhang, *One Step at a Time* (Shanghai: Wenhui, 2006), 27.

the different demands is a complex skill. Their position is shaped in part by the processes though which the IO leaders reached their position and the debts that they incurred on the way.

(S)ELECTING IO LEADERS

Leadership elections create dilemmas for member states. The rules themselves are expressed only in general terms and give no direction about how leaders are chosen. There is no consideration of what the consequences of those processes might be for the running of the organizations. These are three examples.

> The World Bank: 'The Executive Directors shall select a President who shall not be a governor or an executive director or an alternate for either. The President shall cease to hold office when the Executive Directors so decide.' (Article V, section 5)
>
> The WTO: 'The Ministerial Conference shall appoint the Director General and adopt regulations setting out the powers, duties, conditions of service and term of office of the Director General.' (WTO Articles of Agreement, Article VI, paragraph 2)
>
> FAO: 'There shall be a Director General of the Organization who shall be *appointed* by the Conference ... by such procedure and on such terms as it may determine.' (FAO Constitution, Article VII, paragraphs 1 and 2)

The same word 'appoint' underpins different practices across IOs. At the IMF and the World Bank, the EB still 'appoints' the head of the organization; in other cases, such as the FAO, member states actually 'elect' DGs based on the one-state-one-vote principle.

Traditionally the member states insisted that merit should be the sole criterion. How merit was judged became a matter of contention, raising issues of whether there should be a job description or formal terms of reference that candidates should be required to meet. They were never developed. Even if such a job description did exist, it would have been interpreted through a number of lenses that member states would apply.

Individually, some national governments are heavily involved in (s)electing the heads of IOs; they want *their* nationals holding positions as IO leaders whether for issues of national prestige or for representativeness. Even where, as in the World Bank and the IMF, the choice is effectively in the hands of the US President or a small group of European countries, they still want to make their voice heard and seek to influence the process.[9]

---

[9] Staff in the IOs too care who their CEs are; they know that they must adjust to the approach and interest of each new incumbent. Most also understand that who their leaders are makes a

A number of changes in recent decades have complicated the selection processes. First is the democratization of IOs. As more member states become active, as the issues expand, so the emerging powers argue that the choice of leaders should reflect these trends. Not only should all members have an equal vote; all areas of the world should have 'turns' in providing leaders. Groupings of countries, whether regional or representing poor and lesser developed member states, often demand some form of representativeness: if the last leader was from Asia, the next one should be from Africa, Latin American, or Eastern Europe. The richer countries provide most of the funds and argue they want some adequate oversight of the expenditure of those funds. The question is always how to balance these divergent dynamics.[10] Some elections become battles between the developed and the developing member states; the candidate is of lesser importance than the representative issue.

Second is the question of term limits. In the IOs' early years, with limited participation, it was not uncommon for an IO to have the same DG for fifteen to twenty years; they were able to use their contacts and support to maintain sufficient support to guarantee their regular re-election. It was not worth the effort for other member states to try and blast them out of office. Officials who served under them argued that consequently there was little accountability to member states. Now member states have in general set term limits and, accordingly, demand greater accountability.

Third is the question of whether the heads of IOs need to be insiders or outsiders? Should they have experience working in IOs and know the details of the challenges they must meet, or should they be people of distinction, with records of achievement elsewhere, who can use their standing to provide leadership? Choices on these issues can determine the mandate and legitimacy of the eventual winners.

There have been a number of reviews of leadership (s)election processes that raise questions about how they might be done better, with little apparent impact.[11] After a review of procedures in the World Bank, the IMF and the WTO, Miles Kahler suggested they needed a 'selection process that produces

---

difference to the survival and wellbeing of the organization as well as the cause they are serving. They have no formal voice.

[10] Robert O. Keohane and Joseph S. Nye, 'The Club Model of Multilateral Cooperation and Problems of Democratic Legitimacy', in Roger Porter et al. (eds), *Efficiency, Equity and Legitimacy: The Multilateral Trading System at the Millennium* (Washington: Brookings Institution Press, 2011), 264–94.

[11] Miles Kahler, *Leadership Selection in the Major Multinationals* (Washington: Institute for International Economics, 2001); David Peretz, 'The Process for Selecting and Appointing the Managing Director and First Deputy Managing Director of the IMF,' Backgrounder, IEO, IMF, BP/07/01, 2007; Charles H. Weitz, *Who Speaks for the Hungry? How FAO Elects its Leader* (Uppsala, Sweden: Dag Hammarskjold Foundation, 1997); Brian Urquhart and Erskine Childers, *A World in Need of Leadership: Tomorrow's United Nations* (Uppsala, Sweden: Dag Hammarskjold Foundation, 1990); Andresen, *Leadership Change in the World Health Organization*.

consensus on an effective leader through a process of restrained competition'.[12] These are the three IOs where member states do NOT vote. Kahler still argued that the initial stages where there was a search for suitable candidates should be in part confidential, but the later stages, where selections were made, should be more transparent. He wanted the competition restrained because 'an outcome with clear winners and losers within the organization is unlikely to produce legitimacy and effective leadership in an IO'.[13] He argued for less flexibility, believing that a process with formal criteria and job descriptions would erode the practice of pushing for national candidates. Unsurprisingly, member states have been loath to restrict themselves by limiting the candidates to those who have precise minimum qualifications or a list of desirable characteristics.[14] Kahler does identify the key issues: competition, transparency, and the need for a winner who unites, not divides, the organization he or she is then required to manage.

A review of the leadership (s)election process in the IMF, initially written in 2002 and later updated, identified similar weaknesses. There was no clear duty statement; a 'candidate profile' issued in 2007 fell far short of a full job description. There was no formal search, with the process relying on the convention that governments proposed their nationals. There was deal-making between governments, 'trading off one international appointment against another'.[15] The processes, David Peretz argued, lacked transparency 'not least because the formal processes [in the Executive Board] are to a degree detached from the substantive decision-making processes which to a large extent take place elsewhere in direct discussions between the EU, the G7, and within the US Administration'.[16]

The mode of election must therefore be the starting point for any discussion of what authority leaders may wield. The electoral process provides assets, but also acts as a constraint (see Table 3.1).

The range of 'electorates' falls into three groups. First are those where IO leaders are appointed, whether it is the World Bank with its one elector, the US President, or the IMF after a European consultation. Second is the managed development of consensus at the WTO. Third is the process of election, whether at a restricted committee, such as the WHO's Executive Board (EB) with thirty-two members or WIPO's Coordination Committee with eighty-three, or at an open ballot at the FAO, where each member has one vote: a tiny Pacific island has the same vote as China (with the largest population) or the

---

[12] Kahler, *Leadership Selection in the Major Multinationals*, 18.
[13] Kahler, *Leadership Selection in the Major Multinationals*, 80–1 n.
[14] Kahler, *Leadership Selection in the Major Multinationals*, 93.
[15] David Peretz, 'The Process for Selecting and Appointing the Managing Director and First Deputy Managing Director of the IMF,' Backgrounder, IEO, IMF, BP/07/01 (2007), 5–6.
[16] David Peretz, 'The Process for Selecting and Appointing the Managing Director and First Deputy Managing Director of the IMF', Backgrounder, IEO, IMF, BP/07/01 (2007), 5.

Table 3.1. Modes of IO leadership (s)election

Institution	Method of (s)election	No. of leaders since creation	No. who served eight years or more
FAO 1945–	Elected by full membership: one member, one vote	8	4
IMF 1946–	Nominated by EU countries, endorsed by Executive Board	11	3
WHO (1948–2017)[a]	Ballot of Executive Board, formally elected by World Health Assembly	7	3
WIPO 1967–	Nominated by Coordination Committee after a ballot and formally elected by General Assembly	4	2
World Bank 1946–	Nominated by US President, endorsed by Executive Board	12	3
WTO 1995[b]	'Selected' by all members through a rolling process of consensus	6	1

[a] Under the election process for the WHO Director General 2017, the Executive Board will nominate three candidates to go forward to the World Health Assembly for a vote to become the new DG.
[b] The GATT had just three DGs between 1948 and 1993. The last GATT DG, Peter Sutherland, was appointed in 1993 and also served as the first WTO DG until 1995.

USA (with the largest economy). We will deal with each group in turn, before considering how the process shapes the powers, legitimacy, and accountability of the heads of the various IOs.

Appointed Leaders (World Bank and IMF)

The president of the World Bank is appointed by the US President and approved by the EB. That is a historical compromise, the outcome of a 'gentleman's agreement' struck at the 1944 Bretton Woods conference establishing the IMF and the World Bank. At the time the USA insisted that the World Bank should be headed by an American, not only because the USA was the largest contributor, but also because the World Bank lending would depend on American financial markets. Since the USA could not head both institutions, the Europeans would choose the IMF MD. Formally the EB makes the decision; in practice, it has always accepted the nominee proposed by the US executive director. The process of appointment means that there is never an open campaign for the job, although James Wolfensohn had energetically pushed his case; he was reputedly McNamara's choice to succeed him in 1981. Often the selection is a surprise: Barber Conable was a former Republican congressman; Paul Wolfowitz was US Deputy Secretary of Defense. A key point is that, as the position does not require Senate endorsement, the President has a free choice from any background. After all, the

World Bank president does not represent the United States (in contrast, the US executive director to the Bank does need Senate confirmation). There is always extensive speculation about who is being considered; some, such as Obama's choice of Jim Yong Kim in 2012, are complete outsiders.

Some concessions have been made to the membership of the EB. The EB may now interview the nominees, asking them about their views. Alternative names will be bruited in the press; in 2012 they included a number of people with experience as ministers of finance, some of whom had experience in the World Bank as MDs (the second level of management in the Bank below the president). Up until 2017 no US nominee has been opposed in the EB. Whether this US monopoly is sustainable is often questioned. Obama, in appointing a Korean American academic, went some way to recognizing the need for alternative views, but without ceding his right to make the selection. In 2016, more than a year before his term was due to end, Jim Kim lobbied the Obama administration to put him up for the second term ahead of time in case Trump won the presidential election later in the year. He got it.

The line of accountability is clear: World Bank presidents are dependent for a second term on the White House. If they can maintain the confidence there, primarily at the time their reappointment is due, they do not need another source of support. On the other hand, if they are to run the Bank effectively in the intervening periods, they need the support of the other state members, the EB and the secretariat.

The IMF MD is also formally appointed by its EB; the nomination actually comes from Europe. Consequently, there has to be a degree of internal negotiation between the leading European countries. Of the six MDs since 1976, four came from France and one each from Germany and Spain. Competition was often intense. The European prerogative is not untrammelled. When the proposal was to nominate Caio Koch-Weser, a German former MD at the World Bank, there was less than full support from other European countries. Eventually when the Americans objected to it, the nomination was withdrawn, although it would thereafter have been hard for the USA to oppose the next German nominee, Hans Kohler. In 2007, the EB heard presentations from German and Czech candidates before selecting Strauss-Kahn from France by consensus.

Though Europe may nominate, there remains a broader need for support than at the World Bank. There is too a growing demand that the candidate is widely acceptable as part of a rhetoric that the positions should be open to merit. In 2012, Nigeria and Columbia decided to challenge the American-dominated presidency at the World Bank and proposed their candidates. At the last minute, Columbia withdrew its candidate; Nigeria did not. While the US Treasury insisted that the United States continues its leadership role in the World Bank, President Obama had to justify his nomination of Jim Kim, a Korean–American who had worked from Asia to Africa to the Americas, to fend off challenges from some developing countries, and also a few developed ones. At the IMF, the European monopoly was also challenged. The Australian and Canadian governments nominated the head of the Mexican central bank for the position, with no expectation that he would win, just to make a point. The very fact that another candidate was formally nominated was intended as a message that the European monopoly might not go unchallenged at the next vacancy.

The Strauss-Kahn appointment also broke a pattern of preferring central bankers. An executive director noted: 'we moved into this world where now it was considered appropriate that we should have political managing directors, people with political ambitions or at least political backgrounds. I am not convinced that is ideal.' Of course, the MDs were always required to operate in the summits of political leaders; recent appointments suggest greater weight to this part of the role: less technical, more political and diplomatic.

A Managed Consensus Election (WTO)

Consensus is the working principle in nearly all activities at the WTO, hence the preferences for the 'selection', rather than an election, of its DG. At its predecessor, the GATT, continuity had ruled. The first English DG was there from 1948 to 1968. In the following twenty-five years until 1993, two Swiss trade officials, Oliver Long and Arthur Dunkel, were the DGs.

After the WTO had been created in 1995, member states took a more active role in selecting the DG. The chair of the General Council facilitated the process, assisted by the chairs of the Dispute Settlement Body and the Trade Policy Review Body. This 'troika' canvassed opinion among the members before reporting which of the candidates had the greatest level of support. The assumption was that the candidates without support would then withdraw. That required that the supporters of the unsuccessful candidates accepted the troika's calculations. It did not always happen, and the consequences were a cautionary tale that the WTO never wanted to replicate. In 1999 there was a deadlock, with members split between New Zealand's Mike Moore and Thailand's Supachai. A participant explained:

> Basically we don't actually vote as such in WTO. There is a series of informal processes and then the Chair of the General Council announces that based on the consultations so-and-so has got the least level of support and is least likely to attract consensus. So that person is expected to fall out. Eventually you end up with two, and in this case it was Supachai and Moore. The thing is they were virtually equal. Moore tried to claim that he had a little bit more, the Supachai supporters were very suspicious because it seemed that some countries were giving both candidates their vote.

Eventually the deadlock was broken; each candidate was given a 'half' term of three years. It was an unsatisfactory outcome. A veteran state ambassador explained: 'We got this wrong; so we decided to develop a set of formal procedures to avoid stalemate, which often takes a long time to settle.' The General Council did develop a consultative procedure by which the numbers would gradually be whittled down.[17] It still relied on goodwill and consensus via an elaborated process. Pascal Lamy was selected twice, the second time unopposed.

The question of a detailed job description for the DG was raised during Lamy's tenure, but never pursued. The ambassadors thought it would be too hard, not only because all major decisions require consensus support, but also because any duty statement would itself become open to interpretation, dependent on the circumstances and members' attitudes at the time. The belief was that it would reduce even more the necessary flexibility. How DGs operate, and with what authority, is effectively renegotiated by each new appointee and then adjusted as needed on the run.

It was hard to be specific about precise qualities. The complexity of the processes was explained by an experienced ambassador's musings on leadership; he illustrated the problem in developing an effective job description:

> The person himself does not define the candidacy. The candidacy is defined by perceptions and the perceptions vary from country to country... I think what people would like to see—and I'm giving you my personal view—is a director general who is a leader but someone who can build consensus. To lead, he has to know the system. He has to be credible. Members have to trust him. So at the same time, he must lead but not force. It's very tricky. It's a very thin line between leadership and imposition. So if he tries to impose, he's dead.

The 2013 election became another test of the process.[18] Long before the process had even started, we were repeatedly told by trade ambassadors from both developed and developing countries that the next DG would come from a developing country. The common argument was that, as Europeans and developed countries had dominated the position of the previous DGs, it was time for a DG from Africa or Latin America. Nine candidates were put forward by their governments: two from Africa, three from Asia, three from South or Central America, and only one, a New Zealander, from a developed country.

At the WTO, there is always a need to balance different types of support for a candidate. The troika started the facilitating process in January 2013. They held discussions with the General Council on the process and also decided on three tests: First, did candidates have a simple majority of member states;

---

[17] WTO, 'Procedures for the Appointment of Directors-General' (WT/L/509), 2 January 2003.
[18] This detailed account is based on interviews with several participants in the process.

second, did they have the majority support of countries weighted by their share of world trade; third, did they have a geographical spread of support from all geographical areas? Two procedural principles were agreed: there would be two rounds of elimination, and members would be asked for their choices, first five (out of the nine) and then two (out of the five), without being asked for, or needing to provide, reasons for their choices. Further, no negative votes or vetoes would be accepted. Again there was no way that the troika could enforce their recommendations; they had to rely on goodwill.

After nominations, the details of the candidates were circulated, and candidates all had the same opportunities to address the General Council. To ensure absolute fairness, presentations were timed to the minute, and the opportunity for members to ask questions was determined by lot. Candidates also faced a press conference; the transcripts were made public. Implementing strict rules was not easy. One chair recalled:

> I was here in 1999 and witnessed the trauma. So I made sure the process was fair for all for members and candidates. All of them except one tried to overstep the time, so I had to stop them, which I did. One candidate came back, complaining one had got three seconds more, because they had timed it too. Strict rules for member states when they asked questions—one minute each, no statement, no speeches. When some overstepped, I overruled them all. Of course, after the formal process, I also arranged lunches with those left-over candidates and concerned members so that they could talk in more detail. That was informal and I was not involved as a chair.

The troika then, always acting as a group and never individually, met all the 159 members, and asked each member to nominate their first 5 choices. Where members did not have delegates in Geneva, they arranged phone calls with their capital cities. Delegates handed in their selections but had no further conversation. This was approval voting, noting whom they supported without having to choose between them at this stage. On the basis of those consultations, the troika proposed that four candidates should drop out.

That left five—all experienced trade experts. Three were or had been ministers for trade. The other two were trade negotiators. A further round of consultations reduced the numbers to two: from Mexico and Brazil. The members were asked for a third time which candidate they preferred. Although the USA and other developed countries supported the Mexican, they also revealed that they had no objections to the Brazilian if he won support. The selection committee finally recommended the Brazilian, Roberto Azevêdo.

Of course, this brief outline does not cover the reality of the campaigning. Candidates had meetings with the ambassadors at the General Council in Geneva. They crisscrossed the globe to visit countries. The president of Brazil took the Brazilian candidate with her to Durban for the BRICS (Brazil, Russia, India, China and South Africa) summit to try to swing support for him from the other leaders (she got no commitment). Since governments nominate the candidates, they finance their campaigns too. That concerned ambassadors from the smaller countries, who pointed out there was a clear correlation between national GDPs and the order of elimination; only big countries, an ambassador argued, could afford the campaigns needed to win the selection.

The final decision would be based on country as much as individual personality. A candidate from a developed nation was never going to win. The only one, New Zealand's Minister of Trade, who had been a respected WTO ambassador, beat the first cut but did not make the last two. He came from the 'wrong' country.

By the end, the Brazilian had a degree of support across the system. The process settled on a person who was experienced—thirty years in trade negotiations, in Geneva as well as in the capital, and a reputation as an effective ambassador—and with widespread support even from those who did not vote for him. Such divisions as there were seemed to evaporate once his nomination had been announced. In that respect, the lengthy and elaborate process worked.

In neither the World Bank nor the IMF has its head had experience as a member of staff within the organization. After 1995, Kahler argued, the WTO had chosen to adopt this practice too; he argued that the fact that the WTO 'invariably chooses outsiders probably reflects a determination on the part of member governments to prevent collusion between top management and staff'.[19] Azevêdo's selection challenges this conclusion and is a reversion to the DGs under GATT, people deeply immersed in the trade networks. What made him different from his predecessors was that Azevêdo had not been a minister; he had been a civil servant.

He has been working in and around Geneva on trade issues for some time and had deep connections with member state representatives at the WTO and with the secretariat. Expertise, experience, and knowledge of working in the epistemic community were considered important for the job.

Openly Contested Elections (FAO, WIPO, WHO)

In the other three IOs, the election of leaders has a varying degree of openness. In the WHO and WIPO, the elections have been held in a committee that consists of some of the members. The WHO Constitution specifies that the Health Assembly shall 'appoint the Director General' (Article 18c). This responsibility was quickly delegated to the EB whose thirty-two 'persons' were initially to be appointed in a personal capacity and not as national

---

[19] Kahler, *Leadership Selection in the Major Multinationals*, 79.

delegates. By 2000 that distinction had largely disappeared, and they were certainly voting in line with decisions made in capitals. The member states on the EB were themselves selected from different groups of countries; so participation in the election just depended on whose turn it was within the constituency to serve on the EB. Nominally at least, the biggest donors might not have a vote when the DG is elected. In practice, there is extensive consultation.

The WIPO Convention specifies: 'The General Assembly shall appoint the Director General upon nomination by the Coordination Committee.' The membership of Coordination Committee is large (eighty-three in 2016) and they are all state representatives.

The FAO is the only IO among our selected IOs where all members vote in an open contest that includes anyone that a country chooses to nominate. Indeed, the process has been politicized since its early days. The formal selection procedure written in the FAO Constitution is not very different from that of many other IOs: 'The Director General of the Organization... shall be appointed by the Conference.' The 'appointment' has over the years become 'the culmination of a long, high-visibility political campaign to garner support'.[20]

In these three organizations, if a person wants to run, he or she must seek support from his or her home government; there can be no such thing as a private candidature. Where there are contests, they may become part of a broader calculation of national foreign policy, as votes may be traded from one contest to another and deals are often made among countries. Before candidates are able to run, they need to discover whether the conditions are right. Does their country have any other possible candidates? Has it already traded its votes, seeking support here in exchange for a commitment elsewhere in the future? A vote in an IO election, for instance, can be traded for a vote for a position on the Security Council. This form of bartering may be particularly common in Geneva, where there are multiple IOs, mostly represented by a single national office of a group of generalist diplomats who work across IOs, than it is among the more limited number of organizations in Rome. None can be totally isolated from these expressions of national interest.

Some countries choose not to put their nationals into these elections: the United States, for instance, normally does not actively seek to nominate its nationals for the DG position at IOs, as it has usually held a deputy position in most IOs and is able to exert sufficient influence without contesting the top job. China has become an active player in IOs only since the last 1990s. It did not seek leadership before then, but preferred to work within the organizations at the second or third levels (although it had a Hong Kong DG in the WHO,

---

[20] Weitz, *Who Speaks for the Hungry?*, 9.

one step removed). Others are regular contestants; Japan, France, and Brazil are the countries that most consistently provide candidates.

Because they are government nominees, the campaigns are run by governments, both in Rome and Geneva and across the world. Some countries run better campaigns than others; some commit more resources than others too. Candidates meet both representatives of member states to IOs and sometimes relevant government officials too. In Geneva, for example, the mission to the UN agencies of the candidate country will organize activities, and candidates will rush from mission to mission to put their case. They may fly around to the capitals of the more significant countries. The larger the constituency is, the more politicized the process has become, as diplomatic manoeuvre drives the calculations. A country may be happy for a candidate to run with its blessing but not with any substantial resources to fund the campaign. Candidates from a few countries, with the support of their governments, are known to make promises to individual member states—for example, that, in exchange for votes, they will receive more aid in various forms; these promises are described as the 'dowry' candidates bring to the job. One candidate was asked: 'What can you do for us, as your rival candidate has already promised to build an electricity grid for our cities?' The candidate reported: 'I said, "Nothing. I cannot even get my government to pay for my airfares, let alone give you an electricity grid".' It is not uncommon to trade votes with various types of assistance, and 'some governments spend a lot of money backing up their candidates.'

The decisions of how a country will vote in elections are invariably made in the capitals. There are clearly advantages if the candidates are known within the relevant community. In countries that lack depth of expertise, and where the IO may appear less relevant, their representatives at the IOs will make recommendations about the choice of candidates, and even the strategy that can be adopted in the process of election. Elections are not just about the calibre of the individuals.

In the WHO, the EB has thirty-two members. In the three contested elections since 1998, only one outsider, Gro Brundtland, a former Prime Minister of Norway, has won; at the time there was extensive disillusion among member states and the staff with the performance of the WHO and a desire for sweeping reform.[21] After Brundtland chose not to stand for a second term, there was a tight contest to replace her. The number of candidates was finally reduced from nine to two: Dr Lee Jong-wook, a veteran at the WHO for twenty years, who had held various positions including regional director, and Peter Piot, the director of the UNAIDS programme. The EB was split 16–16 for three ballots; then one country switched and Lee won 17–15.

---

[21] Andresen, *Leadership Change in the World Health Organization*, 15.

It was reported that Dr Lee had received 'considerable financial help' to run his campaign. 'There were fears that Lee lacked the necessary political skills, but he showed political acumen in persuading 53 members of the US Congress to write to the Secretary of State, Colin Powell, and to Tommy Thompson, the US Health Secretary, backing his candidacy.'[22] When Lee died suddenly, an acting DG was appointed while another contest was held. This time the preferred choice had wider support: Margaret Chan, then an ADG and before that director of health services in Hong Kong during the SARS epidemic. Two consecutive DGs from Asian countries did not become a political issue until after the election. This eventually triggered discussion whether there should be a geographical rotation of DGs and whether more than one candidate should be forwarded by the EB for the World Health Assembly to consider.

At WIPO, there were only two DGs between 1973 and 2008, both former staff members. Arpad Bogsch, Hungarian–American, had served for twenty-four years from 1973 and Kamil Idris, from Sudan, since 1997. Idris had been re-elected without a contest twice. He had long fallen out of favour with the developed countries, but they had not been prepared to run an alternative candidate who might not win. He was finally 'persuaded' to stand down early after a series of scandals including evidence he had declared an incorrect date of birth. In 2008, nine candidates entered the race to replace Idris. Four of them were internal. The electoral process was simply a series of ballots until one person won a majority of the eight-one members of the Coordination Committee. There was an extensive campaign. Some candidates were well funded by their governments. Much of the campaigning was about second preferences. If the preferred candidate was eliminated in an early ballot, could you consider us next? By the time the Coordination Committee met, no one knew who would win. It was seen as too close. The ballots were run in rapid order. There was little chance to gain further instructions from capitals if the voting had not worked out as anticipated.

The process turned out to be fairly swift. A number of candidates dropped out after the first round. The candidates were soon reduced to three, and then to two. The Australian, Francis Gurry, a deputy director general (DDG), eventually beat the Brazilian, a director, by forty-one votes to forty. That was not the last stage. The outcome of the Coordination Committee ballot became a recommendation to the General Assembly. There was concern that Brazil might try to reopen the ballot there, so over the next few months the winning team sought to elicit expressions of support for their candidate from a wide variety of countries. In the event the General Assembly followed tradition and accepted the recommendation of the Coordination Committee.

---

[22] Paul Benkimoun, 'How Lee Jong-wook Changed WHO', *Lancet*, 367 (2006), 1806.

In the FAO, after eighteen years as the DG, Edouard Saouma (Lebanon) decided to retire in 1993. Eight candidates put their hand up for the position. After four ballots, the number of candidates was reduced to three. The two candidates from developing countries (Chile and Senegal) agreed that whoever was eliminated would direct their preferences to the other. When nineteen of the Chilean's thirty-one supporters duly voted for Jacques Diouf (Senegal), he finally won on the preferences.

Diouf was subsequently re-elected twice. At the time of his second re-election, there was widespread dissatisfaction with the performance of the FAO, particularly among developed countries. Diouf meanwhile had already shored up his support among the G77 and African members. The Indian representative sounded out the American ambassador about support for an Indian candidate; he feared that another Diouf term might results in the 'benign neglect (or worse) of FAO by major donors'. The US ambassador thought the proposition was welcome but tardy, as Diouf had already locked in enough support to win. He argued that 'anything less than a gung-ho candidate with money, energy, time, organization and full national support is not going to make the grade'. No one wanted to propose a candidate unless there was 'some assurance of a successful outcome'. There was not in this case, so no candidate was put forward to run.[23] There was instead widespread abstention in the vote of the conference that re-appointed Diouf, almost equal to the numbers of developed candidates. In a system of one state one vote, the position of donors was weaker, and disengagement was a preferred strategy to running a forlorn hope.

In 2011, there was a field of six candidates but just two ballots. José Graziano da Silva from Brazil won by ninety-two to eighty-eight over a former Spanish foreign minister in a battle that was interpreted as a contest between developed and developing countries and their different views of the FAO's proper roles. He was re-elected unopposed in 2016.

Increasingly active participation of member states in elections has put pressure on the old procedures for choosing leaders. This tension is reflected in the debates about the geographical rotation of IO heads. Regions expect their turn. An irony often escapes the member states that, while insisting candidates for the head of IOs be 'international', they expect geographical rotation of these IO leaders. These issues came to the fore in the WHO when dissatisfaction with existing processes erupted in 2012–13. The debate there can serve as an illustration of the tensions.[24]

---

[23] Cable sent by Ambassador Tony P. Hall to the State Department on FAO Director General Election, 28 July 2004, made public through Wikileaks.

[24] For the debate, see WHO, 'Election of the Director-General of the World Health Organization: Report of the Working Group', A65/38, 3 May 2012; 'Follow-up on the Report of the Working Group on the Election of the Director-General of the World Health Organization', EB134/43, 10 January 2014, and related documents.

A delegate from a developing country tells the story that touches on all the sensitive issues for leader elections: regional turns, participation, and equal opportunity:

> In May 2010 the African group surprised everybody with a draft resolution on the election of directors general through which the rotation among regions would be established. So if today the director general is from Asia, the next director general couldn't be from Asia. He/she would come from Africa for instance... they felt that Africa had never had an opportunity.

These concerns triggered a whole serious of 'very difficult debates', explained one senior official. The perception was that

> the process was skewed in favour of some regions and against others, in particular the Africa region, the eastern Mediterranean region and to a lesser extent the south-east Asia region. They protested that in sixty and more years, no directors-general came from their regions and thus the system was unfair and unjust because of the difference in power and money and so on. The only way to make it fairer is to rotate the post of director general amongst regions.

According to a senior official at WHO:

> They [the African group] suddenly said, 'enough is enough; we want to go with the principle of geographical rotation; and we want a clear decision from the World Health Assembly now and would think of the detail later'. They then put forward the draft proposal on the regional rotation of director general. This precipitated a procedure of mayhem that lasted for two days. It was very bruising for everybody, myself included.

A state representative confirmed it:

> The atmosphere was very tense; there was a lot of distrust. Canada took the initiative of preparing amendments to that draft resolution, stating that the criteria should be the competence, the quality of the candidate. Of course, if you can also consider the rotation, great, but the rotation shouldn't be the first criteria. Then, there was another argument that it is nice to talk about the level playing field, but in practice it's very difficult when you have countries that have so much power, so many resources, against others who don't have any power, don't have any resources. This is where the suggestion of a candidates' forum so that all candidates can meet all members here in Geneva was proposed. Another issue was that electing DGs should be a universal decision, that is, it should be the Assembly to decide who the director general will be, not just rubber stamp the decision of the EB. This was very difficult partly because people are always resistant to change, but also because some felt that by changing this, we would disempower the EB.

Out of these difficult discussions came 'another attempt through a working group at the board to come to an agreement on a revised process', explained a senior official. 'That working group was successful and the outcome was adopted by the board that revised the election procedure and introduced three candidates for the World Health Assembly to vote on.'

One concern was that an open vote at the World Health Assembly would politicize the process. One representative commented:

> We are not against politics, we think it is fine. We have no difficulty with that; people go, oh! Don't politicize this; don't politicize that; we think that everything is politics and even the absence of politics is politics. So we shouldn't talk about politics as being a negative thing or a bad thing, it is part of life and we should deal with that in the best way possible.

For some WHO officials, this was a painful experience too because the debate was not only about procedural issues, but also about politics:

> we are the first international organization as far as I know to have a code of conduct that has just been part of the resolution, a part of the package. It's not binding obviously, but it's like a political statement of good conduct, of good practices, in the overall process of election. In particular the process is not regulated and is not regulatory, regulatable—if that word exists—by the World Health Assembly.

In 2016, the procedure was thus set in motion to elect the next DG to replace Chan: greater involvement and a process where every member state, regardless of size, has a single vote. In March 2017, three names were forwarded by the EB to the Health Assembly for a vote on the new leader.

Rewarding Leaders

Reappointment of DGs to second terms has become a common practice. Once they have stood for election, candidates for the position have become politicians, even if by background they may have had a long career as technical experts. At its most fundamental is a political reality, as an official observed:

> He has to get elected. He had to get elected before. When you do that, you make promises to people. It's a patronage system, but it's not acknowledged as such. That creates an enormous amount of tension and resentment within the house.

DGs have both debts to those who elected them and often a need to be concerned about their re-election. When a DG is elected with a very small margin, he or she faces serious challenges in gaining a broader legitimacy among member states and, sometimes, among its staff too. Sometimes the scars take time to disappear. At WIPO, Gurry had to face a disgruntled section of the secretariat, based in the Staff Association, throughout his first term; they had wanted a different outcome in the election. In the early years, DGs sometimes effectively sought to nominate their successor; as one WHO official noted, if they tried to do so now, 'all hell would break loose because there is a much stronger sense that the member states own WHO'.

In the search for re-election, incumbents had advantages. Not only were they well known, they could constantly tout for votes. One FAO official recalls a flight from New Zealand with a DG for a lunch at a Pacific Island ministerial agricultural conference; he wondered why the DG was bothering, until he realized there were a number of votes around the table appreciating the attention. The DG could make commitments from his discretionary fund—they were very small countries and thus easily satisfied—and leave after lunch with their votes locked in. Most DGs are constantly on the move; their role is to sell the organization to national leaders, to ensure it still has support and funding. In so doing, they will often bolster their own position. If they were effectively immune from action by the principal donors, the ability to behave as though beyond accountability is perhaps not a surprise.

Lack of opposition can make leaders autocratic; the Independent External Evaluation (IEE) of the FAO noted that the DG, Edouard Saouma, 'took autocracy to exceptionally high levels'.[25] The response in the agencies where DGs are elected was to introduce term limits rather than try to blast out an embedded incumbent. Each DG could serve no more than two terms (of four, five, or six years). Even if reappointment for the second term often seems a formality, there was at least a final date on which unsuccessful leaders would depart.

Even so, re-election shapes in part how DGs and the organizations work, and what priorities are adopted. One official explained what happened at the FAO when José Graziano was elected as its DG:

> He's got a shortened term. In 2015, he has to get re-elected. He had to keep people happy. He had made a bunch of promises to a bunch of countries in order just to get elected. He's got to deliver on a proportion of whatever promises he made, unknown to us, and he has to get ready to be re-elected again very quickly. That's a very different set of circumstances from a head of a company who might be required to report to the evaluation committee of the board, or a small number of individuals who have got the job of evaluating the performance of IO leaders and setting their remuneration or making a recommendation to the board. It's an inherently political process and it's a flawed process in terms of managing a modern organization.

That range of commitments and promises can permeate much of what they will have to do, from promising to open country offices to financing an agricultural museum.

---

[25] David Hallam, 'Turbulence and Reform at the United Nations Food and Agriculture Organization', in Patrick Weller and Xu Yi-chong (eds), *The Politics of International Organizations: Views from Insiders* (New York: Routledge, 2015), 203.

Usually, therefore, DGs get reappointed without challenge. In a rare exception, Francis Gurry's re-election in 2015 was contested; he won easily on the first ballot. Most of the time member states do not want to go through the trauma of a contested election, and, as long as the DGs have done nothing to appal the member states, they can be assured of a second term. So, at the WTO, Pascal Lamy and Roberto Azevêdo were reappointed; as was Margaret Chan at the WHO, and José Graziano at the FAO, even though in the last case the original margin of victory had been minuscule.

When leaders are not elected by member states, their relationship with members is very different. Leaders of the World Bank and the IMF are both 'imposed' on the organizations. Whether this USA–Europe agreement is sustainable is debatable. The impact, however, of the existing process means that the heads of the two organizations have a different relationship with their members and EBs from those of other IO leaders. They do not depend for their position on the continuing good favours of member states. Although the president of the World Bank chairs the EB, he may delegate that task. The EB does not dominate the life of leaders. They look elsewhere if they want reappointment.

IO leaders are hard to shift, not least because of the authority that appointed them in the first place. Often the big powers, disillusioned with their performance, have more significant priorities. It is better to let their term drift on. A spectacular exception was the departure of Wolfowitz from the World Bank. Opposition to Wolfowitz came in part from the staff; there was a public letter of condemnation signed by a wide array of country directors. That of itself would have had no impact except on internal relations. When executive directors started an investigation into accusations that he had given special treatment to his partner, it became both trigger and excuse. The edifice crumbled, and he left under agreed terms. When Wolfowitz was under attack in the World Bank, primarily from European executive directors, the UK did not join the push. For Blair, said one close observer, it was not worth expending political capital or undermining his relationship with Bush, who had appointed Wolfowitz. It was enough, observers said, that the UK executive director did not actively support the Bank president. In the bigger scheme of capital cities, the presidency of the Bank was not that important.

That calculation was even more applicable in the smaller IOs such as WIPO and the FAO; the lack of challenge to long-term DGs was not a sign of satisfaction, rather a calculation of the costs of moving against an incumbent, and particularly ones that could rely on a phalanx of grateful smaller or developing countries. Put simply, it was not worth the effort.

This analysis of leadership selection processes suggests one counter-intuitive consequence. The more open the electoral system and the broader the electorate, the more restricted the pool of candidates is likely to be. Those nominated will usually be members of the existing epistemic network grouped around the subjects. They can more easily illustrate that they have the technical expertise and they will know the country experts, whether in the capital cities or in the local national missions. By contrast, when IO leaders are 'selected', they are usually chosen for their experience and record in other environments in the hope that their success elsewhere can be replicated in the IO. Thus, when the process is restricted, insiders never win; when it is open, outsiders rarely do.

LEADING INTERNATIONAL ORGANIZATIONS

The treaties or articles of agreements that created IOs often say little about the way DGs should work or about their responsibilities. As Pascal Lamy put it: 'there is no job description for this job'.

As the formal rules tell us little about the potential powers of the leaders, we need to understand how the politics works. The terms of agreement that establish the organizations say no more than that a president or DG will be appointed and be responsible for the management of the secretariat. There were good reasons for the lack of detail when IOs were being created, not least an awareness that quite how the organizations would work was yet to be appreciated. The scope for action is left to the players to define, within a framework of explicit agreement and implicit expectations. As the levers of influence are contested, and as some leaders show greater skill and aptitude than others, so their influence changes within the same organization, and even within the term of a single leader. The leaders in different organizations have over time followed diverging paths. The rules do not change; expectations and influence within those rules do.

That scope will depend on the political position of the heads of IOs: on the process by which they were chosen, on the degree of discretion members are prepared to cede, on their own personal and institutional ambitions, and, most importantly, on their ability to act as an effective politician, diplomat, and manager. It can never be decisively formulated. The questions we therefore seek to illustrate are how the influence of leaders may vary over time within a single organization and why they differ between organizations: what are the features that either empower or restrict the leaders?

The leaders of all IOs have a number of roles they must fulfil.

- As diplomats, they must represent the IO in diplomatic forums, interact with heads of government, and 'sell' the mission of their organization to the international community.
- As politicians, they must work with member states, whether representatives in national capitals or ambassadors and delegates on the spot, to ensure that some progress is made in fulfilling the tasks of the IO.

- As managers, they must manage diverse multilateral organizations that are often dispersed round the globe and with staff drawn from different cultures and traditions.

Of course, these roles are not distinct. Leaders are conscious of each of them all the time. However, the categorization does allow us to consider each role and explore how the leaders work, what options and strategies they can use, and how their roles vary from organization to organization.

The managerial role in all cases is clear. All IOs grant their leaders the responsibility to appoint and manage the secretariats. Any other influence depends on their skill in trying to guide members and facilitate agreements between them. They usually have to do so with tact and finesse. It is soft power, exercises in diplomacy, not formal authority.

Diplomatic Role

IO leaders are expected not only to lead but also to represent the institutions. There are four distinct functions:

- to persuade national leaders of their case, as a means of getting the necessary political support; that includes attending international summits and gaining support from key states;
- to attract the attention of international and economic communities to generate both the legitimacy needed for their cause and the financial resources to carry them out; increasingly the latter come from private foundations or through dedicated donor funds;
- to work with peers in other IOs and in the UN;
- to work with the broader community.

The heads of the World Bank, the IMF, and the WTO attend meetings of the G8 and G20, where they have access to the world leaders and are expected to advance 'noble' causes that countries often support yet are reluctant to fund. So they must manage multilayered, multinational networks to achieve their objectives. Lamy's appeal to the G20 for a standstill on protectionist measures was his own initiative as DG of the WTO; it was not a proposal that had been considered by the General Council. He was able to persuade the G20 to issue a proclamation warning against the dangers of a revival of protectionism.

A FAO officer explained why this was important.

> Our former DG attended the summit last year, and I do not remember whether he made a statement or not, but he attended. This year, I tried to get us invited to the summit and had done a lot of work on it. The summit would be attended by the relevant ministers from G20 and people from UNCTAD, World Bank, OECD, IMF, WTO, etc. It was difficult to figure out where the former DG

stood on a particular issue, but he was acutely political. The current DG knows exactly what he thinks on specific issues. He has also got strong political views, but he is a bad politician. He does not realize that what we are doing here is not about specific issues, but to have an opportunity to tell Obama, Putin, all the rest, what we think about these issues and what they should do about them.

Many ambassadors to the WTO acknowledged their DG's ability to talk in those forums but argued it did not actually cut through knots. One ambassador's reaction was dismissive.

Well, normally these conversations in summits are very brief. The ministers don't sit down and discuss the issues with the DG. They give him five minutes and ask what he thinks about world trade. They listen. 'Oh thank you very much. Bye.' That's it. The DG then issues a report. The press uses that report and says that the DG said this and that. They make a lot of hype but it doesn't change much of what we do here. In fact, I get instructions from the same minister: the one who talked to the DG. The DG may say G20 reached decisions on this or that. I get the same instructions, regardless of the ground-breaking statements that they made in the G20, because they're all subject to interpretation. It's like this standstill. Nobody is going to introduce protectionist measures, etc., etc.! Everybody does it all the time. People say that; they don't really do it.

Whether by addressing the G20 Lamy was able to reduce the reluctance of any individual states to negotiate seriously on the Doha agenda was questioned. Some ambassadors resented his attempt to bypass them; they had disliked the way that Peter Sutherland as DG had bypassed them to close the Uruguay Round. They were determined to circumscribe the role of the DG,[26] insisting that whatever general statements were made at summits they would await altered instructions from the capitals before they changed their position. This access is selective; the heads of the WTO, the World Bank, and the IMF were there on most occasions; the DG of the FAO had to negotiate attendance; all were there as a matter of grace.

There is always the dilemma. Many IO leaders are international personalities, formerly senior politicians or diplomats who do know the leaders. They may have ready access. When Peter Sutherland was leading the GATT in the final negotiations of the Uruguay Round, he worked closely with senior US officials[27] and did on occasion, when threatened by a senior businessman, ring President Clinton to deflect the criticism; Clinton returned the calls. Lamy had worked with European leaders when at the EU. Zoellick had been the Trade Representative for the USA. These IO leaders were not bluffing; they could contact national leaders. One DG, when asked whether he talked to

---

[26] Stuart Harbinson, 'The World Trade Organization as an Institution', in Weller and Xu (eds.) *The Politics of International Organizations*, 27.

[27] Craig VanGrasstek, *The History and Future of the World Trade Organization* (Geneva: WTO, 2013), 59–63.

national capitals, answered: 'Of course I do, but they [the ambassadors] hate it.' DGs also need to be conscious of their limitations; as one WTO official commented, Ruggiero 'had one thing right, which is you can't back the US into a corner, you've got to keep the US onside'.

The attention from national leaders on issues troubling an IO, at the G20 or on the end of the phone, is likely to be limited. National leaders sign off on declarations and make promises to push items through domestically. Their attention nonetheless was often fleeting; there are usually more pressing demands on their time.

IO leaders are often on the move. In part, they enjoy the accolades; it is also an essential role to communicate with national ministers. Who will see them in capitals? The more senior the national leaders to whom DGs have access, the greater is the scope for influence. It is a sign of the priority that the country gives to the issue. The presidents of the World Bank or the MD of the IMF sometimes see prime ministers, at least as a formality. They definitely can meet their governors—ministers of finance or treasurers, always senior members of national government. By contrast, DGs of the FAO will meet a minister of agriculture, always some way down in the orders of precedence and less able to drive proposals through a national government. In the case of WIPO, who is seen will reflect the interest that country has in intellectual property.

On occasions, leaders of IOs are also expected to mediate conflicts among states or align the support from NGOs. It becomes a particular problem when the IO is exercising independent power in the face of national challenges: the WHO's advice on travel arrangements during the SARS epidemic is one example. The DG had to insist on her right to tell it as it was; later she had to face the complaints from some members who felt that the IO had exceeded its remit and should have been more sensitive to national domestic interests.

Direct connections can help DGs on bilateral issues that do not necessarily cover the full membership. They can contact key actors. On important matters, the IMF MD can contact the Secretary of Treasury directly and IMF senior officials also keep direct contact with senior officials at the US Treasury. When big issues arise at the IMF, they are soon discussed at levels that are way beyond the ED's pay grade.[28] This may in part explain why one of the US positions (executive director or alternate) is often vacant; it is not really needed in the way that executive directors for other countries are.

One of the key capacities is to be able to communicate his or her mission to the international community in general. If a leader cannot explain his or her mission clearly and succinctly to the public, it is a lost cause even before it has been launched. While the WHO's DG Hiroshi Nakajima could present his 'holistic, dynamic model of health', a commentator argued that 'even

---

[28] Randall W. Stone, *Controlling Institutions: International Organizations and the Global Economy* (New York: Cambridge University Press, 2011).

Dr Nakajima's most dedicated staff acknowledge that his severe difficulties in communicating are a major handicap for a United Nations leader'.[29] Others are diligent in being the 'voice' of their organization. Lamy's 200 plus media interviews in a year were all about explaining the role and benefits of the WTO to a wider world.

Heads of IOs may tread the world stage with national leaders, commune with ministers, and speak on behalf of their organization and its interests. Occasionally, just occasionally, those connections may turn out to be crucial in shaping an agreement. In bilateral discussions, as Paulson's story shows,[30] a DG may act as an effective intermediary. For the regular activities of IOs—the IMF's surveillance, the World Bank's projects, WIPO's treaties, the WHO's aid in epidemics—the bulk of the work is undertaken at official level. Effective diplomacy can strengthen any DG's hand; it is a necessary, if not by itself a sufficient, condition for success in achieving an IO's ambitions.

Political Role

There is little direction in the treaty agreements for determining the relationship between DGs and the member states they serve. There are some minor variations from one IO to another.

> At the World Bank: 'The President shall be Chairman of the Executive Directors, shall have no vote except a deciding vote in case of an equal division. He may participate in meetings of the Board of Governors, but shall not vote at such meetings.' (IBRD Articles of Agreements, Article V, section 5, paragraph (b))

> At the FAO: 'The Director-General or a representative designated by him shall participate, without the right to vote, in all meetings of the Conference and of its Executive Committee and shall formulate for consideration by the Conference and the Executive Committee proposals for appropriate action in regard to matters coming before them.' (FAO Constitution, Article VII, paragraph 5)

After having enjoyed the glare of a G20, IO leaders have to return to the routine interaction with the executive directors and national ambassadors, back to the constant process of negotiation with a group of people who are, within their own political systems, middle-ranking diplomats but who within the IOs regard themselves as the master of the IO and its leaders.

---

[29] Fiona Godlee, 'The World Health Organization: WHO in Crisis', *BMJ* 309 (1994), 1424; see also Fiona Godlee 'The WHO: Interview with the Director General', *BMJ* 310 (1995), 583–6; Fiona Godlee, 'WHO Director General Faces Leadership Challenge', *BMJ* 314 (1997), 993.

[30] See Chapter 5.

It has always been a process of negotiation. At the World Bank, one early step underpins the president's influence in the EB. The second World Bank president, John McCloy, accepted the position only after it had been agreed that all the initiatives to be considered by the EB would originate with the president and the secretariat, thus giving presidents a monopoly in terms of selecting and developing proposals. This agreement, nonetheless, was never accompanied by a change in the rules.[31] Such understandings shape the exercise of influence by leaders; they are based on the traditions, not the rules, of the agencies. In theory, at least, they can be contested. Most of what DGs do now has been developed, negotiated, or finessed in practice, rather than stated in formal terms.

An observer of leaders at the IMF and the World Bank compared styles. Strauss-Kahn, he argued, was better able than Jim [Wolfensohn] 'at managing his frustration with us middle-ranked bureaucrats' who constituted the EB. Ruggiero, the WTO DG, his staff recall, would be great company on the road, where he was welcomed by national leaders, but became glum as the plane began its descent into Geneva. He complained: 'When I go to Paris or I go to Washington I see Prime Ministers and Presidents. When I'm in Geneva I have to ask permission to go to the toilet, and the members say, "Yes, but only two minutes!"'[32] There is always a level of suspicion. Faced with a perverse motion in the World Health Assembly, Margaret Chan burst out in frustration: 'I have ten seat belts on me and I can't move an inch; the bottom line is that the membership does not trust the secretariat.' (A Brazilian delegate sang back a tune from Evita: 'You know we have always loved you.') However, the tensions were clear.

Leaders of IOs must be in a process of constant negotiation with the representatives of member states who officially decide what the IO will do. Yet, unlike domestic politics, where the head of any national organization will be accountable to a single minister, the IO leader must answer to 150 or more members, of unequal power and size, with varying interests and commitment to the IO, and often with very different opinions about what the IO should do. The members may be organized into a series of blocs, sometimes with overlapping memberships. The constellations of support for IO action may change from topic to topic. At worst it can lead to constant gridlock; at best the situation requires a skilled negotiator to identify the common ground and to assist the members to reach it. In this sense, the leader of an IO must be a politician, a builder of coalitions, a conciliator, and a councillor. While working in a non-hierarchical system, DGs must be able to rally members

---

[31] Edward S. Mason and Robert E. Asher, *The World Bank since Bretton Woods* (Washington: Brookings Institution Press, 1973); Jochen Kraske, *Bankers with a Mission* (Washington: World Bank, 1996).

[32] VanGrasstek, *The History and Future of the World Trade Organization*, 506.

behind their policies, agenda, and strategies. This requires them to have the political skills to work with those who share their ambitions as well as those who hold different ideological beliefs, and with both those from like-minded countries and those from quite different political and cultural backgrounds. They often have to assimilate contradictory demands and ambitions. They have to work within the existing arrangements, often 'a political architecture that corresponded to an economic reality of the 1970s rather than now'.

They work with small groups to develop trust and support. One official bemoaned the difficulty of gaining agreement: 'There are too many moving parts and parts that you're not even aware of, so it would be very hard. From our DG's perch, he can do a fair amount. Part of his strategy that has worked pretty well is calling in ambassadors for lunches and talking to them about these very fundamental issues.' Close connections with some delegates, and working with the chairs of the significant committees, allow DGs to build up the personal and institutional links that they require to start building a consensus. One DG commented that 'this week I have visited the Brazilian ambassador, the Egyptian ambassador, and the Algerian ambassador. I did this deliberately because I was campaigning for a meeting to get a result.'

All IOs involve negotiations that face stalemate from time to time. This should neither surprise the chief officers nor frustrate them, because, as one DDG explains:

> as a director general, you have to have a sense when it is my opportunity actually to do something and when it is not; when a director general sees himself more than just a kind of a good officer, a mediator, but acts as an active participant, this can really rub some members the wrong way, no matter how critical the conclusion of the negotiation is.

The skill is acting proactively while not being seen as pushing for an agenda. The member states want DGs who are leaders; they are not sure they want them to lead. One DG noted: 'It's a job of influence and they sometimes lend you an authority while making it clear that it is on lease, not given.'

At the WHO, Chan's style was deliberately low key and consultative. An ADG mused:

> I am never quite sure how much of it is member states who want to involve themselves, how much is her involving them. Anything I do, she speaks about the member states. 'We will be directed by member states on this. On this we consult with member states. On this we make the decisions because it is internal.' She is very clear when she will take direction, when she feels she has received direction that she has to implement. She will never take for granted that she has an open mandate to do what she wants.

IO leaders have some institutional advantages. They will often determine the agenda that is discussed by the EB or governing committees. This arrangement may be official. The World Bank's EB has never rejected a proposal put by the president, although the governing committee at Singapore did send back Wolfowitz's anti-corruption strategy in 2006 for redrafting. Of course, the president is aware of what the board thinks and will not send to it any proposal that is unlikely to get its support. As the World Bank's MD Shengman Zhang advised Wolfensohn: 'The Board may not help you accomplish anything, but it can make it impossible for you to achieve anything.'[33] It needed to be adequately managed. Another World Bank official agreed:

> It was always important to try to convince a president that his best friends in a government, his most important allies, are really the executive directors because they are here all the time. Wolfensohn never quite understood that he could have a meeting with a minister and it would go just beautifully. Then, half hour later, he would encounter in the next board meeting an ED who essentially said to him that we are going to cut back on the budget and do these things, none of which were the issues that were raised by the minister. He never understood that ministers don't want, in their one brief encounter with Wolfensohn, to get into an argument with him. They turn around and tell their executive directors, now you chew him out on this and so on. Wolfensohn never quite understood that. He always thought it was something personal by the EDs. In Wolfensohn's early days he had real problems with the EB, because he came from the place where the Board was made up of people he had personally selected from his own friends. The idea of a Board of twenty-four people, who represent governments of all sorts that are not personally beholden to him, was very hard for him to understand.

Also at the WTO there was a level of frustration:

> Ruggiero, Lamy, and Supachai all say: 'I'm the director general of the WTO, when I travel I meet presidents, I meet prime ministers. Do I have to deal with these guys?' We used to say to them, 'you may not like these ambassadors, you may think they're just playing around half the time, but these are the guys who are writing the telegrams on a daily basis back to their capitals, and whether you like it or not, the capitals will look at you through the eyes of these ambassadors so you'd better get on side with them and start kind of using the network'. They didn't like it.

All leaders need to appreciate the different interests that those they meet represent. Ministers and state representatives may come from the same country but what they seek to gain from a meeting with a DG is determined in part by their position. Leaders must combine their activities as diplomat and politician to determine how best to reconcile these diverse stands and turn them to the benefit of the organization.

MDs at the IMF have their own vehicles for exerting influence. The MDs are always aware that they need to have heard views that represent opinions in

---

[33] Zhang, *One Step at a Time*, 27.

capitals, not just those of EDs. They can then provide the 'Summing Up', a statement at the end of the debate that has been written by the secretariat to represent the anticipated views of the member states; it acts as the decision document, providing the authority for action. Members can challenge the conclusions, but seldom do. The ability to chair and summarize puts influence in the MD's court.

Leaders of IOs have a number of more informal advantages. They have multiple 'principals' with diverse views. Some are more important than others. For a long time the QUAD (USA, EC, Canada, and Japan) was crucial in determining the outcomes of the GATT. The USA, as donor and principal shareholder, is the big player in the World Bank and the IMF, both situated down the road from the White House and the US Treasury. When the Board discusses items, the MD's advisers keep track of the balance of opinions and how they reflect the voting powers of the members. In other IOs the DG is often the one person in the room who knows where everyone stands on an issue. Often member states will trust the secretariats more than they will trust each other (even if they will never say so in public).

IO leaders can act as a broker of ideas. They will know what opinions are accurate, and whether these ideas are manageable or practical. They have access, in theory at least, to the institutional memory of their organizations, knowing what was done in the past. They must be, and be seen to be, constructively neutral between members. As an international civil servant, leaders cannot be identified with their nation of origin. Nor can they be seen as promoting the cause of any section of the members. While they retain that neutrality, they may be trusted by the members; if they lose that trust and are seen as advocates rather than brokers, their task is made all the harder. Thus, leaders must always pursue a balancing act. If they are not just the passive recipients of competing demands, they need to be able both to initiate and to react. It is easier to illustrate what goes wrong than what goes right.

One World Bank executive director gave an example:

> Everyone agrees that corruption is a bad thing and we need to deal with it, though there were many different views about how best to do that. He [Paul Wolfowitz] was at one end of the spectrum: a complete zero tolerance and cut off anybody or any country where there's corruption. You can go right the way down to the other end of the spectrum: the only way to improve things is to engage and that sometimes involves accepting standards that you don't like. It is a very difficult question, as there is no right answer. At the Board, by and large, people agreed with him that it was time for a review of the issue, but many also thought this was not where the centre of gravity of the shareholders was. The Board really struggled to influence him in trying to reach a consensus, but the tension between the management and the board was stronger over the time and it had become clear the organization did not operate properly, in addition to policy differences. On a Friday board meeting, we could not agree with him; he just announced: 'I am

going to call this meeting to an end and we do not have to have this conversation.' It was amazing, as I thought we were reaching a decision, but clearly it was not the decision he had wanted. He just ended the meeting. This was the time when finally a lot of tensions got out into the open that had been simmering.

Paul Wolfowitz, as the president of the World Bank, might have won the battle on this occasion; he quickly lost the war, as his agenda did not quite align with that of the Board or the staff. Boards may often be reactive; presidents still had to get their assessments of probable support right before they could develop policies that were of widespread interest.

In the WTO, the Doha Round had ground to a halt. Negotiations were stalled primarily because of an impasse between major players. Lamy wanted to get them moving and tried to present a draft on which members could work. There were precedents. In 1994 the Dunkel draft, presented by the then DG of GATT, Arthur Dunkel, had proved to be the catalyst for reigniting the negotiations and eventually bringing the Uruguay Round to a conclusion. His advantage then was that all major trading countries wanted to conclude the round and were prepared to make concessions. Not this time. An ambassador considered Lamy's role in trying to push ideas forward.

> If you need someone really to help us through, that's when you measure how good the DG is. Pascal [Lamy] was very useful in some moments. Even in 2008, he was very important. He was a very useful tool in trying to make things advance at that point in time. When we had that moment of impasse and talks essentially collapsed, from that point on, I think he got desperate, because he didn't see a way out. He tried forcefully to find this new path. In trying to do that, I think he disregarded sensitivities and he tried to push further than he should have. That's when he lost credibility with the major players. That's when, essentially, things got completely stuck. There is a very thin line between leadership and imposition. Members accepted his role as a leader, and resented when he tried too hard to broker some deals. He became too much of an alchemist, if you want to have my opinion. That's when he lost control and lost credibility.

Several ambassadors endorsed the view and also added that Lamy had overreached.

When Roberto Azevêdo was interviewed to be the DG of the WTO, he explained how he saw the DG's role in negotiations. He was a long-term trade expert and ambassador. So he spoke with experience of the perspective of member states and expressed an attitude as much as a process: his was an insider's view.

> When I've helped to unlock stalemates, I didn't know [what would emerge] until we started the conversations. Listening to the delegations: what is it that they are saying? What are the driving forces behind them? What did they do in similar situations in the past? Even at times, I know the negotiator's holding something back.

Even those things are helpful. And then after a lot of conversations, interactions, and dialogues, you begin to notice a little thread that is common to every position. At that point in time, if they trust you, and if they know that you are trying to achieve a balanced solution, a creative solution, a viable solution, they begin to listen to you and examine your proposals, a way out here and a way out there, and all of a sudden a solution that didn't exist before then materializes. Then people begin to engage and you have complete different dynamics and you may end up with a mutually satisfactory solution to everyone.[34]

A nudge here, a push there, an idea, a form of words: these are essential for a DG's role. It is about process. Meanwhile, when member states do not want to move for domestic reasons, the frustration throughout the WTO is evident.

The process can be difficult for DGs in any IO. 'What is frustrating in doing your job with no result is the size of the effort you have invested. All jobs have merits and purposes. The problem is when you do it or when you believe you do it properly and there is still no result.' Directors-generals can lead and persuade; the member states finally decide. In some IOs they will agree most of the time; in others the director-general role is much more contingent on a multiplicity of often unpredictable forces.

Managerial Role

The formal powers of IO leaders in terms of managing the organization are clear.

The World Bank: 'The President shall be chief of the operating staff of the Bank and shall conduct, under the direction of the Executive Directors, the ordinary business of the Bank. Subject to the general control of the Executive Directors, he shall be *responsible for the organization, appointment and dismissal of the officers and staff.*' (IBRD Articles of Agreements, Article V, section 5, paragraph (b))

The WTO: 'There shall be a Secretariat of the WTO (hereinafter referred to as "the Secretariat") headed by a Director General. The Director General shall *appoint the members of the staff of the Secretariat and determine their duties and conditions of service* in accordance with regulations adopted by the Ministerial Conference.' (WTO Articles of Agreement, Article VI, paragraphs 1–3)

The FAO: 'Subject to the general supervision of the Conference and its Executive Committee, the Director General shall have full power and authority to direct the work of the Organization.' (FAO Constitution, Article VI, paragraph 4)

---

[34] Roberto Azevêdo, press conference during the WTO DG selection processes.

To manage the organizations, which are diverse and sometimes decentralized and very large, IO leaders need help. They are able to get it from two groups. The first can be described as the 'political appointees', either those who assist the leader in the daily grind (the *cabinet*) or those senior officers who serve 'at the leader's pleasure'; they are the deputies and vice presidents (VPs)/ADGs. The second group are the tenured career secretariat staff that make the organizations work. Of course, the two groups are not absolutely distinct. Many VPs and ADGs were appointed from within the ranks to head divisions of the organizations and are career officials who have become institutionally less secure when promoted to higher ranks. In this subsection we first examine the contribution of the core support, the *cabinet* and deputies (with appropriate reference to VPs and line managers where they are relevant) and then consider those who deliver the IOs' services: the VPs, directors, and other programme staff in the secretariat. In each case we seek to identify the key links between these groups and their DGs in considering the support they can give to the DGs.

Assisting IO leaders. In immediate terms, help comes from their *cabinet* (in the French sense of the institution). It is generally a small team, headed by a chief of staff, who works for the DG and acts as a link between the DG and member states and between the director general and the secretariat.

The chiefs of staff often act as de facto DDGs and are important because they will range across the whole organization. Their interests reflect the DG's interests. They are usually experienced. In the WTO, Stuart Harbinson, a former chair of the General Council while serving as ambassador for Hong Kong, became chief of staff for DG Superchai. Lamy brought his *chef du cabinet* from Brussels; Arancha Sanchez stayed for the entire eight years that Lamy was DG, acting as adviser, troubleshooter, and filter. She annoyed the continuing staff but served Lamy well, heading a small team drawn from both the WTO secretariat and outside. Each member covered a part of the DG's jurisdiction and could be both adviser and the DG's eyes and ears. If they did not act with tact, they could cause problems. When directors were not told of any amendments to their proposals, they grumbled they were left out of the processes. When Azevêdo became DG, he appointed Tim Yeend, the Australian ambassador to the WTO, as his chief of staff. All chiefs of staff had standing in their own right and were knowledgeable on trade issues.

At WIPO, Gurry appointed Naresh Prasad, an Indian IP expert, who was always a key member of the DG's senior management team, with responsibility *inter alia* for liaising with the regional groups of members. In Gurry's second term, Prasad was given the status of an ADG. At the FAO, the *cabinet* managed the DG's diary and provided advice on the issues that were coming across his desk; as the DG was often away from Rome, the linkages they facilitated became important for anyone who wanted an opinion or the approval of the DG. Its process of reviewing documents sent to the DG could lead to dysfunction:

> When such documents are not properly prepared, the *Cabinet* re-writes them in order to ensure that the form and content are harmonized with the mission and strategy of FAO. As a consequence the departments often do not feel the ownership of such documents and draft them with the expectation that the *Cabinet* will review and finalize them.[35]

The process thus became counterproductive. Too large and intrusive an office for the DG could slow processes down. At the WHO, Ian Smith was always at the side of Margaret Chan and eventually formally given the ADG status that his influence warranted.

Cabinets are essential assets for the DGs. Problems arose when they either sought to freeze out staff or intervened in ways that undermined the competence of the secretariats. Wolfowitz brought to the World Bank his advisers from the State Department who had no experience of the Bank or any other IO. These people acted as gatekeepers, so fiercely loyal to the American administration and Wolfowitz that they became known as the Rottweilers. The peremptory demands they made of VPs and others, often without any obvious appreciation of what the World Bank did, was a principal reason for the alienation of Wolfowitz from his senior staff.

The depth of expertise lies within the staff; none of the *cabinets* is anything like large enough to provide an alternative bureaucracy. Nor should they be. DGs will all have their ways of managing the pressures. Some allow their chiefs of staff to act in their name; their influence always relies on an understood delegation; they have authority only because they speak for the DG. Some travel with the DGs, keeping open lines of communication. Often senior staff talk to the chief of staff, in the knowledge that some problems can be solved without taking up the DG's time and that usually the messages will be delivered.

The second group to provide assistance is the senior management team, DDGs and ADGs (in WIPO, the WHO, FAO and WTO), the MDs and VPs (in the World Bank) and the deputy managing directors in the IMF. These are the officers above the rank of director in all IOs; they are appointed by the head of IOs, sometimes with the endorsement of their Councils or EBs They serve to an extent at the pleasure of the DGs. Many are internal appointments, and thus career international civil servants. Some have programme and institutional interests that they will advance; so, unlike the *cabinets*, their interests are not synonymous with those of the DGs.

---

[35] FAO, *Final Report Executive Summary: Office of Director General Review*, 19 March 2010, 9. At its largest, the ODG contained thirty-five people.

The World Bank has between one and four MDs; their thirty or so VPs with line responsibilities (some regional, some functional networks, some administrative) will report to a MD and through them to the president. WIPO has four DDGs and three ADGs. Each of them has delineated line responsibilities. There is little real distinction between DDGs and ADGs, except the former are paid more and the member states have to approve their appointment, while they will merely note the ADGs (and there is really no difference in practice between those two processes). The WHO had just one DDG, who looked after internal management, particularly when the DG was away: 'whatever is internally prepared goes through many discussions with him and then he decides when we can go to the DG. There is a very good trust that he is preparing the ground.' The line responsibilities are taken by ADGs. The WTO has four DDGs; as befits a small organization, there is no intermediary level between the deputies and the directors who are the career line managers. The IMF too has no equivalent of the VP/assistant rank. Its deputy managing directors oversee the work of the directors.

While IO leaders may not have job descriptions, their deputies do. DGs allocate them supervisory responsibilities, often managing sections of the organization, with some additional cross-organizational functions. One DG explained: 'I do not have a job description, but they [the deputies] do because I gave them one.' Their role and contribution to the organization as well as trade negotiations to a large extent depend on what responsibilities the DG allocates them. With a number of directorates to oversee, even if without complete line authority, DDGs do have the opportunity to make a difference.

These DDGs fulfil a representative role. In 2011, the four DDGs at the WTO came from Latin America, Asia, Africa, and the USA, to complement a DG from Europe. When the new DG was selected from South America, the new team again had one deputy from each region. Few in the system thought that the WTO needed four deputies; the GATT had had only one, acting as a chief operating officer. When the WTO was created, members could not decide who should be the DDG or which part of the world this individual should come from. They chose the easiest option—having four DDGs, representing all regions. There was a serious debate in the late 1990s about reducing the number. At the last minute the USA baulked when it saw a danger that in future it might not have one of them. The General Council is prepared to leave the number where it is in exchange for the representational benefits. Both Lamy and Azevêdo chose to advertise for DDGs, rather than rely on contacts or nominations; the last two US deputies were former US ambassadors or senior counsels to the WTO, well known in local trade circles and respected. Although the process is not official, the nominees would have been approved by their states of origin. The WTO ambassadors just shrugged when asked why they had approved a budget for four deputies that in their view were not used effectively. The issue of deputies at the WTO is beyond the normal responsibility of trade ambassadors. It is political.

WIPO's DDGs and ADGs are also representative: one each from Africa, Latin America, Europe, the USA, and South America and two from East Asia. Unlike their counterparts at the WTO, but similar to those at the WHO, they all have specific line responsibilities and specific policy portfolios, in addition to their management responsibilities. They are thus required to be technically competent, and most are experts in specific IP fields.

One issue for these deputies as part of the senior management teams is how to balance being international and being expected to represent their 'region' or country. DGs do sometimes use their connections in capitals to convince national leaders to support multilateral agenda; they also expect these deputies to work for the organization with their loyalty to multilateral cooperation. Two DDGs at two IOs, both American nationals, provided contrasting responses to the question how they got their job. One replied without any hesitation: 'I was appointed by the White House; it is an unwritten understanding that the United States will have some sort of right to a deputy director general position; so I got this through a political process in Washington.' The DDG from another IO had a similarly quick if completely opposite answer: 'I was chosen by the director general; I am a deputy director general for this institution who happens to be American... there has always been an American as a deputy, not an American deputy. This is an important distinction.' Reflecting on his status, he added: 'it is really important to maintain your integrity by not working for a government and by not having corrupt influences dictating how you do things. Once you lose your integrity, you cannot get it back.' Their approach to the task reflected their self-perception. The former was constantly concerned with US interests and was not averse to using his contacts in the US Congress to oppose some of the initiatives being undertaken by his DG. To say the least, this seriously undermined the integrity and effectiveness of the senior management team. The second saw his role as fulfilling whatever functions the DG requested; he had the contacts in Congress too but his connection was not utilized; that was the DG's decision. This is an issue of more than self-perception. It is one of how to behave as international officials, not domestic ones, at IOs, even when they are political appointees.

The high echelon officials at IOs serve at the pleasure of the heads of IOs, even those who have risen through the ranks. At some IOs, they are part of the package through direct elections of DGs, while others are chosen by DGs separately without formal approval of member states. In both cases, there is an understanding that the continuity of those above the rank of director depends on the DG. Deputies will serve set terms and know that, if they are to be reappointed, it will be at the behest of the DG. Some are concerned about the possibility of losing their job. Others are not. Shengman Zhang, who served the volatile Jim Wolfensohn, argued: 'as a deputy, you cannot always worry about your own interest or be afraid of losing your position'.[36]

How these management teams are used depends on the DG. At the WTO, Lamy kept the same four deputies, and the same chief of staff, for his full eight years. It provided unprecedented stability. If a DG wants to move them around, they can accept the decision or resign. After a change in DG, some deputies are given no responsibility and can be seen to be 'serving out their term'. Wolfowitz assured Shengman Zhang, the key MD under Wolfensohn, that he was needed and respected, then cut him out of the chain of command and kept him in the dark until Shengman chose to leave the World Bank. Zoellick promoted two women to MD rank; Kim removed them both. When Wolfowitz clashed with the VP of the Middle East and North Africa, Chrik Poortman, he offered him a position as country director in an obscure part of the world as a means of forcing him to resign.[37] Other VPs were cut loose or offered no serious alternative.

When Brundtland became DG of the WHO, she asked for and received the resignations of all her ADGs. To end the practice that the five permanent members of the UN Security Council all had their deputies, she changed the title to executive directors and broke the nexus with the UN representation. The title reverted to ADG after she had left the office. In the FAO, the outgoing DG appointed two new deputies in the last months of his term. Although several of the ambassadors noted that it was an odd thing to do—indeed, some thought it improper—they did not seek to oppose the appointments when the DG informed the Council of the decisions, as he was obliged to do. To break the cycle, the new DG asked for the letters of resignation from all his DDGs and ADGs. He got none, so he had to await the end of contracts before he could replace them with his own appointees. Over the next years, almost all left before the DG's re-election.

How much responsibility is given to the deputies who do not have line functions is always a matter of judgement for the DG. IO leaders need to delegate if the management is to run smoothly; the levels can vary even within the regime of a single leader. In the GATT, Arthur Dunkel delegated internal matters to his leading deputy: 'Mathur chaired the selection and promotion committee; I interfered only when the committee could not decide between two people.' Wolfensohn refused in his first term to give full authority to any single deputy. He did not want to follow the example of his predecessors, who had allowed Ernie Stern to run the Bank on a day-to-day basis. In his final years he found a deputy he trusted. Shengman Zhang became the principal, sometimes the only, deputy; he was in effect the chief operating officer who

---

[36] Zhang, *One Step at a Time*, 112–13.
[37] Xu Yi-chong and Patrick Weller, 'Chrik Poortman: A World Bank Professional', *Public Administration Review*, 69/5 (2009), 868–75.

dealt with management and recommended promotions. He could withstand his boss's occasional volcanic temper. That level of delegation has become rarer. Leaders want to remain across the principal management issues.

At the World Bank, a senior official noted:

> What everyone has always said is really necessary is a chief operating officer or a deputy and the presidents have never been willing to give that authority. Essentially Shengman became that, but it depends on the personal relationship with the president. Whenever board members encouraged this idea of the chief operating officer, not all the presidents have been willing to concede that. Without it, the president has to manage over some thirty VPs.

Brundtland at the WHO, building on her experience as a prime minister, tried to integrate her executive directors into a cabinet system, but it never seemed to work. The relationships have to be worked out occasion by occasion.

The WHO DG has some specific additional challenges. The regional directors are appointed by, and responsible to, the states in the region. Their appointment and tenure depend on the support not of the DG but of local member states; some regional ADGs have served a number of consecutive terms. The WHO is thus in many respects a federation. The reason for local autonomy was that one regional body, the Pan American Health Organization (PAHO), based in Washington, pre-dated the establishment of the WHO. When it became a component of the world body, it retained a degree of independence and became the model for other regions.

Consequently DGs of the WHO have to manage the regional offices by persuasion, because they cannot direct. DG Margaret Chan established a global policy group that contained all the regional directors.

> The global policy group is a really serious attempt to look at corporate issues as one group. If Brundtland was someone who said I don't want to deal with the regions, I want to go past them, Margaret Chan is completely the opposite. She said the only way we are going to make sense of this organization is to work hard on these relationships because it is a question of building trust. I think many of us tend to think about it in terms of structure, but actually I think it is much more to do with past relationships and if you make those work you can make anything work.

The management team in each IO brings resources but not answers. Some argue that 'the main purpose of the deputy director generals is basically to represent the interests of the key players within the membership'. Yet it is less so in practice. Some DGs may use their position as conduits to their region; others merely are allocated responsibilities across the IO. Their presence alone fulfils the representative function. Deputies see themselves as part of the institution, as political appointees in the sense that they are appointed by the DG, after more (as in WIPO) or less (as in the FAO) formal consultation with the member states. That said, when deputies are the nominees of member states or regional representatives, they are hard to remove, even when they fall out with the DG and campaign with members of the US Congress to oppose his re-election. How useful they are as a part of an executive team is often questioned. The responsibility to use them is a challenge for all IO leaders.

Managing staff and secretariats. IO leaders are expected to manage the organization with few formal limitations. At the World Bank:

> In appointing the officers and staff the President shall, subject to the paramount importance of securing the *highest standards of efficiency* and of *technical competence*, pay due regard to the importance of recruiting personnel on as wide a geographical basis as possible. (Article V, section 5, paragraph (d))

So the president is responsible for the appointment and management of the staff. The staff must be international; in addition to competence, recruitment must pay some attention to geographical representation. The World Bank is often described as presidential, a one-person rule in which the directions and whims of the president can shift an organization's directions. Some presidents were seen as bullies, rude and impatient with staff, ruling the organization by fear, impregnable in the certainty that their position was secure, although the worst of those regimes may now be in the past. Management of IOs has never been that easy.

IO leaders tend to head sometimes large, and often bureaucratic, organizations that have their own history, culture, codes of expectations, and criteria of appropriateness.[38] These bureaucracies can enable and assist the leaders;[39] they can also thwart and undermine through their dysfunctional bureaucratic cultures.[40] Bureaucracies often do not work by command. The staff of IOs can be a great asset: dedicated, creative, experienced; or they be a dead weight, disinclined to do more than a minimum. Leaders need to know how to encourage the staff, work with them and maintain their support, both active and passive. Leaders cannot do everything; they have to mobilize those officials who have the skills, the institutional knowledge, and the local connections. They must learn who to trust, and who not to alienate. An ambassador stressed how important it was: 'If he can't manage the staff then demoralization sets in. Motivation levels go down, infighting starts, so the DG is very important in terms of staff.'

---

[38] James G. March and Johan P. Olsen, *Rediscovering Institutions* (New York: Free Press, 1989).

[39] Xu Yi-chong and Patrick Weller, *The Governance of World Trade: International Civil Servants and the GATT/WTO* (Cheltenham: Edward Elgar, 2004); Xu Yi-chong and Patrick Weller, *Inside the World Bank* (New York: Palgrave Macmillan, 2009).

[40] Michael Barnett and Martha Finnemore, 'The Politics, Power and Pathologies of International Organizations', *International Organization*, 54/4 (1999), 699–732; Michael Barnett and Martha Finnemore, *Rules for the World* (Ithaca, NY: Cornell University Press, 2004).

The degrees of interest in management vary. One experienced IMF executive director argued that 'Lagarde was one of the first interested in how this place was managed'. She was the first to ask questions at the IMF about who was the client, what can we bring to the party, and other managerial probing questions. She appointed a deputy with similar priorities. To other MDs, the executive director claimed: 'the Fund was a black box'. At the WHO, J. K. Lee wanted to maintain a distance from staff, while Margaret Chan was seen as a micro-manager, interested in the detail. There is no one proper way to manage.

There are a number of tools available. Heads of IOs can reorganize the secretariat as a way of determining priorities, shaking up their staff, and breaking down silos. The World Bank, more than any of the others, seems to be in a constant state of organizational flux as presidents change. Some reorganizations destabilize the organization, as staff worry about their positions and their futures more than about the immediate demands; the World Bank's 1987 reorganization, in which everyone had to apply for their own positions, became a byword for dysfunction. Wolfensohn introduced a system of matrix management as a means of integrating the twin demands for subject expertise and regional connections. Jim Kim wanted to put the emphasis back on knowledge and redefined priorities in terms of Global Knowledge Networks. He hired several managers from outside to run the networks and then got rid of them before he reverted to an earlier model. The World Bank's regularly issued organization charts are evidence of the frequency of changes in units and their leading personnel. At the WHO, Brundtland wanted a more cohesive team, reminiscent of the cabinet system she had led in Norway, but found the conditions very different in trying to develop any concept of collective responsibility. Gurry wanted the WIPO structures to represent the outcomes that the organization provided and changed the titles of the principal divisions. As an ambassador noted:

> Upon taking office in 2008, Francis Gurry faced an organization in serious trouble as some member states felt that 'WIPO had failed to focus on its core activities of managing patent, trade mark and copyright activities and had become distracted with promotion, grand gestures and internal politics'; there were series of investigations of the use of WIPO funds and building contracts; and divided member states and the secretariat. The situation for the organization was so dire that something had to be done to make it work. The new DG initiated a reform at the organization.

Hiring staff is an option; in most organizations the DGs cannot fire them. As one senior manager noted: 'This is a horribly difficult place to manage: Look, if you have a hotel that everyone checks into and doesn't check out of, you have therefore a lot of problems handling professional development, motivation etc.' DGs agreed their powers were far more limited than they would have liked.

By contrast, in organizations where the functional differentiation was distinct, as in the WTO or FAO, where units have a strong logic and have developed silo characteristics, structural units and their directors have been more stable since 2000.

DGs' degree of involvement with the staff will vary. In the past they could be remote. Few in the World Bank even sighted McNamara, let alone had a conversation with him, during his entire tenure of thirteen years, even though the changes at the institution were felt by everyone. Some seek to be accessible. Brundtland started with a plan for a 'cafeteria policy'—initially she wanted to be accessible with her presence at cafeterias; her global travelling made this promise unsustainable.[41] A long-serving WIPO staffer remembered the early leaders: 'The Director General was like a deity. You would never address the DG. You would say "sir". Most of the staff were intimidated. Today the DG is called by his first name by everybody, even staff members. He gets emails.'

Perceptions of access may differ. An organization can be hierarchical and a DG may still be accessible in the cafeteria and in town hall meetings with staff. Whether a degree of remoteness is a result of formality or necessity is debated. At the WTO, one DG was so invisible and ineffective that a director joked that he did not even recall having him as a boss. How DGs choose to convey messages or instructions can cause gripes within their organization. The tests that senior staff often use include: the degree to which they have access when they need it; the means by which requests and instructions are conveyed from the DGs' offices; and the responses they might get when that information or advice is forwarded.

In the World Bank, VPs could see Wolfensohn if they had an important issue; they had a direct email connection and he would respond. In his last years as president, they would report to the MD Shengman on a regular basis, and talk to the president as required. Wolfowitz worked through his personal staff, drawn in from the US government, and with no experience in the Bank. Zoellick would meet his senior team every morning at 8.30. It provided a good opportunity for them to talk to one another (which they were otherwise often too busy to do), but that did not translate into easy individual access to the president.

In the GATT/WTO, Dunkel had been easily accessible to directors. Lamy was more remote; deputies and directors stated they could see him if there was something essential. With his experience of government in Paris and Brussels,

---

[41] Andresen, *Leadership Change in the World Health Organization*, 21.

Lamy was accustomed to a style of management that relied on his own *cabinet*, so requests used to come through his *cabinet*, and particularly through his *chef du cabinet*. He would ask for papers; some directors found it frustrating that they often did not get a response. Direct discussions with the DG were rare; they were left to manage their areas. Whether the DDGs were included in those requests for information was unclear. The directors were the sources of information and lengthy experience.

DGs of IOs nominally have to appoint staff on the basis of merit; they also have to satisfy the demands of members for national representation. Ambassadors will come with the names of their own nationals for vacancies, sometimes insisting that their countries are underrepresented within the ranks of the secretariat. Some DGs will simply refuse to listen to representations; Lamy always stood out against such considerations. Others knew that disappointed members could make life difficult in other arenas.

Sometimes, too, ambassadors could not avoid being drawn into staff discussion. After the WHO experienced a serious financial crisis in 2010–11, in part because of a 30 per cent appreciation of Swiss francs when contributions came in US dollars, the organization went through a series of hard reforms. There were job cuts in both HQ and country offices. According to an ambassador:

> the staff may be international from different parts of the world, many come with strong backing from their government so you [as DG] deal with those governments as well when you take action against your staff; you have to be really careful in how you treat a particular person. So when WHO decided to downsize, there was a lot of heartburn around there. There were many private meetings between DGs and ambassadors. In principle, we do not intervene, but in practice, we do.

We asked DGs how much time was committed to management; one responded he spent about 15 per cent of his time on management issues; it was the one area where it was easier to delegate to a trusted deputy, although that circumstance will vary over a single term too.

DGs may direct staff; but doing so by itself can no more ensure positive support in an IO than in any national bureaucracy. DGs need to persuade the staff to follow them. History shows that formal powers alone are not enough to mobilize that support. There is a record of IO staff openly opposing their leaders: country directors of the World Bank signing a petition against Wolfowitz's continued tenure; FAO staff walking out of an annual meeting as a response to Graziano's reduction in their conditions; the WIPO staff association constantly complaining about Gurry's leadership. Of course, if staff want to achieve anything, the support of IO leaders for initiatives is a *sine qua non*, but they will protect their own interests against those of their leaders.

CONCLUSION: MAINTAINING THE BALANCE

Michael Moore, a former Prime Minister of New Zealand who became DG of the WTO, grumbled: 'you're not a director nor are you a general'.[42] It is not that IO leaders cannot direct, just that there are limitations in all areas of activity.

If leaders have little formal power except over their staff, they still have a mélange of mechanisms through which they can exert influence as long as they retain the trust of members and staff and a degree of legitimacy that permits them to use the levers they have. Their power through chairing meetings, their ability to apply the knowledge the secretariats can generate, their ability to mobilize networks, the capacity to negotiate, the application of expertise: these assets have a chance of working only where leaders can combine both trust and legitimacy.

There are varying degrees of independence, from the WTO at one end of the spectrum to the IMF at the other. That depends on the levels of participation of member-state representatives in the day-to-day activities and the extent to which proposals require the consent of members. These situations can change when the IOs are transformed. As the political, rather than primarily technical, imperatives have begun to dominate the WHO, the DG has had less room to initiate and has needed to spend more time in generating widespread support. In the FAO, the gap between members and DGs has been distinct for some time.

If member states trust their leaders to work on behalf of the IO as a whole and not any single state, they may be prepared, within limits, to give them some scope for initiative; but only on lease. If that trust breaks down, stalemate tends to follow. IOs will often wallow in the doldrums when the principal members distrust the leaders yet do not have the ability or the desire actually to remove them.

As elected officials, DGs have constituencies to nurse. More member states have sought to become active, but they are not all committed to the same vision of what the IOs should achieve. The greater the participation, the more diverse the membership, the more organized the electoral groupings, the harder the balancing acts become. Interests become more differentiated. Most IOs now espouse a public intent to be member driven. Many have tried to restrict the capacity of IO leaders to take independent action. The freedom IO leaders once had, when they could serve several terms, occurred in another century and can now be but a memory.

IO leaders need skills to maintain the diverse relationships in the modern political environment. Modern communications have ensured that everything

---

[42] VanGrasstek, *The History and Future of the World Trade Organization*, 518.

they say is readily accessed and open to (mis)interpretation. One DG was surprised how carefully anything he said in public was analysed, 'because what I say doesn't matter; ultimately it is what the member states decide'. That is a little disingenuous. DGs help shape that agenda, particularly in those IOs with limited oversight and a lack of senior ambassadorial interest.

The task is hard, but evidence shows it is far from hopeless. It is possible to construct support for initiatives, but only by understanding the complexities of the regimes they service. As one DG reflected:

> I don't think there is any inherent power; power has to be earned. Someone in this position could come in and say whatever they like, but if they start saying that from Day 1, they are not going to have any credibility. You have to earn that trust and you have to have a power of persuasion that is credible. Then you can say you have an influence.

Julio Lacarte Moró, involved in the GATT/WTO since its foundation in 1947, drew a similar contingent conclusion in 2013. He commented: 'In the real world the director general carves out his role according to his charisma, professional strengths, ability to interpret governmental trends and interests, and personal relationship with the accredited ambassadors.'[43]

---

[43] Cited in VanGrasstek, *The History and Future of the World Trade Organization*, 518.

4

Secretariats and Staff

The mantra, 'a member-driven organization', is used by member states to insist that they are the masters of International Organizations (IOs) and secretariats are no more than secretaries, serving the masters. Member states, and only member states, will make decisions about what an IO will do, as an ambassador to the World Trade Organization (WTO) explained: 'That's the culture in WTO: the secretariat works for us; we don't work for the secretariat.' The mantra may have originated in the WTO; it is now emphasized across IOs. Of course, it is far too simplistic. Member states alone cannot drive organizations; they need help. Some discretion must be delegated to the secretariats, even if only the ability to 'interpret' their masters' wishes when they are ambiguous or uncertain. That will differ from organization to organization. To what extent the secretariat is delegated with what discretion, when that occurs, and why the variations exist are the subjects of this chapter.

Secretariats acknowledge the formal authority of the member states. They will advise and assist, brief and support. They will operate within the parameters of their delegated authority. They often do more. The secretariats we consider here sit along a spectrum, from those international civil servants (ICS) at the WTO, who are seen as primarily reactive at the one end, to those who dominate the intellectual agenda, as those at the IMF. The ICS in each secretariat have different relationships with their state 'masters'. Few can seriously assert they have no influence. What influence ICS could insert and whether it is legitimate provoke constant debate.

To understand the relationship between the secretariats and both member states and IO leaders, and thus to identify what influence they may have, we follow a number of steps. We need to provide a profile of the people who make up the ICS whose impact we seek to explain: Where do they come from? Are they careerists? What is the pattern of appointment? What is the national representation and distribution of staff?

Then we will ask what factors allow them to exercise influence and how it varies from institution to institution. What are the expectations? What should the ICS do? How does expertise empower ICS? How do the practices, routines, and standard operating procedures provide them with opportunities? Are there distinct cultures that vary from IO to IO and what implications do such cultures have? Does working with external organizations provide potential for influence for ICS?

In each case we not only ask what opportunities are provided to ICS but also consider whether bureaucratic assets can also work to the detriment of the IOs. Can established practices and expertise lead to conservatism, expertise to the promotion of bureaucratic ideas, culture to revolt and the protection of self-interest?

We conclude by identifying the qualities that secretariats require if they are both to serve their member states and to influence the outcomes of their IOs.

UNDERSTANDING INTERNATIONAL CIVIL SERVANTS

Much of the academic literature, particularly those studies that utilize the principal–agent analysis,[1] tries to identify the tensions in the relationship between member states and ICS. Assuming that the member states, as principals, know what they want, the studies ask to what extent the secretariats, as agents, either pursue their own interests or fail to deliver what their principals want. There is an assumption that the agents have some scope for discretion, even if almost any exercise of independent initiative is interpreted as dysfunctional.

Whether secretariats *should* have influence may be a normative question, but they do, and, we contend, were always intended to. The challenge then is to explain how they gain that influence and what they do with it. There is, of course, an extensive literature explaining why bureaucratic position brings power in national governments, in what form and through what channels. Some power is exercised *through* elected political masters; the civil servants define problems, offer solutions, advise decision-makers, and implement policies; anonymity hides their influence and the degree to which they shape decisions.[2] Other influences come directly as a consequence of *delegated* authority; civil servants work in the name of their masters, sometimes because the latter want to distance themselves from specific dilemmas.

The impact of civil servants is based on those characteristics that empower bureaucracies, whether national or international. Officials work through

---

[1] Darren Hawkins et al. (eds), *Delegation and Agency in International Organizations* (New York: Cambridge University Press, 2006); Manfred Elsig, 'Principal–Agent Theory and the World Trade Organization', *European Journal of International Relations*, 17/3 (2011), 495–517.

[2] Jeffrey M. Chwieroth, '"The Silent Revolution": How the Staff Exercise Informal Governance over IMF Lending', *Review of International Organizations*, 8/2 (2013), 265–90.

routines that tame the unmanageable, shape the understanding of problems and break them into pieces that can be solved with standard operating procedures. Professional expertise determines what questions will be asked and through which prisms problems are perceived. Continuity of employment provides an institutional memory and a narrative that defines what has worked before and what might be possible in this case: the officials are conscious of the past, sensitive to the present, and aware of the need to chart a future for the organization. Neutrality ensures that they should be able to work effectively for whomsoever time and chance has placed in authority above them and underpins the trust and legitimacy on which they rely. Departments develop organizational cultures that create modes of behaviour and expectations to which new inductees are expected to conform. These cultures will often be contested and mutate. They are always a powerful force in shaping the ambitions and responses of the secretariats.[3] Long-standing connections, both within and between organizations, provide the oil that makes institutions work; they speed up responses outside formal channels.

The existence of these characteristics is not controversial. They would be recognized and accepted as providing the *potential* for all officials in government bureaucracies to exercise influence. Indeed, it would be difficult to visualize a large institution where these capacities do not exist. Ministers may decide policy; they do not make it on their own. Who exercises initiative will depend on circumstance and on personality.

Bureaucracies within IOs are obviously in a different situation from national civil services. Member states are not ministers with a single view, and there is no authoritative figure to equate to the prime ministers or presidents who can cut through to make final decisions. As one former IO staff complained: 'To understand the daily life of an international civil servant, consider the troubles of a national civil service, multiply by the number of the member countries and square it.'[4] In terms of the ease of getting clear decisions, he has a point. ICS deal with a range of members, all of whom have standing but are of different weight. Decision-making can be serpentine. Accountability is diffuse, because normally no one state member can act on its own.

As a consequence, some academics argue that no lessons drawn from the experience of national governments can then be applied to IOs.[5] We argue,

---

[3] For our earlier studies, see Xu Yi-chong and Patrick Weller, *The Governance of World Trade: International Civil Servants and the GATT/WTO* (Cheltenham: Edward Elgar, 2004); Xu Yi-chong and Patrick Weller, *Inside the World Bank* (New York: Palgrave Macmillan, 2009).

[4] Hans Mouritzen, *The International Civil Service: A Study of Bureaucracy: International Organizations* (Aldershot: Dartmouth 1990), p. xii.

[5] Robert I. McLaren, *Civil Servants and Public Policy: Comparative Study of International Secretariats* (Toronto: Wilfred Laurier University Press, 1980), 27.

to the contrary, that IOs are institutions in the same way as government departments are institutions: bureaucracies designed to develop and deliver policies. If that exercise of power in national governments is a consequence of bureaucratic form and procedure, why should we be surprised if it also occurs within an IO? It will just work differently.[6] The ambiguities they must manage are just as real. Like governments, member states raise expectations, pursue inconsistent objectives, have inadequate funds to do all they propose, and justify their positions after they have acted. ICS must manage a complex and changing environment where the demands themselves are unclear and the interpretation of what they need to achieve is open to dispute.

ICS also have the potential benefit of their own separate legitimacy. They do not nominally represent states (at least they should not, even if, as we will show, it is not always that clear cut); they are often required to take an oath of allegiance to the international body that they will NOT represent their country of origin.

To understand the impact of secretariats, Reinalda and Verbeek stress the value of middle-range theory. They note that the contributors to their work have utilized bureaucratic politics, two-level analyses (looking at the interplay of organizational and national domestic concerns), epistemic communities, group think, and core executive studies, to appreciate the impact of secretariats.[7] In their edited volume, theoretical eclecticism allows analysts to identify many of the phenomena that can be found within any organizations: the significance of expertise, self-interest, environmental pressures, and spatial impact. If our concern is to explain why the secretariats in IOs do what they do, then we need to use the available constructs to open up the different parts to analysis.

There is, too, a need to be wary of oversimplifying by assuming that in each IO there is only one position. We need to explore the contests and disputed territory within organizations and explain why they occur, as well as looking at the differences between them. Of course, we are not concerned with ICS alone; none of them works in a vacuum. We want to understand how they relate to member states, the heads of IOs, and the network of organizations outside. We need to identify the impact that different characteristics have: large or small secretariats, centralized or not, merit-based or geographically representative, tenured or not, general or specialized expertise.

---

[6] Stephen Bauer, 'Does Bureaucracy Really Matter', *Global Environmental Politic*, 6/1 (2006), 23–49; Per-Olof Busch, 'The Secretariat of the Climate Convention', Global Governance Working Paper, no. 22 (October 2006).

[7] Bob Reinalda and Bertjan Verbeek (eds), *Decision Making within International Organizations* (New York: Routledge, 2004).

STAFF PROFILES

The staff are the permanent manifestation of an IO. They tend to serve longer than any single leader of the organization or any state delegate. In these aspects, they are like the career civil service of any nation state.

Understanding the role of the international staff requires us to limit those about whom we will talk. As we are concerned with the way that the IOs operate, and the relationship between the three sets of players—state representatives, the heads of IOs, and secretariats—we need, when referring to the staff, to identify those who will interact, occasionally at least, with the other players and who can thereby have an influence on the organization's decisions. Therefore, we have chosen to concentrate primarily on the three levels of the bureaucracies below the heads of IOs.

In the previous chapter, we discussed the process of appointment for the principal line managers who were also political appointees: vice presidents (VPs) at the World Bank, assistant directors general at the Food and Agriculture Organization (FAO), the World Health Organization (WHO), and the World Intellectual Property Organization (WIPO). They were appointed by the DGs, but their line responsibilities meant they had interests to promote, projects to protect, members to serve; consequently they were potentially powerful figures in determining what the IO should do. The right of the DG to remove them was a given, but that does not prevent them from arguing a case or working with member states.

In all IOs, there is a distinction between professionals and general supporting staff. By tradition, all the six IOs had a similar tenure system for their professionals—merit-based career civil servants. Some offered more rigid tenure than others.[8] Below the senior management, the rank of director is common across UN organizations and so provides a degree of comparability for our purposes. Many directors have a view that is broad enough to understand some of the dynamics that drive the IOs. If we go lower, that broad view is less consistent, if nevertheless often interesting; ICS are more focused on the particular programmes for which they are responsible. The exceptions are those at the centre of the organizations, in the coordinating units or the support groups for the heads of IOs, where they must have a more strategic scope.

So our discussion here can relate both to appointed and to career officials (professionals, not including general support staff); the defining characteristic is what they do, rather than how they are appointed. Besides, occasionally the

---

[8] The tenure system at the WTO and WIPO has become a controversial issue, as one senior official discussed it: 'I find this tenure system bizarre, because you'll find it many times, once people get a regular contract and they're grade 10 [the highest professional non-managerial position], they'll just cruise.' The tenure system makes it very difficult for the management to restructure or revitalize the organization. Increasingly, IOs are pushing for contract systems.

distinction between political and career appointments is far from clear. Vice presidents (VPs) at the World Bank are largely appointed from within, with the common understanding that, once they have stepped up to the VP level, they in effect surrender the protections they had as a director. In the World Intellectual Property Organization (WIPO), several deputy directors general (DDGs)/assistant directors general (ADGs) too had risen from inside the organization. In contrast, at the Food and Agriculture Organization (FAO) we were told that most directors would not aspire to become an ADG, or expect to be appointed; at the same time, many of them were on rolling annual contracts, with no guarantee of continued employment. In the WTO, those above director rank are outsiders. Directors, the rank below DDGs in the WTO and the International Monetary Fund (IMF), and, where they exist, the VPs or ADGs in the other IOs, are usually seen as the key line managers, the people who know the detail, who oversee programme delivery. In the IMF and WTO, both smaller institutions, there is no intermediate layer between DDG and the directors.

The directors and those below them in IOs are often career officials, protected from arbitrary dismissal. At the WTO, long-term serving directors are the international depositary of knowledge in an often highly specialized field, and have served for a long time in the one position. In the World Bank and the IMF they are seen as the crucial elements in shaping and delivering policy. A Bank official described the job of Country Director (CD) as 'the best job in the Bank', because the holder of the position had the authority and scope to interact with the client states, often in the national capitals a long way from his or her supervisor.[9] Few are recruited from outside. Directors at the IMF are the key professionals, with long service in, and deep knowledge of, the institution.

In the terms of the IO constitutions, the instructions to the DGs are similar across IOs. DGs are to appoint staff on the basis of merit—the most qualified they can find to do the job. At the same time, IOs are encouraged to take account of the distribution of staff in terms of their countries of origin. For instance, the FAO rules require:

> In appointing the staff, the Director General shall, subject to the paramount importance of securing the highest standards of efficiency and of technical competence, pay due regard to the importance of selecting personnel recruited on as wide a geographical basis as is possible. (Article VIII)

All the IOs will retain detailed figures that chart the countries of origin of their ICS.[10]

---

[9] Xu Yi-chong and Patrick Weller, 'Agents of Influence: Country Directors in the World Bank', *Public Administration*, 88/1 (2010), 211–31.

[10] See, e.g., WHO, Human Resources Update: Workforce Data, as at 31 July 2016, issued 19 September 2016; it includes distribution of staff by gender, grade, geographical representation,

How professional expertise and geographical representation should be balanced is a matter of contention. One DG saw the need for member states to 'grapple with this Gordian Knot, which is inherent in a multilateral organization'.[11] There are a number of ways to deal with it. The World Bank and the IMF argue they recruit on merit by scouting the best universities in North America and Britain for doctoral candidates, primarily in economics. Many will be from developing countries.[12] The IOs' statistics stress countries of origin; the qualifications illustrate how their talented people have been educated elsewhere. Qualifications and competence have always been given greater weight than geographical representation at the WTO too. Careful selection would, in the long run, pay large dividends in the form of efficient and sound operations.

> The staff is just first rate. It is unusual for international organizations to keep people of this high calibre. The cynical view is: we get around diversity by hiring people from ten graduate schools. There is little pressure to hire outside from the merit dimension.

Management of the IOs is aware of the desire of many member states that their nationals should be on the books of IOs. Heads of IOs are also constantly reminded and frequently lobbied by member states when vacancies are to be filled. Member states may ring to 'encourage' the DG to employ their nationals. The executive directors in the World Bank and the IMF can often act as cut-outs, passing on messages but insisting they do not support the demands. In other IOs, while such requests are considered as part of the game, the resistance is strong. The head of an IO told us:

> Do they come and ask me to hire their people as directors or something? Of course, they do. Here, it is no-go. It was not totally a no-go before I came in but I completely streamlined the system. It is totally transparent. If they want their nationalities to get a job, they can send them to apply for it. There is only one condition: I put only super experts on the things we handle.

While DGs refuse to entertain such pressure, they do take the country of origin seriously when the candidates have the same qualification. 'After all, we are international organizations and this is what we should do.' In some IOs, the protections for merit are more limited. At the FAO, candidates for vacancies are compared to the lists of nationalities currently serving in the secretariat.

---

age, and location. For similar details, see also Director General, *Annual Report on Human Resources*, WIPO Coordination Committee (October 2016).

[11] Director General, *Annual Report on Human Resources*, WIPO Coordination Committee (October 2016), 3.

[12] See the discussion in Jeffrey M. Chwieroth, *Capital Ideas: The IMF and the Rise of Financial Liberalization* (Princeton: Princeton University Press, 2010).

If an application comes from a country that is above the average, then, regardless of quality, the applicant cannot be shortlisted without a special dispensation from the DG's office. There is no record of one ever being granted, so merit is qualified before the interviews even begin.

At other IOs, national representatives will ring, not just to ask for more representation at the IO, but to demand that 'this person' be granted 'that position'. When their demands are not satisfied, they can make life difficult at the next meeting, just to make a point. A former DDG at WIPO remembers:

> I have seen instances where countries whose requests were not met, for whatever reason—and it has happened with both developed and developing countries—would take obstreperous positions during the open formal meetings, purely as a consequence of the fact that their requests had not been met.[13]

There can also be questions for ICS who are deemed to be close to member states as to whom they owe loyalty. As IOs have become more decentralized, that becomes more of an issue in country offices where some locally hired ICS have closer connections with local political elites than with their HQ colleagues.

Most international civil servants, once appointed, are career officers in the IO unless they are promoted to higher rank. Whether kept there by ambition, commitment, or superannuation benefits, many will spend up to twenty or thirty years in an IO. Turnover tends to be very low, despite claims that the IOs are badly managed and that the perks of the job are constantly reduced. Staff will expect to survive most of the immediate crises and presidents. Most will hope to stay there for the rest of their careers; the common UN retirement age is 62. They will, therefore, have a past, a present, and a future: that career trajectory means that they carry into any project ongoing histories, relationships, and resentments.

Between IOs, the more technical the area of policy is, the stronger their position may become. The WTO's position on market access or dumping, or WIPO's work on trademarks or patents, can become so technical that its staff are indeed the guardians of 'the knowledge', its history, application, and problems. Any proposals they make are likely to be based on established practice and a long list of precedents. Of course, protecting that career has implications too. Continuing staff concern about their careers may influence internal debates if they are unwilling to take risks for fear of upsetting their superiors.

---

[13] Geoffrey Yu, 'The World Intellectual Property Organization: A Comment', in Patrick Weller and Xu Yi-chong (eds), *The Politics of International Organizations: Views from Insiders* (New York: Routledge, 2015), 166.

THEIR FORMAL ROLE

The head of IOs has the responsibility of recruiting and managing the personnel at the secretariat. Once recruited, all staff must metaphorically check in their national passports. They are required to commit to serving the international community and not to promote or advantage their countries of origin. The point is made explicitly in the original constitution of the organization, or/and in the handbook of the secretariat. For the FAO, for instance,

> The staff of the Organization shall be responsible to the Director General. Their responsibilities shall be exclusively international in character and they shall not seek or receive instructions in regard to the discharge thereof from any authority external to the Organization. The Member Nations and Associate Members undertake fully to respect the international character of the responsibilities of the staff and not to seek to influence any of their nationals in the discharge of such responsibilities. (Article VIII)

A few may not. Those who are on short-term contracts and on secondment from their government maintain close ties with their country of origin. The principle nevertheless remains important.[14]

In most constitution and formal rules, the secretariats are generally coupled with the DG, who is responsible for their management. The formal powers are described as 'trivial'.[15] Changing the provisions of the constitution is rare, because of the need to build a consensus. Most of the time, the secretariats have to operate within mission statements or constitutional guidelines that were prescribed at the time of their foundation, while having to deal with new activities that member states choose to pursue. Nevertheless, changes do happen, even if they are changes in practice and attitude. Since the mid-1940s, the missions of the IOs have become broader, the number of member states has increased, the secretariats have expanded, and the staff have been relocated more and more across the globe. Many of the changes have been a response to the ambitions and demands of member states, sometimes without proportionately expanding the capacity of member states to oversee their activities.

So we need to look elsewhere to determine what potential they have and how they may vary from place to place and time to time.

---

[14] In contrast to our six IOs, the International Atomic Energy Agency (IAEA) has two-thirds of its staff on secondment from their governments. There is no formal requirement for switching the loyalty to the organization and multilateral cooperation. Yet, it is difficult for the staff to make a real difference when national loyalty comes in the way in conducting activities at IOs, even at the IAEA.

[15] Kenneth Abbott and Daniel Snidal, 'Why States Act through Formal Internationals Organizations', *Journal of Conflict Resolution*, 42/1 (1998), 9.

Expectations

Based on the extensive literature on the influence of bureaucracies, we can make some assumptions when asking what influence the staff may have.[16] First, secretariats are there for a purpose; from the very beginning state members recognized that they needed some continuing support in IOs, in contrast to those bodies that were merely conference secretariats. Some critiques from state members imply the staff have invented a role for themselves. Rather the ICS were given a core role by their very existence. The issues were on what terms and with what degrees of independence that role should be exercised. The functions of IOs have developed and expanded, in response to the demands of the member states; so too in parallel must secretariat support. The key factor, we argue, is their ability to fulfil these additional requests and still maintain the trust of member states.

Second, bureaucracies are neither necessarily benign nor malign. They can be either or both. While it is necessary to appreciate that all bureaucracies have the capacity to develop dysfunctional characteristics, they do not always do so. Indeed, they may need to use all their skills, and to expand their activities, just to deliver the support required. How IOs respond to new challenges, and how the ICS develop their practices, will be determined by the leading players at any given moment. Their motives and actions can always be disputed. What some see as tardiness or obstruction, others will regard as the proper exercise of due diligence and proper process.[17] The selected path is not predetermined, but all the time the key players, whether state representatives or ICS, will have to be conscious of the historical limits and expectations within which they work.

Member states delegate functions to the DG and the secretariat. Like legislatures they can authorize, oversee, and comment, but they cannot themselves deliver those continuing responsibilities that underpin IO activity. Delegated responsibilities provide the foundation for secretariat influence.

The WTO secretariat supports both judicial and negotiating functions. The former include the Dispute Settlement Procedures and the Appellate Board, where appeals against improper trade actions are considered. The Appellate Board has standing members. Members of Dispute Settlement Panels are appointed to consider particular cases. Where the interested parties cannot agree on a membership (which is often), the DG of the WTO appoints the

---

[16] See, e.g., Derek Beach, 'The Unseen Hand in Treaty Reform Negotiations', *Journal of European Public Policy*, 11/3 (2004), 408–39; Steffen Bauer, 'Bureaucratic Authority and the Implementation of International Treaties', in Jutta Joachim, Bob Reinalda, and Bertjan Verbeek (eds), *International Organizations and Implementation* (New York: Routledge, 2008), 62–74.

[17] See, e.g., Manfred Elsig, 'The World Trade Organization at Work', *Review of International Organizations*, 5/3 (2010), 345–63; Tana Johnson, 'Looking beyond States', *Review of International Organizations*, 8/4 (2013), 499–519.

members after a recommendation from the secretariat. The secretariat advises and supports the panels. It will often draft the initial findings. When a decision is brought down, it is accepted by negative consensus—that is, it is agreed unless everyone decides to reject it. As there is always a winner, that condition is unlikely ever to be fulfilled. So these are cases where the secretariat acts in support of a judicial and independent function and where its choices are crucial.[18]

There is a contrast between the role of the WTO secretariat in Appellate cases and the role in the more informal processes where trade negotiations are undertaken and where its input is more muted.[19] The WTO is primarily involved in negotiating agreements that will eventually be binding on the members; they are consequently always conscious of their interests and suspicious of the ambitions, even the motives, of the secretariat.

Similarly, in the WHO in times of crisis the secretariat, in support of the DG, acts to coordinate responses to outbreaks such as SARS or Ebola. These responses included travel warnings. During the SARS epidemic, the WHO issued a travel warning to Toronto. Before the crisis was over, questions about the appropriateness of the WHO's actions surfaced when member states did not agree with and resented the WHO's decision. Whatever the justification, Toronto complained it had not been adequately involved in the decision-making. Member states seemed to agree and designed an advisory committee to assist in future cases. Delegated authority works when outcomes are what states like!

In the IMF, the staff serve a diagnostic role, seeking to determine where the problems lie and developing a dashboard of measures that might be negotiated. Diagnosis does not require consent, even if there are fears that area departments were 'unduly captured by countries'.[20] Their surveillance reports and crisis proposals often cut to the heart of national interest, but they require a level of detail and expertise that transcends any member state. Sometimes the delegation is explicit. When there was a review of the special drawing rights (SDR) basket of currencies, the MD, Christine Lagarde, reported to the EB:

> The *staff* of the IMF today issued a paper to the Executive Board on the quinquennial review of the SDR. A key focus of the Board review is whether the Chinese renmnbi (RMB)...also meets the other existing criterion...In the paper, the IMF *staff* assesses that the RMB meets the requirements to be a freely 'usable' currency and, accordingly, the *staff* proposes that the Executive Board

---

[18] Stuart Harbinson, 'The World Trade Organization as an Institution', in Weller and Xu (eds), *The Politics of International Organizations*, 34.
[19] Harbinson, 'The World Trade Organization as an Institution', 37.
[20] IMF, *Evaluation Report: IMF Performance in the Run-up to the Financial and Economic Crisis* (Washington: Independent Evaluation Office of the IMF, 2011), 19.

determine the RMB to be freely usable...The *staff* also finds that the Chinese authorities have addressed all remaining operational issues identified in the initial staff analysis. I support the staff's findings. The decision of course...rests with the Executive Board.[21]

The Secretariat provides an independent recommendation that is then separately endorsed by the MD and the EB. This is similar to what happens at the WTO: 'we as ambassadors walk 90 per cent of the way; of course the final decision is made by the minister and the government'.

In WIPO, the organization manages the international scheme for registering patents. It is continuous, routine, and profitable, and it is expected to be independent of the interests of any particular member state. That kind of activity attracts attention primarily when it goes wrong.

In the World Bank, the FAO, and the WHO, much of the activity involves in delivering, or overseeing the delivery of, particular programmes. Often the work is decentralized and technical. The programmes can be vaccination schemes, budget assistance, notification of danger in health pandemic scares, or technical assistance for fisheries and agriculture. There is far too much activity for the members to oversee, even if they thought they should be into micromanagement, which they usually do not.

The World Bank EB agreed very early that it would consider only those papers that were brought up from the president and prepared by the secretariat. It was a self-denying ordinance that meant that the EDs themselves would not prepare and circulate papers for the review of their colleagues. The initiative was effectively passed to the secretariat to shape the papers. The EB has not rejected any project proposal put before it by the staff. In practice, the staff ensure as a matter of prudence that any proposal has the support at the board and will liaise with the EDs from the countries affected by a proposal. As a proposal has probably had a gestation period of twelve months or more, from the time the idea was initially suggested to the occasion when it is presented to the board, it is somewhat of a fait accompli by the time it is there. Consequently, the EB accepts most project proposals without discussion.

Observers note:

> States sometimes lack technical expertise, credibility, legitimacy and other resources to make policy on their own. The greater the need of states, the larger the gains from specialization and the more likely states are to delegate to IO agents, even though large agents' capabilities also increase the possibility of shirking by those agents. States may delegate routine loan decisions to the World Bank and the IMF.[22]

---

[21] Statement by Christine Lagarde on the IMF Review of Basket of Currencies, Press Release no. 15/513, 13 November 2015.

[22] Hawkins et al. (eds), *Delegation and Agency in International Organizations*, 14.

It sounds mundane, even prosaic; an obvious step. But who determines what is routine? It goes to the core of oversight and delegation. In this case, loans are routinely negotiated, with member states acting as clients who have needs. The delegated discretion is not exercised independently of members but by officials working with them as clients rather than as supervisor or principal. The staff will make sure that whatever they propose to do will get the support from the Board of Directors, often before they take the proposal to the board.

This delegation includes those people, such as research people, who, by the nature of their work, have a lot of independence and autonomy. One chief economist at the World Bank explained:

> We have an annual presentation to the board on the research programme, what we have learned over the past, what are the key aspects of our research, and also all our flagships—by the way, we have several including World Development Reports. We take them to the board for discussion but not for approval. There are comments, but the board also understands that it is a research product and it is by the Bank staff. So there is no pressure to change. We nonetheless believe this is an important consultation process.

At another IO, a senior official described how it worked in organizational terms:

> Our programme of work and budget is formally approved by member countries; it is specified down to what we refer to as an organizational result. So it's at a fairly high level in terms of results-based management. The member countries know, for example, that we plan to put a certain amount of money into global agreements and international instruments, and that we plan to put a certain amount of money into support for policy studies and policy advice... So they've got the bigger picture. Once the budget is approved, the actual deliverables, in terms of outputs of specific studies or specific meetings or whatever, are prepared by the secretariat and it's put into our programme system, which in principle the member countries can look at. But they do not approve it. So our responsibility is to produce a result as approved by them. How we produce that result is, strictly speaking, a management decision rather than a governance decision.

Delegation empowers the secretariats to shape decisions and debates.

In all IOs, there is an organizational expectation that ICS will be neutral *between members*. The capacity to act as an impartial arbiter or intermediary is a principal reason that IOs retain support. ICS must be trusted to serve all the member states and listen to their concerns. An early judgement on ICS still has force.

> In order that they should be in a position to carry out the task entrusted to them, it was essential that—without arrogating to themselves any authority of their own—they should approach problems from an elevated viewpoint, taking into

account the interests of all, not being content with any 'particularist' point of view and not favouring anybody.[23]

Indeed, the more diverse the positions states hold, the more state delegates are willing to ask the secretariat to use its discretion. When two parties negotiate, neither is neutral; the secretariat is the best third party, who can help bring about compromises and agreements. Member states are often suspicious of the other members; they are in a negotiation and will not want all their ambitions and limitations known. The secretariat is more likely to be aware of what each member state wants. When the staff provide advice, they will know how far various parties can be pushed and what their bottom line will be. It is not necessarily that the delegates always have confidence in the secretariat; it is that they trust other members less. State delegates may be more prepared to accept a proposal drafted by the secretariat because, as one delegate said, 'it is easy to agree if you do not have to say yes to another country'.

When new issues come up, state delegates, especially those from developing and small countries that do not have the expertise or manpower to undertake research, tend to ask the staff in the secretariat to provide assistance and explanations. The secretariat staff will do so, confidentially explaining the issues and implications and scrupulously ensuring that the confidences of the member states are not divulged.

None of these qualities implies that ICS do not have views. Indeed, they are paid to have distinct ideas that are not in line with one state but are in the interests of multilateral cooperation and the mission with which they are entrusted. ICS should be biased only in favour of the mandate, not specific countries or positions. Persistent impartiality is the key to successful cooperation and the key to the maintenance of the legitimacy of ICS; often states trust ICS more than they trust each other in negotiations on the basis that they will deal honestly and confidentially with each member and the acceptance that they are international in their allegiance. When trust breaks down, the whole operation in an IO is under threat (see the discussion in Chapter 5).

The expectation of what ICS should do varies across IOs. In the World Bank, directors normally work with EDs as proposals are developed; in the IMF, the EDs are informed of proposals, but not aware of the discussion or divisions that preceded them. In both institutions, the continuous presence of EDs is regarded as a necessary, but sometimes burdensome, part of the infrastructure.

At the other extreme, at the WTO, staff know that any assistance they may be able to offer or any influence they may have has to be muted and largely unseen. 'We go through the motions of pretending that members make all the decisions' was one observation of an experienced director. The challenge at

---

[23] Georges Langrod, *The International Civil Service* (New York: Oceana Publications, 1961), 39.

WIPO is to get ambassadors interested in its issues. Within each IO the questions of what staff will or should do is contested.

On procedural issues, the expectations are that staff will emphasize the importance of bringing divergent views together, particularly when the objective is to reach an agreement: 'we can't allow the perfect to be the enemy of the good', said one staff member. ICS seek to identify conditions that will allow agreements to be made, by a form of words, by a well-designed informal consultation. Their influence is exercised through persuasion, logic, and persistence; after all, no negotiating rounds finish quickly, and the secretariat has to seek to maintain interest and momentum.

Of course, as officials repeat all the time, they have no power to coerce, no sanctions to threaten; they 'cannot move body politics to something states do not see as important'. ICS serve the system, but how that system should be interpreted is the subject of their internal debate. The developing question is how openly they should do it and what initiatives they should take to make it work.

Much of the debate on principal–agent theory assumes that the principals know what they want and can readily judge whether the agents have in some way thwarted their intentions. Only in rare cases in most IOs is that even barely true. It assumes a commonality of intent that is now under challenge. If it was once possible to argue that all member states were committed to the mission of the organization, now the commitment is more diverse, and there is constant disagreement between members and groups of members. The secretariat can both act as a bridge and assist in developing a more coherent view, if the members want them to, and even more so when they provide general instructions.

BUREAUCRATIC ASSETS AND SKILLS

The secretariat provides the support that underpins all of an IO's activities. It has the continuing presence that lasts longer than any leader or group of state representatives. That continuity gives it potential influence; its members are far more likely to be aware of the history of the organization. Like all bureaucracies, IO secretariats have the advantages of expertise, routines and its standard operating procedures, and, more generally, organizational culture. We discuss each in the next sections.

Expertise

Secretariats bring assets without which the IOs could not operate: levels of expertise in the relevant disciplines, continuity that comes with a career service with long memories, a detachment from the interests of any one state member, a perspective that appreciates the interests of all its member states, and an ability to facilitate agreement. These assets mean they can assist their political and managerial masters, but can also give them the capacity to shape the directions the organizations take.[24] The secretariats' expertise, experience, and memory can be combined with the basic characteristics of all bureaucracies: operational networks, standard operating procedures, continuing access to clients, decades of experimentation on which to draw, the ability to describe what has been tried, successfully or not, over the history of the organization. There will inevitably be far more ICS to tackle these issues than any one member can possibly commit to the issue; secretariats have more people with longer expertise than any of those whom they will serve.[25]

All the IOs are based on some expertise, on their ability to make a contribution in areas that rely on a fundamental basis of evidence, be it medical, legal, scientific, or economic (and then either macroeconomic or developmental). The staff's standing and legitimacy depend in part on the quality of their contribution, judged by their peers in the epistemic community outside, and to which the experts in the organizations consciously relate.

The workings and their proposals will be filtered through a dominant intellectual screen. The IO's central discipline frames the questions asked, and can determine which evidence is seen as persuasive. Of course, all the IOs hire a number of people from other disciplines, but the latter often feel that, if their proposals are to progress, they need to appreciate the language of the dominant discipline. As a consequence, most staff talk a common language that also helps to define issues and to approach them in a way that is consistent. A common language does not assume a common set of proposals. Heated debates and contested interpretations can exist even within those confines.

At the World Bank and the IMF, the dominant discipline is economics, although, when the Bank primarily funded infrastructure projects in the 1960s and 1970s, it was also the realm of the engineer. The World Bank publishes more on the economics of development than any university, and its research staff are required to place their work in good academic journals, at the same time as ensuring that it is useful for their colleagues in the field. Its recruitment programme, for young professionals, recruits the best Ph.D. graduates from the best universities. The internal debate at the IMF is shaped by its recruitment patterns too; most have a common foundation, even if they may not

---

[24] Sean Gailmond, 'Expertise, Subversion and Bureaucratic Discretion', *Journal of Law, Economics and Organization*, 18/2 (2002), 536–55; Jarle Trondal and Frode Veggeland, 'The Autonomy of Bureaucratic Organizations: An Organization Theory Argument', *Journal of International Organization Studies*, 5/2 (2014), 55–60.

[25] John D. Huber and Nolan McCarty, 'Bureaucratic Capacity, Delegation and Political Reform', *American Political Science Review*, 98/3 (2004), 481–94.

agree how action should be taken.[26] The prevailing intellectual dominance creates pressures on staff to conform to established norms. In a review of how the IMF responded to the global financial crisis, its Independent Evaluation Office (IEO) reported that the internal 'incentives were geared towards conforming with prevailing IMF views [and] several senior staff members felt that expressing strong contrarian views could "ruin one's career". Thus, advice tended to "gravitate to the middle".'[27] Yet, a number of senior officials at IMF strongly disagreed with the interpretation:

> IEO said that we were unable to catch the crisis because of the group thinking. That is, we think as a group, all with new classical training. I would like to ask them: who were the two economists who caught the crisis before it happened? One was Raghuram Rajan. He was the chief economist here. The other was Nouriel Roubini, now at the New York University. The Board may think it is an issue and IEO may think it is an issue. To me, it is not. Issues are debated in such a fierce manner internally amongst the staff that it is absolutely unbelievable and it is extremely helpful so that when you go to a country or you go to the Board on a policy issue, there is virtually nothing that you haven't heard before in the internal debate. Then there is back and forth and it is really, really helpful. Now it may be true that dominant personalities dominate but that is by the very definition of a dominant personality. They would dominate in politics as they would dominate the debate; I was teaching in Chicago when Milton Friedman dominated the thought process for a while.

This being said, professions do make a difference. In WIPO, the lawyers predominate and in the WTO the trade economists rule.

The WHO has a medical culture; as one staffer there said, doctors are used to triage, to deciding what can be done and what is beyond hope, and thus making decisions without too much over-analysis and agony. When the WHO EB members were health experts serving in their personal capacity, they used to argue that it was a technical organization and that issues were technical ones and should be managed that way. Increasingly, member state representatives serving at the Board may or may not be health experts. So the culture has changed, even though at times people would still like to see the WHO run by experts, not by political pressures.

One WHO official interprets the problem differently:

> It is much less of a medical culture than it used to be. I think the difficulty in management that is particular to health is that health divides up in so many different ways. This started as a very normative organization; it was an organization of technical experts required to produce technical expertise; people came here for advice. Then you needed a department of XYZ. It then morphed. The demands changed, particularly as more developing countries became

---

[26] Chwieroth, *Capital Ideas*.   [27] IMF, *Evaluation Report*, 19.

involved—'we want a health and development organization that will help us deal with development issues at country level'. They are much more concerned with helping ministries of health and a variety of partners around national priorities where you don't need technical specialists that much. Squaring those two slightly different demands is something we have never quite cracked. You have to do both. We are not going to pull out of either, but you have a HQ which still very much operates in normative technical expertise level and strangely that structure is mirrored in most of the regional offices, whereas their role is actually much more concerned with negotiation, planning, and strategies at a country level.

The FAO too is divided between subdisciplines: fisheries, agriculture, forests. Both it and the WHO can be seen as a combination of specialities that work within silos. The World Bank and the IMF staff have more common ground. They can traditionally be switched between regions and across functions. But, even there, the growth of the World Bank's involvement in the environment, education, health, and governance has brought the need for additional skills and qualifications.

In a desire to be apolitical and non-partisan, professionals couch propositions in technocratic terms, based on disciplinary best practice at the time. Technocracy may determine the shape of proposals, sometimes too much so. There is a complaint that IOs have been controlled by bureaucracies that 'increasingly lock themselves into a single, technocratic way of perceiving and addressing social issues, regardless of the costs and consequences that this course of action might have according to other points of view'.[28] Keohane and Nye argue that, the more a given organization is technically specialized, the less it is exposed to political uncertainties and then the more influence international civil servants may be able to exert.[29] With their expertise, international staff can have a pervasive influence in establishing the intellectual climate and thus setting the framework within which the questions of policies are raised and discussed.[30]

Many at the secretariat nevertheless cleave to the notion that technical expertise *should* determine what is done. One WHO official commented wistfully:

> WHO rightly or wrongly has seen itself as a technical, not political, organization, with a secretariat that had a lot of freedom and manœuvre, so most of the work could be achieved by our network of experts and collaborators. And to that extent

---

[28] Marco Verweij and Timothy E. Josling, 'Special Issue: Deliberately Democratizing Multilateral Organizations', *Governance*, 16/1 (2003), 2.

[29] Robert O. Keohane and Joseph S. Nye, 'The Club Model of Multilateral Cooperation and Problems of Democratic Legitimacy', in Roger Porter et al. (eds), *Efficiency, Equity and Legitimacy: The Multilateral Trading system at the Millennium* (Washington: Brookings Institution Press, 2001), 264–94.

[30] Peter M. Haas, 'Knowledge, Power and International Policy Coordination, Special Issue', *International Organization*, 46/1 (1992), 1–390.

we do it. We report back to our governing bodies that meet a total of two weeks a year and then they go home and we continue with our work. In the last thirteen years WHO has been more overtly politicized and member states are taking back the organization.

Another official never accepted those 'good old days':

> In an organization dominated by health specialists, there is somehow this notion that the priority setting can be a technical function. If only you get the matrix right, if only you get the planning framework right, it will come out; there will be some way of doing a survey which will translate into real priorities. Actually it is a political process.

At each stage of decision-making, state delegates rely heavily on the competence of highly qualified and widely dispersed staff to identify, develop, and recommend proposals for actions, and to evaluate and oversee their implementation. ICS, particularly their heads, consequently will have an active role in shaping the decisions. The debate is: to what extent, in the WHO, FAO and WIPO, is the greater scope for initiative due to the technical specialization, rather than to less continuous or rigorous oversight?

At one level the contribution of staff is clear. Staff write and publish substantive reports that highlight the issues IOs can and should take on and work out long-term strategies for the organization as well as in their specific fields. The World Bank's Development Report is the most obvious case. Each year, a team is assembled to choose the topic, do the research, and produce a substantive report that is widely circulated. The report states that it does not reflect Bank policy, but it does identify Bank thinking and often foreshadows future Bank priorities. *Development and the Environment* (1992), *Building Institutions for Markets* (2002), *Making Services work for Poor People* (2004), *Development and Climate Change* (2010), *Jobs* (2013), and *Digital Dividends* (2016) are just some of the topics, often controversial, always significant. They are but a small part of the extensive publications provided by IOs. Statistics may describe how countries are doing, whether from the FAO or the WHO, sometimes creating controversy. Policy evaluations identify where programmes have succeeded or failed. These expert publications provide a voice for the members of the secretariats. However widely they may be read, the intent is clear: to set the agenda for future action, and in the process doubtless to inform their member states.

IO secretariats can also use their expertise to become the principal depositary of information both on international trends and on the ambitions and prospects within each member state. As IO membership has expanded in areas where a high level of technical competence is required, so new members have to understand what is at stake. Many of the new members are from small or less-developed countries. They require assistance. So IOs such as the WTO on trade issues and WIPO on IP, will send missions out to the new members to explain the implications of their areas, to advise how new customs systems or IP regimes might be developed. The term used is the anodyne Technical Assistance. It sounds, and in international terms is, non-political. But it allows the secretariat to inform and educate new members into the benefits that can be drawn from their participation in the IO. Its staff will espouse the general mission of their organizations. WTO staff will see the need to liberalize trade, WIPO staff the advantages of IP. In explaining the benefits, they will inevitably identify how their organization can assist. They can in effect socialize new members into the organization.

The imbalance becomes most apparent when the secretariats are briefing some key programme committees. The dependence of state delegates on secretariat support was noted at the FAO when the Independent External Evaluation (IEE) argued that the rotation of membership in the key Finance and Programme committees on a regional basis meant that the delegates did not develop the skills needed to provide strategic leadership. The secretariat wrote the papers and developed the proposals. At the meetings, the members tended to read prepared statements in reaction to proposals from the secretariat.[31]

New areas of activity strengthen their capacity. With the creation of the WTO, the secretariat was granted another responsibility—the Trade Policy Review Mechanism allows the secretariat to collect information on the implementation of trade agreements. The Marrakech Agreement specifically states that the economists in the secretariat's Trade Policy Review Division prepare the report and the Trade Policy Review Body, which consists of all member states, 'takes note' of the reports. In the reports since the early 2000s, the secretariat has broken new ground—that is, after collecting and analysing the information of trade practice in that country, it has also made recommendations, a function similar to that of the IMF and World Bank.

When the World Bank expanded into new areas of activity, including the environment and social security, as these became issues of concern for their client countries, it needed to recruit staff to meet the new demands. A decision to introduce programmes in areas of governance added a further need for new skills; the governance hub was symbolically developed within the Poverty Reduction and Economic Management division of the Bank, to stress that good governance was essentially an economic initiative. The WHO had never exercised its right to develop treaties. When Brundtland wanted to develop international action on tobacco, the WHO secretariat proposed that it be tackled through treaty negotiations. The idea of using a new vehicle for coordinated action came from within.

---

[31] David Hallam, 'Turbulence and Reform at the United Nations Food and Agriculture Organization', in Weller and Xu (eds), *The Politics of International Organizations*, 199.

There is nothing sinister in these developments. They are a product of a multitude of IOs working in circumstances where member states often do not have the capacity to provide subject expertise. Diplomats will be in contact with capital cities. The principal negotiating positions may be determined there, but will often still be of tangential interest when compared to pressing domestic problems. When conditions change, the ICS assist.

Indeed, secretariats often followed that adage of the former DG at the WTO: 'if you [state delegates] do not agree, we would fill the gap'. Where needed, they use their expertise to suggest ways ahead. At times this allows the secretariat to present, even push, some of its own preferred solutions. WIPO has a broad range of committees; a former DG was known to ask the secretary of the committee to insert some directions or suggestions into the debate when the meeting was deadlocked. The balance between seeking to assist the development of a consensus and pushing an agenda where none existed is hard to identify. Finding a form of words is the secretariat's proper role.

WTO staff in particular would never openly express such a proposition, but the quiet belief was there. 'Because it is a member-driven organization, we have to exercise our influence indirectly; and it would rather undermine the point of the exercise to tell you how to do it'. Besides, many were sceptical about the idea that members could drive: 'A member-driven organization is one that has one foot on the brake and the other on the accelerator, with one hand indicating right and the other left, and trying to go forward and in reverse at the same time.' Some used the caricature in Lamy's office to make a point: 'that is a nice sculpture of a tree and a car crashing into the tree with many at the driver's seat'. 'They [member states] insist this is a member-driven organization and then come and ask us to teach them how to drive,' said another. Few of the member states would openly agree, but the staff, while accepting the members have the right to drive, believe the wheels need greasing and there must be assistance in sorting out machinery.

In other organizations there were cases of what an officer called 'serial ventriloquism'. In the WHO, an officer drew distinctions in the way the system worked:

> I think some of the bigger issues tend to be generated more by member states than by the secretariat. It is not exclusive; there is a back and forth. With resolutions, which are the kind of lower-level agreement, a lot of the proposals come from the secretariat. And there is a process of ventriloquism whereby I, running a programme, want to get more resources, so I go to my national representative or somebody who I think will be sympathetic to my cause and I give them a script which they then read out in the World Health Assembly. And then it is member-state driven. So there is a process of serial ventriloquism. Whereas I think that is less the case when it comes to really big issues; it is much more the member states driving.

Sometimes member states are too divided to mobilize adequate collaboration. In the FAO, the IEE report had criticized the quality of the oversight provided by member states. So the members decided they would develop a response to the report without the assistance of the secretariat. They floundered. They did not have the expertise, resources, or detailed knowledge needed. Nor could they agree on priorities. After some months they asked for help, and a team was drawn from the secretariat to assist in the development of the Immediate Plan of Action that laid out the next steps to be taken. It was an indication of the asymmetry of information. Members' oversight is reactive. This was not a conspiracy but evidence of how multiple members, with constantly changing personnel, have limited capacity to develop the comprehensive united view needed effectively to oversee a worldwide organization. When the FAO is interpreted as a series of silos, each requiring its own specialized expertise, then the problems are merely exacerbated, since few within the organization have a detailed cross-institutional perspective either.

In the WHO, the member states wanted to ensure that the financial reform was 'member driven'. So the World Health Assembly asked the secretariat to develop a member-driven process. There was a year of internal negotiation, of testing ideas with the regional branches, before the DG and the secretariat brought a proposal to the Health Assembly for ways of dealing with financial problems. An observer commented that 'the DG initiated the reform precisely to allow state members to drive the process', but it had to be developed within the organization first, needing both time and expertise at the top of an extensive organization. A membership with both diverse opinions and limited capacity provided the officials with their clout.

As organizations take on new activities, the benefits of a common discipline become less certain. There is an administrative downside to an organization run by technical experts. A reliance on technical expertise can create problems when competent people are promoted beyond their levels of expertise. Technical skill does not readily translate into managerial knowhow. As a WHO official noted:

> There is a tendency for people in senior positions to move up on the basis of their technical skills rather than on their managerial competencies. So people tend to get into managerial responsibilities because they are extraordinarily good technical people, which obviously then causes some problems in that most of the managers are in fact enthusiastic amateurs rather than professional managers... So therefore we always have this tension. When we have 8,000 plus staff, managing a $2 billion annual budget, and working in 180 locations, you need to be able to manage that well and effectively. Enthusiastic amateurs usually don't, unless they have been given some further training.

The need to balance technical expertise with managerial and political skills is a constant refrain in all IOs. They can hire the latter, but will they understand the organizations and their capacities?

Routines and standard operating procedures

Institutions are sets of routines and standard operating procedures, based on both formal and informal rules, established but not immutable. ICS follow these routines to identify issues, disaggregate problems into manageable components, and propose new outcomes. That is why institutions are so essential; ICS can learn lessons from the past and provide continuity of practices, rather than treat everything *ab initio*. ICS follow precedent and experience when they manage new issues, even if they are slightly different. In so doing ICS can control and frame the emerging issues constructively.

So, before the World Bank's EB will consider any new proposal, it will have a long history. A need will have been identified, sometimes by the client country, often by members of staffs who are always on the lookout for ways the Bank can assist. A proposal will have been worked out, assessed by various levels of management and agreed with the client. The staff usually run the proposal past the ED, who represents the client country. Only after all these internal steps have been completed (and the average time for preparation of World Bank loan documents is a year or more) will the proposal be presented to the EB, or, as often happens, be approved without discussion as part of the delegated powers.

In the FAO, most new proposals may come from staff. In the WHO, where activity often takes place in the regions, staff are the proponents of new ideas. In the World Bank, the FAO, and the WHO, senior officers repeat the same belief: 'In this organization, you can get things done if you know how to work the system, if you understand what is feasible and who to talk to, and if you are prepared to take the initiative and work at it.' A number of examples are given where good ideas were developed, often without contact with member states.

Officials also sit at the centre of the IOs to draw together the different threads of policy activity. For instance, the IMF's Strategy, Priorities and Review division not only oversees the preparation of papers for the EB, but also ensures they both meet the established criteria and are consistent with existing practice. The division provides summaries to the EDs of the different positions held by member states before a debate is held in the EB. It drafts in advance a formal 'Summings Up' for the MD. If accepted, and it usually is, it becomes the authoritative decision that directs future actions. Again, there is nothing sinister in such an activity, but the hand that holds the pen can influence the outcome. These are what coordinating departments or offices do; in the preparation of these documents there must be a degree of discretion: to agree that the papers go ahead, to discern the feeling and consensus of the meeting. Without it no conclusion will take place.

IOs' management has to determine which tasks are delegated to what level or regions, as Chapter 7, on location, describes. IOs sit along a spectrum from centralized to decentralized, and vary in terms of what is decided and where, both geographically and organizationally. The issue to be explained here is where and why those decisions are made and how the location and content of those decisions is determined.

At each stage of decision-making, a wider degree of initiative may be needed, and member states rely heavily on the competence of a large number of highly qualified and sometimes widely dispersed staff to identify challenges, develop projects and recommend proposals for actions, and evaluate and oversee their implementation. ICS, particularly the senior officers, consequently not only have extensive interactions with state representatives, but also are able to have an active role in shaping the decisions.

Many senior officers at all these IOs have worked in the system for twenty or thirty years. Their long experience allows them to appreciate what has or has not worked in the past. They have access to, and sometimes are, 'the files', the communal memory of the organization's experiences and experiments. That information can be brought into play whenever a new scheme is proposed. Of course, it may not determine outcomes; organizations change their approaches and their incentives, but information is the key to decisions. It was explained to us by a state representative chairing a committee:

> when we were in some key negotiation process in a Ministerial meeting or at the Council meeting, some issues came up; you brief this director on it; he quickly understands what the issue is and how it worked and all that; good directors in this place are hardwired for both the substance and the diplomacy and we have got a huge institutional wealth here.

Indeed, the reliance on the secretariat becomes evident when members of the secretariats assist committee chairs. Many of the state representatives are not subject experts in agriculture, IP, or health. They are busy covering a range of UN institutions, often with political agendas that are more susceptible to diplomatic skills. So experts with detailed understandings of technical subjects, based on cross-national knowledge, deal with non-expert missions reliant on irregular connections with the experts back in their capitals. When they have to take a lead role, as chair of a committee, they represent the organization. Some subject knowledge and an appreciation of the options becomes even more essential. At the FAO, in the past, chairs were elected for a single meeting and had no chance beforehand to become familiar with the issues to allow them to guide a meeting; they relied on the secretary. Even since the practice has changed, so that they hold the position for a series of committee meetings and can thus develop some depth of knowledge, they will still rely on the secretariat to draft the papers, prepare the agenda, and, while the committee is in progress, advise on possible ways ahead. In 2003, a director of the WTO commented: 'the more technical the area, the more intensive and complex the information, the greater the need of the chair for assistance from ICS'; they were after all hired because of their expertise and knowledge over various trade issues.

To provide an example of the processes the staff can use, we can reconstruct a typical process for a multilateral negotiation group at the WTO. It is all based on informal rules and expectations; nothing is set in stone. It depends on actors reading the wind and appreciating what might be possible. The first meetings are often dedicated to a statement of positions; in the terms of a senior official, it is 'a classic bazaar: hard-boiled ambassadors arguing about bits of national interest and often paranoid about what others want'. After a few meetings, the secretariat will be asked to provide a compilation of views, organized under a series of headings to show which are matters of general concern. Some items will be quietly dropped. Second, the secretariat will provide a structure for discussions, noting a series of themes under which the issues can be organized for further debate. While the precise form will be for the secretariat to determine, it will be 'user-friendly'. The newer the subject, and the more complex the issues, the greater the scope the secretariat has for shaping these directions. After each discussion, the issues are gradually refined, the points of agreement identified, and areas where further discussion is required noted. At each stage the chair of the committee will be given a checklist of points for discussion and decision. Third, the secretariat will provide a concepts paper that is the first step towards a draft agreement; it might define the conceptual terms, provide a framework of what an agreement might look like, and provide some options on the way to tackle tricky issues. Fourth, the concepts are translated into legal language that provides the basis for the rules that will apply if the agreement is signed. Those parts of the text that are still not agreed will appear in brackets; bit by bit the secretariat will provide formulations of words until agreement is reached. It will be described as a technical exercise; it requires political sensitivity.

In the development of drafts, the secretaries necessarily develop a dual loyalty. ICS will serve the two masters: the IO in general and the committee that they are assisting.[32] On the one hand, they answer to the chair of the committee whom they advise on tactics and for whom they develop drafts; they need to maintain the confidences of members about what their bottom lines will be and where there is scope for negotiation. On the other hand, they work in a hierarchy where they answer eventually to the DGs. Keeping a balance is a skill.

This description portrays a classic secretariat at work: officials providing support for a negotiation and assisting in the process; their particular interest is to keep the negotiations going, to keep the delegates talking. Yet at every stage there is a need for the exercise of judgement, about what issues should be left in, about how far an issue can be pushed, about when the time is right to provide a clean text. Even if nominally all these are decisions to be made by the

---

[32] Harbinson, 'The World Trade Organization as an Institution', 11.

chairs of the committee, who are state delegates, in many cases they rely on the secretariat for advice and proposals on how to move forward. An experienced state delegate described one occasion when

> the biggest problem among members was trying to figure out how to develop some idea. And it seemed hopeless; it seemed like there was a big gap between members. Then the secretary, an old friend of mine, leaned over to the chair and whispered in his ear. Next thing the chair proposes this language. 'Oh, yes, it's fine.' I know it came from my friend and he didn't need to take credit for it. He wasn't pursuing an agenda, but he was lubricating the process with his wisdom, his knowledge of the people, his experience.

Control of information is a responsibility of, and provides opportunities for, ICS. In all IOs they are required to collect, analyse, or disseminate information in order for the collective actions to take place. This is a double-edged sword for member states—it creates dependence on ICS, but cooperation cannot take place without that authority. However, control of information, often the ability to access information, places ICS in a commanding position, because they must select and filter. 'Since the supply of facts is infinite, finders must exercise discrimination in their accumulation, or in other words, choose facts with a view to their analytical arrangement.'[33] Economists seek and interpret economic data; doctors look for medical explanations. That is the way they are trained, which determines their instinctive response to a challenge. The principal–agent literature often treats ICS negatively—that is, the agent takes independent actions by hiding information from principals, or misinterpreting the mandates to justify their own preferences or to evade principal control mechanisms. Information allows ICS to 'reinterpret' their responsibilities on the basis of their knowledge and their precedents.[34] However, IOs are created for the positive reason that states realize that some actions must be taken that would be too costly for them to do themselves. Collecting and analysing information can be and is an effective way to facilitate cooperation, because ICS can use that process to propose new ideas, suggest new alternatives, and shape the final outcomes.

The secretariats seldom get the credit but often receive the blame. When there is gridlock, then suddenly it is attributed to the secretariat. Members unhappy with the proposals of other delegates can disguise their discontent by attacking the secretariat. 'If they do not like the outcome, they blame the process,' said one experienced hand. One deputy DG at WIPO recalls times when he

---

[33] Charles Kindleberger, 'Economists in International Organizations', *International Organization*, 9/3 (1955), 339.

[34] Darren Hawkins and Wade Jacoby, 'How Agents Matter', in Hawkins et al. (eds), *Delegation and Agency in International Organizations*, 199–288.

sat on the podium, in meetings, listening to the abuse thrown at the secretariat, yet always keeping a calm demeanour and working with the chairperson and delegates to achieve compromise outcomes... A delegate from a large developing country actually said the secretariat was the most inefficient ever known in the history of international organizations and that nothing good had come out of WIPO since World War II. No one offered any defence of the secretariat.[35]

It was always easier to blame the secretariats for the failure of negotiations, rather than other member states. At the WTO, being used as a convenient scapegoat is part of the facilitator's role—'we do not mind being a punching bag'. It may help reach an agreement if state delegates do not blame one another. Every other participant's picture must be partial. Member states have ambitions but will often not impart all their demands to other members, lest they undermine their negotiating position. Only the secretariats can understand every member's bottom line in negotiations. Member states' resources are often too limited to integrate even all their own activities of one IO, let alone service them across the whole spectrum of institutions. For many ICS, shrugging off such abuse was just part of the process. Without them acting as brokers of the disparate ideas and coordinating all participants, progress of negotiations is difficult.

Difficulties can occur even within an IO when there is little interest in what is occurring elsewhere. A director of the IMF noted he saw no point in daily meetings of senior staff, because 'many of them are not interested in what I'm doing and I'm not interested in what they're doing'. That indeed can create its problems too. An evaluation of IMF performance noted:

> An important organizational impediment that hindered IMF performance was its operating in silos, that is, staff tend not to share information nor to seek advice outside their units. This has been blamed for the IMF failure to 'connect the dots' in the run-up to the crisis. The silo behaviour is a long-standing problem; it occurs between departments, within departments, within divisions, and even within Management, adversely affecting IMF staff's ability to learn lessons from each other's experience and knowledge.[36]

The existence of dedicated silos was common in all institutions. ICS at the centre have the resources to concentrate their attention on the broad picture as others come in and out of the debates. They need to know what is happening across the organization, to integrate the different demands, to ensure some consistency. They can make the connections between demands and assist member states as they grapple with technical complexity. It is the relationship between the secretariat and the members in carrying out its responsibility of

---

[35] Yu, 'The World Intellectual Property Organization', 169.
[36] IMF, *Evaluation Report*, 18.

coordinating actions among member states, rather than 'rules' themselves, that underpins its potential influence.

The secretariat too may often be a conservative force. The tasks they undertake can readily be seen as the tasks they should be doing. They can become resistant to change. A VP at the World Bank argued that sometimes important initiatives during his time of service came from outside; the staff were less keen to innovate (and sometimes faced problems when they tried).[37] Often that change is necessary. In WIPO, for instance, there was a dramatic change in the source of applications for patents. Whereas once they primarily came from the developed world, they are now coming from the East (China, South Korea, and Japan). Consequently, there is now a need for fewer staff with the traditional languages and more with skills in Chinese and Korean. Those changes can threaten easy staff assumptions about how jobs should be allocated.

Culture

Any organization will develop its own culture. That may have benefits and disadvantages. An awareness of how things are done over time can morph into a belief that this is how things ought to be done and inculcate an institutional conservatism. Officials look at their peers, who are both their colleagues and their rivals for promotion, and judge their performances. They develop standard operating procedures and their own jargon.[38] (The WTO is referred to as 'the House' by its staff in any interviews, for example.) They are always conscious of a future that will stretch beyond the horizons of those national governments and executive directors who are temporarily put in the position of oversight.

We need to appreciate how ICS see themselves when they interact with their leaders, their member states, other IOs, and their own colleagues. We need to understand their beliefs, interpretations of practices and ambitions, for those beliefs will shape the way ICS understand and manage the problems they must solve.[39]

---

[37] Jim Adams, 'Reform at the World Bank', in Weller and Xu (eds), *The Politics of International Organizations*, 58–81.

[38] For a brilliant early example, even if they never use the term organizational culture, see Hugh Heclo and Aaron Wildavsky, *The Private Government of Public Money: Community and Policy inside British Politics* (London: Macmillan, 1974).

[39] Valentina Mele, Simon Anderfuhren-Biget, and Frederic Varone, 'Conflicts of Interest in International Organizations: Evidence from Two United Nations Humanitarian Agencies', *Public Administration*, 94/2 (2016), 490–508; Sean Gailmond and John W. Patty, 'Slackers and Zealots: Civil Service, Policy Discretion, and Bureaucratic Expertise', *American Journal of Political Science*, 51/4 (2007), 873–89.

Organizational culture serves a multiple of purposes. It determines how people are expected to behave and what they are likely to do in any given set of circumstances. The concept then leads to the application of explanatory ideas such as Groupthink, whether that implies there are no alternative ideas espoused or whether the pressures are bureaucratic. As noted in the IMF *Evaluation Report* cited earlier, staff believed there was pressure to conform. However, too often culture is treated as though it has two characteristics: it is identifiable and constant, and it is unified. Neither proposition is really observable and neither is logical.

First, within each IO the question of what staff will, or should, do is contested. Over the decades, there have been changes in the culture of all IOs. The WHO shifted from being technical to more political. WIPO shifted from being one providing services to rich countries only to one with development as part of its core business. The World Bank was once an empire of engineers; now it is an arena for economists, sociologists, environmentalists, and health and education specialists. There were battles too about particular strategies within each IO. Chwieroth charts the debates about fiscal liberalization within the IMF since the early 1970s, a battle fought between the gradualists and the big bang advocates. It was not a question about whether it was required; all agreed it was. The issue was how it should be achieved.[40] At the WTO, the Slater report, commissioned by DG Michael Moore in 2002, identified two groups within the secretariat: a more traditional group that sought to work within the 'member-driven' mantra and was primarily comprised of the old GATT hands, and a younger group that thought the secretariat should play a more active role and initiate where necessary. The two views are still relevant in today's operation.[41]

The challenges to the traditional cultures emerge from new areas into which the IOs have expanded; some ICS believe they should exercise their expertise more explicitly. Member states are ambivalent in most IOs and would, at least publicly, still strongly disagree in the WTO. Culture can seldom be regarded as unified or settled. Change agents want a different culture.

Second, culture shapes how others see them. An experienced ED compared the World Bank and the IMF by defining the way they worked.

> The IMF is like the Marine Corps; it is primarily about crisis response, or at least when there is a crisis it is its primary role. They get on a plane very quickly. They are very organized, there is a team leader, there is one person who speaks, everyone arrives, parachutes in, they've got a clear line back to HQ and they can do that very quickly and very efficiently. They will be there, they will have a

---

[40] Chwieroth, *Capital Idea*. See also Ngaire Woods, *The Globalizers: The IMF, the World Bank, and their Borrowers* (Ithaca, NY: Cornell University Press, 2006).

[41] Terry Slater, *Strategic Organizational Review: Structure and Staffing Resources of the World Trade Organization Secretariat* (Geneva: WTO, 2001), 98.

view and it will be a disciplined and coordinated view. The World Bank is much more like a pluralistic university: lots of ideas about development, people competing with each other for resources to develop their ideas and to solve poverty, poverty being such a broad topic almost anything is justifiable. They will be a month later with a large team, everyone will have a view, they are more likely to find the right answer eventually, but it will be much more messy process. They will also resent the fact that the IMF was there first, committing World Bank money.

Of course, these images also create expectations for staff on how they should behave: they prescribe standards and practices.

The World Bank too changes with the times. A VP recalled:

> When I came to the Bank under McNamara we had what we called country programme papers which laid out our strategy which we did not share with the board. There has actually been a lot more sharing of information with the board and what they now get on strategy. It is true they do not approve them but we have to listen to what they say or we will pay down the road. I think it is an important distinction to make clear that the management is responsible for running the programmes and the board notes them, so that conflict of interest is handled properly. My worry is that, if you went further, if the board started to approve strategies, that would get them directly involved in management issues.

There were limits to which he thought practices should change. The World Bank and the IMF may be called the Bretton Woods twins, but they are not identical twins, even if they are too often treated as such.

Rather than refer to culture as a single component that determines the activities of staff, we prefer to break the idea down into a series of factors that may influence the outcomes. Each contributes to the culture, but some differentiation allows a better appreciation of the way that the IOs work. That can be illustrated by a further comparison. An ambassador to the WTO contrasted his expectations of the WTO secretariat with those in other IOs:

> I had a talk once with our ambassador—he is not there anymore—to FAO. It was at the time that we were litigating cotton here in WTO. FAO was holding a seminar about the value of econometrics studies in agriculture. That was a critical issue that we were discussing here in the litigation process in WTO. So I called my ambassador at FAO and I said, 'what the hell are you guys doing there? I don't want this seminar. I don't know what's coming out of this. Most likely something will come out which I will not like.' I suspect this was a seminar sponsored by European countries and the United States. 'How is that going to help me? I don't want that seminar.' Our ambassador in Rome said, 'well, but it is organized by the secretariat'. I said, 'Precisely. Tell the secretariat to shut up. They're not to say anything. They can't do anything without your approval.' He said, 'well, that's not the way it works here'. I said, 'then change it'.

Of course, the practice at the FAO did not change, in part because the secretariat at the FAO was expected to take the initiative, and in part because member states needed their support. The secretariats at the two institutions had very different cultures. Nor was the FAO exceptional. Other IOs with less-dedicated oversight mechanisms expect greater freedom to initiate. In Geneva an ambassador to the UN agencies who had previous experience with WTO explained:

> In WTO, the secretariat is there to serve. That's the culture of WTO. The secretariat works for us. We don't work for the secretariat. In these other organizations, the secretariat just goes out doing stuff, not consulting, not talking, not asking anything. It's internally driven, so it's primarily the secretariat which is determining the details of the work plan.

A WHO officer compared the operations of different secretariats.

> WTO is a secretariat which facilitates negotiations between its members; the secretariat has extraordinarily little autonomy to do its own work. WHO was completely at the opposite end of that spectrum. It had a secretariat which was autonomous and able to do stuff in countries with a relatively light guidance from its member states and stakeholders. It has shifted a little way along that spectrum, and there is now a debate as to how far that shift should go.

Institutional culture may determine to whom ICS talk. Secretariats may be forums for contested ideas. Member states are often unaware of the details. At the IMF, there is always a process whereby debate in the secretariat shifts from 'a constructive anarchy to an army', from a position where 'everyone has their own view, they put it to the table; then we discuss and debate it until they slowly become one view', explained a senior official at the IMF. The IMF had 'a culture of internal review'.[42] When conclusions were reached, the time for dissent was over. After that, staff could not 'freewheel without getting their wings clipped'.

EDs in the IMF were sometimes conscious that proposals put to them had been contested within the secretariat, but they were not told what those debates were, what arguments were pursued, or why one had triumphed over the others. It was hard to find out too. The debate at the World Bank was much more free-flowing, but internal disagreements still had to be kept in-house. When new staff argued for the right to speak out, said one VP, 'I reminded them they worked for an institution'. In other words, 'academic freedom does not extend beyond the time the decision is reached while everyone who has equity in the outcome is present and participates in the

---

[42] Luc Hubloue and Orasa Vongthieres, 'Governance at Work at the International Monetary Fund', in Weller and Xu (eds), *The Politics of International Organizations*, 102.

debate to come to the decision'. Then there was a hierarchy that needed to be heeded.

That can lead to the danger of an orthodoxy within an IO that is hard to challenge. In the IMF

> self-censorship appeared to be a significant factor even in the absence of overt political pressure. Many staff members believed there were limits as to how critical they could be regarding the policies of the largest shareholder—that 'you cannot speak truth to authorities' since 'you're owned by these governments'. Moreover, staff perceived that, in case of disagreement, management would end up endorsing country authorities' views instead of those of staff.[43]

Two consequences then emerge. There are debates within the secretariats, the details of which are not exposed to the delegates of member states, and sometimes the preferred response may be revised through a lens of what the staff think will be acceptable to those state delegates.

Internally it is often asserted that the staff would not come out and criticize their management or the decision, because they have to 'walk on eggshells in the all-powerful management'. Some IOs, we were told, 'were run by fear'. If that is true in individual cases, it does not seem true of the staff collectively. The staff at the World Bank openly revolted against Wolfowitz's demands and treatment of individual staff, and perhaps terminally undermined his standing. Dissatisfaction with the directions adopted by President Kim is often in the press.[44] When staff claim that President Jim Kim 'doesn't understand the Bank' or that 'we are not the UN', they are of course defending the traditional functions of the World Bank against the new initiatives that the president wants to introduce and which offend the previous belief about its proper function.[45] The culture determining what the World Bank should do is deeply entrenched. In the FAO, the staff organized a walkout from committee meetings after a new DG had in their view removed some of the benefits of working at the FAO on the grounds that they were not available to other workers and ICS should not be unduly privileged. He also brought many of his own people into key positions. It was as much the way he had treated the staff as what he did that offended them. At WIPO, the Staff Association was the centre of continuing opposition to the DG Gurry's initiatives of reform, publicly appealing to the member states about the policies he had introduced; that opposition reflected many of the divisions that had been endemic in the organization for a decade or more. In these cases the staff take as a given that they are the custodians of both the proper activity and the proper procedures

---

[43] IMF, *Evaluation Report*, 20.
[44] See, e.g., Claire Provost, 'A World Bank of Trouble', *Guardian*, 4 December 2014.
[45] Andrew Rice, 'How the World Bank's Biggest Critic Became its President', *Guardian*, 11 August 2016.

for their organization; it is part of the culture that they seek to defend. It becomes hard for IO leaders who might want, as one put it, 'to drag this old lady into the twentuy-first century' because they want to change what people do and often the way they do it. Staff can obstruct and wait out their leaders, and they have done so. Secretariats cannot be assumed to be passive recipients of often ambiguous instructions from divided member states; they will always have some influence.

NGOs AND EPISTEMIC COMMUNITIES

Any exploration of the procedures of IOs in isolation is limited too. There are always other forums in which ICS must act, usually as a representative of the organization to which they belong and without member states looking over their shoulders. Continuous activity leads to connections built within and across organizations; it gives ICS influence through their contacts.

Staff within the IOs will build up networks of people, which will often cut across the traditional structures. These networks will not only be within the IO but may also extend to other IOs, to the departments of national governments, to NGOs with an interest in what they do, with news reporters who cover the IO. A phone call can often break an impasse; a message can discover information; a favour can lead to better access to a national government. All bodies work through such informal connections and provide scope for achievements that would otherwise prove much more intractable.

NGOs are now a constant, if sometimes uncomfortable, reality for IOs. Some IOs have invited them to attend their formal processes, but others try to keep them at arm's length. The WTO General Council argued that, as NGOs have nothing to bring to the bargaining table, they are loath to talk to them, even if they have standing at WTO conferences. In 1996 the General Council passed a resolution to delegate a new set of responsibilities to the secretariat: 'The Secretariat should play a more active role in its direct contacts with NGOs' through 'various means such as, *inter alia*, the organization on an ad hoc basis of symposia on specific WTO-related issues, informal arrangements to receive the information NGOs may wish to make available for consultation by interested delegations, and the continuation of the past practice of responding to requests for general information and briefing about WTO'.[46] However much the trade professionals deplore the advent of NGOs to the anteroom, even if not to the negotiating table, they are now stakeholders. With this new set of responsibilities, the secretariat acts as a filter of demands from NGOs,

---

[46] Charles Bellmann and Richard Gerster, 'Accountability in the World Trade Organization', *Journal of World Trade*, 30/6 (1996), 63.

shielding state delegates. For the WTO, such delegation is possible because its staff are all located in Geneva and are small in number.

For other IOs, staff scattered around the globe in regional offices must deal with a multiplicity of NGOs of all persuasions. At the WHO, hundreds of representatives of NGOs will register at the World Health Assembly. Many are allowed to speak, but cannot move a motion. They seldom have difficulty in finding a delegate who will do so on their behalf. WHO officials divide them into Public Interest Non-Government Organizations (PINGOs), such as Oxfam, and Business Interest Non-Government Organizations (BINGOs), which often include industry user groups that are seen as Trojan horses for industry interests. There is deep suspicion between the groups that further exacerbates the challenges the ICS face. When the secretariat proposed a world health forum to discuss international issues, the PINGOs opposed the idea, because it might provide a platform for business interests; for them, no forum was a better option. At the World Bank, the '50 years is enough' movement in the 1990s shook the Bank; a multitude of NGOs are now dedicated to observing and commenting on its actions. The Bank has staff with explicit responsibilities for managing relations with them. Staff are conscious of their continuing activities.

ICS are also part of epistemic communities—that is, of networks of people interested in the same topic. Some will be official, some academic, others media. The secretariat may reach out to the favoured few to assist them in developing ideas that can then be developed internally. The Trade in Services Agreement in the Uruguay Round required new ways of conceptualizing the issues in a way that could then be translated into trade terms.[47] Electricity reform, particularly the capacity to unbundle the industry, depended both on intellectual developments and on its translation into a World Bank template. ICS do not work in isolation; nor do they await instructions about how their problems might be solved. Consultants and academics work with World Bank staff. The staff at the World Bank, the WHO, and the FAO include a number of former academics who found the immediacy and relevance of these bodies to be more challenging than the more disengaged academic enterprise. Their links with universities, consulting firms, and think tanks can remain strong. They are testing grounds against which some ICS want to benchmark the quality of their work. There is constant debate and interplay with people outside. The World Bank has been described as a moving seminar; the ideas are not all internally derived. The ICS exchange papers, discuss issues at conferences and workshops, and develop proposals.

ICS also work with their colleagues in other IOs. Sometimes this interaction may be official. The Uruguay Round required the Group on the Functioning of

---

[47] William J. Drake and Kalypso Nicolaidas, 'Ideas, Interests and Institutionalization: "Trade in Services" and the Uruguay Round', *International Organization*, 46/1 (1992), 37–100.

GATT to consider the question of global coherence and relations with the World Bank and the IMF. ICS in IOs also collaborate. The WTO, WIPO, and the WHO combined to develop a common policy paper on innovation and medicines. Ruggie describes the global compact of IOs but notes the difficulty of sustaining such links. He argues that networks have become the 'response of choice domestically and internationally, as social actors come to grips with the multidimensionality of globalization together with the knowledge and resource constraints individual actors face'.[48] How, he asks, are these networks to be accountable, and if, as he acknowledges, they cannot be governed 'strictly through rules-based accountability systems', what kind of staff should be recruited to service them? He foresees the increasing use of networks and the difficulties they create for traditional lines of accountability and organizational culture.

Bureaucracies increasingly work though networks of connections as well as hierarchy. In those circumstances, ICS can select the people with whom they wish to interact and on what terms. They can provide opportunities for new ideas and new procedures, independent of the governing boards.

CONCLUSION

There are, therefore, a number of conditions for an effective secretariat; its staff

- must be prepared to maintain a low profile;
- need consistently to act as neutral intermediaries that are prepared to assist all member states;
- must get it right most of the time to maintain credibility with all members.

The issue is not whether they can have an influence, but how that influence is applied, consistent with the member states' position as nominal masters.

The staff are hired for their skills, but must retain their independent international standing if they are to be trusted. The latter condition is vital; it gives IOs a standing that cannot be achieved by any national body. The staff should owe no residual obligations to the country from which they were recruited, or to any single powerful state. Within the policy community that includes 'officials in other government bureaucracies and international organizations in different issue-areas' and 'the public',[49] the secretariat must maintain strict

---

[48] John Gerard Ruggie, 'global_governance.net: The Global Compact as Learning Network', *Global Governance*, 7/4 (2001), 371–8.
[49] Keohane and Nye, 'The Club Model of Multilateral Cooperation and Problems of Democratic Legitimacy', 266.

impartiality if it wants to have any impact. Then, in the eyes of state delegates, its legitimacy may be intact so long as the ICS stay within their remit and do not favour specific countries at the expense of others. But that remit varies from organization to organization.

The pressures are different from those on national civil servants. One WHO official contrasted the WHO with the Centre for Disease Control (CDC) in Atlanta, USA.

> WHO is less strong technically but it is able to access virtually any technical organization in the world. I don't know any technical organization, if we have gone and asked for help, that has ever said: 'no, we are too busy; we won't help you'. WHO has a mandate which no other organization has. So it can pull things together. It does not belong to any country, so it is really seen (no matter how much we get criticized for this or that) as a fair broker for both sides of any issues, more than any other organization that I know. Yet, it is more complicated organizationally: country offices, regional offices, HQ with quite different groups. The internal workings, the internal politics, the internal management is much more complicated here than CDC. Also, funding for CDC comes from the US government; funding for WHO comes from 193 countries plus donor organizations.

The WHO may not be as efficient as the CDC, but it brings a clout because it is multilateral, does not represent interests of a particular country or group, and is able to manage cross-country issues that no other organization can.

In an international organization, the member states are 'organized', but the staff is the 'international' component.[50] ICS draw their legitimacy from two sources: formal rules and prevalent practices and perceptions. Formally, since all IOs are treaty-based, treaties recognize the legitimate role of ICS in pursuing multilateral cooperation. For example, the Marrakech Agreement that established the World Trade Organization clearly identifies the member states' desire to ensure 'the efficient functioning of the WTO Secretariat'. Within those parameters, ICS draw their legitimacy from their credibility, impartiality and neutrality, to 'a generalized perception or assumption that the actions of any entity are desirable, proper, or appropriate within some socially constructed system of norms, values, beliefs, and definitions'.[51]

IOs cannot work without an effective and active secretariat. The example of the response at the FAO to the IEE report is evidence. Member states tried to develop a response independently but could not and were forced to seek staff assistance. They had neither the history nor the expertise to understand all that the organization did or how it could consider or implement the report's proposals. WHO member states wanted to develop member-driven financial

---

[50] Inis Claude, *Swords into Plowshares: The Problems and Progress of International Organizations*, 4th edn (New York: Random House, 1971), 191.

[51] Hawkins and Jacoby, 'How Agents Matter'.

reform processes and asked the secretariat to devise them. In contrast, the WTO members reacted to the prominence of the GATT secretariat in the Uruguay Round to argue that now the secretariat should serve them.

So this chapter has sought to identify how different secretariats are able to mobilize influence and to chart whether they do so more or less openly. Secretariat capacity can be seen as a function of several forces. Some are external: the commitment and interests of member states; their capacity and determination to use the IO (rather than use procedures to put everything on hold); the degree of cohesion among the multiple member states; the prominence of the issues at a given time. It is possible to locate each of the secretariats along a spectrum, but their precise positions would be constantly shifting.

A WTO official tried to describe his understanding of the ideal relationship:

> It is not that we are manipulators or anything; we do not think of ourselves as some of Machiavellian puppet masters that can control destinies. We do not have power, but we do have influence if we use it carefully. What we can do is to facilitate people finding solutions, helping kick in ideas informally. Very often delegates come to us and ask for advice, quietly, off the record—about how they should pursue a certain issue. A lot of this comes down to trust and confidence between us and the delegates of member states.

Trust, confidence, expertise, knowledge, information, persuasion: these are the intangible, often nuanced, skills that are crucial to the constructive workings of any functioning IO.

That is the nature of bureaucracy. It is uneven in performance, across time and certainly across organizations. What is not reasonable to argue is that secretariats have no influence; that the principal–agent gap can ever be non-existent, or that changes in, or expansions of, the activities of the secretariats do not occur as an IO broadens its remit. Even the most constrained of secretariats makes decisions that have identifiable consequences; at different levels and by different means, they always will.

5

Agenda Setting

Agenda setting and agenda management are key elements for the effective operation of international organizations (IOs). They are also at the centre of political manœuvring among member states and between states and IOs. Agenda setting concerns the framing of issues and the prevailing norms; it sets out boundaries for what is and can be done in work programmes and how the objectives can be achieved. More importantly, it is about distribution of resources. Consequently, it inevitably involves and affects those who desire to defend the 'status quo'—the 'gatekeepers' of the existing practices—and those who advocate changes to the institution. Is the issue of foreign investment in farmland a concern of the Food and Agriculture Organizaation (FAO)? Who should set rules on ensuring adequate access to medicine—the World Health Organization (WHO), the World Trade Organization (WTO), or the World Intellectual Property Organization (WIPO)? Does development have anything to do with 'governance', especially anti-corruption? The international community has been facing constantly emerging issues. Who should decide what IOs do and how the agenda is debated among the players?

Agenda setting is recognized as a problem but one without a solution in sight not only at the WTO, where it often takes as long, if not longer, to negotiate an agenda as to reach an agreement, but also in other IOs, where the agenda is closely tied to the willingness and capacities of members to translate IO missions into political realities. Agenda setting is a competitive process with players striving to get their issues on the agenda at the expense of others; it is a process 'determined by power dynamics'.[1] Instead of taking power as given, recent studies have focused on the different capacities of players in shaping the agenda: those with 'the ability to create, mobilize, or disseminate policy ideas';[2] those with capacity to influence others' choices and policies, and

---

[1] See the discussion in R. Charli Carpenter, 'Governing the Global Agenda', in Deborah D. Avant, Martha Finnermore, and Susan K. Sell (eds), *Who Governs the Globe?* (New York: Cambridge University Press, 2010), 202–37; Cecilia Albin and Ariel Young, 'Setting the Table for Succeed—or Failure?', *International Negotiation*, 12 (2012), 37–64.

[2] Olivier Day, 'How Do Policy Ideas Spread among International Administrations?', *Journal of Public Policy*, 32 (2012), 53–76.

those who are able to build coalitions. The range of players who can shape the agenda-setting process in IOs has widened over the decades. It includes now not only large and powerful states, but also the head of an IO, the international bureaucracy, and chairs of international governing bodies.[3]

In addition, the number of the so-called international advocacy groups, particularly 'non-state' players, has exploded. They are having significant impact in agenda setting in many IOs with their extensive cross-country networks, engaging in lobbying and influencing member states and the secretariat, and building support alliances across countries and groups.[4] That some NGOs are able to take advantage of political opportunities in defining problems, building a profile for an issue, mobilizing support, winning international recognitions, and shaping the agenda process in IOs has become controversial among member states and international civil servants (ICS).[5] What is their role in the formal agenda-setting process across IOs? How do they interact with member states in multilateral arenas? How do member states see the role NGOs play in agenda-setting processes?

This chapter focuses on the interaction among the three groups of players—member states, the head of IOs, and the secretariat—in an agenda-setting process. Agenda setting is 'made up of various elements, including problems, solutions, participants, and opportunities'.[6] It is about how interpretations of problems and options for solutions compete to be selected. We are less interested in what each IO does in terms of programmes and projects than the agenda-setting process in which actors exercise their capacities, whether tangible or non-tangible, such as negotiation skills, knowledge, and an ability to persuade. Its results may legitimize ideas, players, functions, and actions, telling the world what should or should not be done and what actions and behaviour are considered as appropriate. Agenda setting in all IOs has evolved over the decades; the general trend is towards 'a back-and-forth iterative process'. We seek to understand who becomes involved in agenda setting; what capacity and opportunity they have in shaping the agenda; how ideas are identified as a matter of concern for policy; who proposes and supports them; and to what extent the process is open to players that are not necessarily at the agenda-setting table. Is the process one of principal–agent, or rigidly hierarchical, or

---

[3] Jonas Tallberg, 'The Power of the Chair', *International Studies Quarterly*, 54/1 (2010), 241–65; Spyros Blavoukos and Dimitris Bourantonis, 'Chairs as Policy Entrepreneurs in Multilateral Negotiations', *Review of International Studies*, 37 (2011), 653–72; Jarle Trondal, 'The Autonomy of Bureaucratic Organizations', *Journal of International Organization Studies*, 5/2 (2014), 55–69.

[4] Margaret Keck and Katherine Sikkink, *Activities beyond Borders* (Ithaca, NY: Cornell University Press, 1998).

[5] Jutta M. Joachim, *Agenda Setting: The UN and NGOs* (Washington: Georgetown University Press, 2007).

[6] Joachim, *Agenda Setting*, 2.

even the reverse, a case of 'ventriloquism', as we were told by a number of senior officials across the six IOs?

This chapter starts with a discussion on interpreting mandates. All IOs are given a wide range of responsibilities by the initial treaties that created the organization as well as by member states over their development. This variety of specific things an IO can and should do has to be interpreted by those involved. Second, we explore the potential role played by the key players in agenda setting, be they IO leaders, ICS, member states, or non-state players. The third section examines how competing multilateral institutions changed the politics of agenda setting in IOs. The conclusion stresses how pluralistic agenda setting has become. It is not the sole prerogative of powerful member states but is open to a much larger range of influences.

INTERPRETING MANDATES

All IOs were created with a set of formal mandates. While the original mandate sets the broad parameters for the operation and developments of an IO, it never provides specific programmes; nor does it set priorities. Thus, as IOs evolve, their formal mandates are always subject to interpretation. Competition in interpreting the original mission and in specifying programmes and priorities is part of the agenda setting in all IOs. Some IOs have broad mandates, while in others the mandate is relatively narrow. The six IOs in this study can be placed into two groups: the FAO, World Bank, and WHO have broad mandates that can and have to be interpreted when work programmes and projects are decided, often in a flexible way. The International Monetary Fund (IMF), WIPO, and the WTO have relatively narrow mandates. For instance, the IMF was created to promote 'international monetary cooperation' and 'exchange stability'. WIPO's responsibilities include the implementation of several international conventions and treaties, each of them covering specific issues regarding intellectual property rights. The WTO by definition is about trade. When issues are to be brought on board, they have to be justified within the parameter of 'monetary cooperation', trade, or intellectual property rights.

In contrast, the WHO Constitution proclaims its very ambitious objective of 'the attainment by all people of the highest possible level of health' (Article 1). In its preamble, health is defined 'as a state of complete physical, mental and social well-being and not merely the absence of disease or infirmity'. The Preamble of the FAO Constitution stipulates four main responsibilities: (*a*) to raise levels of nutrition and standards of living, (*b*) to secure improvements in food and agricultural products production and distribution, (*c*) to better the condition of rural population, and (*d*) to contribute towards an expanding world economy and ensure humanity's freedom from hunger. Like health and diseases, nutrition, food, and agricultural products are all loaded concepts, each of which covers a wide range of issues, while freedom from hunger and the welfare of rural populations do not have a single set of indicators to measure them.

These broadly defined objectives and responsibilities have seldom been amended, yet they are not only subject to interpretation in the process of deciding these IOs' strategic directions, policy programmes and specific projects, but also must adapt to the changing international environment. There are many examples of the contested interpretations as IOs have expanded. At the World Bank, for instance, what development means is constantly debated: in its first fifty years, 'bricks and mortar' were at the core of development and therefore the centre of the Bank's main business. Since the 1990s, other issues have been argued to be as important, if not more, as those infrastructure projects. Should priority be given to social programmes, such as education, or to economic development? Was health part of the jurisdiction of the World Bank? Was it the Bank's mandate to engage in anti-corruption, to improve the governing capacity of developing countries, to address social and economic inequality? The definitional issues are at the core of the debate at the WTO too—what is considered as trade; is trade facilitation part of trade? There is also the issue of priority. What should be the priority for the FAO—food, agriculture, or nutrition? If it is agriculture, should the priority go to farming, forestry, or fishery? How to interpret and define the broadly defined mandate is the core part of the agenda-setting process in all the six IOs.

In addition, each of the IOs is asked to play two roles: to provide global public goods (for example, negotiating and deciding common rules, regulations, and standards and generating and disseminating knowledge and information in their specific field, known as normative work) and to provide support to their member states (for example, providing specific services needed by member states—assistance work). At some IOs, such as the IMF and WTO, it is accepted that negotiating rules and standards and monitoring their implementation are the core of their operation. At the three technical institutions, the FAO, WIPO, and WHO, there has always been debate over the balance between normative work and technical assistance to member states. It is not only a question of whether normative work or providing assistance should be the priority, but also a question of what each entails. That is, if the normative work should take the priority, what norms are to be debated and negotiated? If providing services takes precedence, what kind of services should IOs offer, to whom, in what form, and how to fund it? Answers to these questions are seldom agreed among states.

The common argument is that the rich countries tend to demand that IOs focus on normative works while the poor countries demand assistance. The logic is that when countries do not have indigenous capacity in the field of health, nutrition, IP protection, or other aspects of development, they would like IOs to help develop local capacities or even assist taking on these tasks, and thus technical assistance is their preferred agenda of IOs. The political reality is much more complex, and the division between rich and poor is never straightforward. That is, not all technical assistance is welcomed in developing countries, while norm-setting can be politically divisive among many rich countries too.

Take the WHO as an example; there has been a long-held and widespread view that the WHO should focus on normative rather than assistance work: 'WHO was created as a UN technical agency...[it] was meant to serve as a reservoir of expertise and knowledge at the service of countries needing a hand...supplying advice, analyses, and best practices, though stopping short of directly implementing health programmes.'[7] Yet, countries seldom agree on what normative work the WHO should engage in and what the priorities of the normative work should be. Should the WHO 'promote and conduct research' and develop standards on infectious or non-communicable diseases? Should it focus on diseases or health systems? When the WHO, under international pressures, took on the negotiation on regulating breast-milk substitutes, there seemed to be consensus. Yet, when the agreement was eventually passed at the World Health Assembly in 1981, the vote was 188 to 1. The USA was the only country that opposed the code, on the grounds that the WHO was interfering in global trade.[8] It took extensive political manœuvring for Brundtland and her senior management team to place tobacco control on the negotiation agenda, and Margaret Chan and her team to start engaging in studies on the health impact of sugar consumption. Tobacco and beverage companies and farmers opposing the negotiation on tobacco controls and guidelines on reducing sugar intakes are predominately from rich countries.[9]

Thus, it does not make sense to see the issue of normative and assistance work as one of the rich versus the poor countries. Rather, the balance is between norm entrepreneurs and norm protectors.[10] This contest can be about big ideas and new issues, but more often than not it is about specific work programmes and concentrations. When a few countries or groups demand that IOs focus on standard-setting on the global health system, on good governance, on good farming practices, or on effective protection of IP

---

[7] Jack C. Chow, 'Is the WHO Becoming Irrelevant?' *Foreign Policy*, 9 December 2010.

[8] Fiona Godlee, 'WHO in Retreat: Is it Losing its Influence?', *BMJ* 309/6967 (1994), 1491–5.

[9] For the role tobacco companies played in undermining the WHO and its DGs, see Gian Luca Burci and Claude-Henri Vignes, *World Health Organization* (The Hague: Kluwer Law International, 2004), esp. 105–6.

[10] Ethan A. Nadelmann, 'Global Prohibition Regimes: The Evolution of Norms in International Society', *International Organization*, 44/4 (1990), 495–526; R. Charli Carpenter, 'Setting the Advocacy Agenda', *International Studies Quarterly*, 51/1 (2007), 99–120.

Agenda Setting 145

rights, the push could come from both rich and poor countries for the same as well as different reasons. Even when there is a united front among one group of members to support certain agenda or priorities, the views of most member states cannot be simply assumed on the basis of whether they are large or small, rich or poor. As one senior official at the WHO explained:

> Some of the North European donor countries like to tell us: WHO needs to focus and its unique role is normative and standard-setting, which it is; great. However, we have 194 member states and when they talk about a comparative advantage, most would say, 'we want WHO in the country'. Increasingly, there is a third voice from the emerging economies, 'which tell us: no, there is a third way of looking at this: we want WHO to be the influential actor in global health governance; we want you as an organization to start showing how all these various bits fit together'. All want WHO to stick with its comparative advantage, but member states see that comparative advantage in radically different ways.

An ambassador provides another angle:

> We are all for the normative work, but you also have got to teach us how to do it. Otherwise, what is the point of the normative work? You set the bar over there and ask me to jump. If I have never done any pole vaulting and I see the bar there; then you tell me that I have failed to cross it. But unless you actually go and train people and help them jump over the bar, it is useless to have the bar set up in the first place. You have to help countries develop national capacities, as the international community cannot replace national institutions.

At the FAO, debates on the mandate and the proportion of the normative versus assistance work have occasionally divided not only member states but also member states and senior management. We see changes of the 'mandate' of the FAO throughout its history, from being the 'world food authority' under the first DG, to technical standard-setter and promoting 'the right to be free from hunger' in the 1950s and 1960s, and to 'an activist organization with a role in operational activities for development' in the 1980s and 1990.[11] Normative work on food security shifted at least three times between 1974 and 1994, from the global and the national to the household and the individual, from a food-first perspective to a livelihood perspective; and from objective indicators to subjective perceptions.[12] Until the late 1990s, much of the FAO's fieldwork was part of the work programmes of the United Nations Development Programme (UNDP), while those at HQ concentrated on normative work. When UNDP resources dried up, some argued that the FAO should focus on normative work, such as technical standard-setting. Others,

---

[11] Charles H. Weitz, *Who Speaks for the Hungry? How FAO Elects its Leader* (Uppsala, Sweden: DAG Hammarskjöld Foundation, 1997), 10.
[12] Simon Maxwell, 'Food Security: A Post-Modern Perspective', *Food Policy*, 21/2 (1996), 155–70.

however, insisted that the FAO help members develop national capacities in sustainable agriculture and fishery, good food and nutrition. Standard-setting is seldom technical only; it is often highly political. Should the FAO engage in work on stamping out illegal fishing, or on setting standards for responsible practices in fishing in line with conservation at the same time, or on standard setting on school lunch programmes? What about soil management, veterinarian practices? All these issue areas can come under the purview of the FAO. There is no consensus on these issues either within states or among member states in IOs.

Balancing normative work and providing actual assistance and support have never been easy, even for those IOs that are seen primarily as delivering 'things'. The World Bank, for instance, was authorized to 'do development'—'to assist in the construction and development...by facilitating the investment...to promote private foreign investment...to arrange the loans... [and] to conduct its operation'.[13] Doing development requires an understanding of development. Normative work was undertaken in the 1960s under George Wood, who argued: 'You can't have a development agency unless it has as its fuselage the loans which are being made, but one wing has to be project work and the other wing has to be economics.'[14] In the following decades, normative work might have been accepted as part of the big agenda of the World Bank, but the understanding of 'development' has constantly changed. As noted, basic infrastructure projects were replaced in the late 1980s and the 1990s when economic policies and policy designs became the core of the World Bank's work programmes. By the late 1990s, some of the old prohibited topics emerged as priorities, such as anti-corruption, good governance, and rule of law. 'I decided in 1996 that I would redefine the "C" word not as a political issue but as a something social and economic,' James Wolfensohn announced. 'That got me under the wire of the Articles of Agreement.'[15] Governance programmes followed.

Interpreting the mandates and balancing the two delegated responsibilities to all IOs—normative and assistance work—are ever evolving. They are shifted not only by power and might, but also by the process where players have interacted. With their technical expertise, both the FAO and the WHO have been pressured to engage in normative work. Many member states also want and need substantial fieldwork. The mismatch of the demand between those who contribute resources to IOs and those who need assistance is undoubtedly a factor highlighting the debate over agenda setting and shaping

---

[13] International Bank of Reconstruction and Development (IBRD), 'Articles of Agreement', Article I.

[14] Jochen Kraske, *Bankers with a Mission* (Washington: World Bank, 1996), 134.

[15] Quoted in M. A. Thomas, 'The Governance Bank', *International Affairs*, 83/4 (2007), 742. For the detailed discussion, see Xu Yi-chong and Patrick Weller, *Inside the World Bank* (New York: Palgrave Macmillan, 2009), ch. 6.

its process. What has complicated this process since the early 1990s is (*a*) an increasing number of players who demand to have a say on IO agenda setting, and (*b*) many more multilateral institutions that compete for agenda, resources, and support of members.

WHOSE INITIATIVES

Who shapes and decides the agenda for an IO is always a political question. We know that (*a*) states jealously guard their prerogatives; states vary in their capacity to participate in IO activities; states often do not agree with each other on what they would like IOs to do or achieve; those representing the member states involved in agenda setting come from different backgrounds (diplomats versus technical experts) and with different viewpoints and capacities; (*b*) the head of an IO matters in agenda setting, as each one comes into office with different visions, skills, capacities, and willingness to lead; and (*c*) the secretariat or ICS play an important role in shaping the agenda, even at the WTO, which occupies one extreme of the spectrum of 'bureaucratic independence'.

In the world of multilateral cooperation, states have also created several intergovernmental organizations in each of the primary areas where the six IOs in this study have jurisdiction. As these IOs compete for international attention, coverage, and resources, opportunities are created for member states and other players to shape the agenda of these IOs in one direction or another. For instance, the FAO is expected both to engage in normative work and develop technical standards in three broadly defined areas—agriculture, food, and nutrition—and to act as a source of support to its members (Figure 5.1). Member states also created the World Food Programme (WFP) as the world's largest humanitarian agency, delivering food aid, and the International Fund for Agricultural Development (IFAD), which focuses exclusively on rural poverty reduction, raising the poor's productivity and income, and improving their quality of life.[16] The line of responsibilities among these institutions has become murkier as member states choose which institutions can serve their purpose while these organizations compete to expand in size and activities.

On health issues, the WHO is considered as the authoritative normative health agency within the UN system; the World Bank also makes loans to 'strengthen health systems', with programmes of health, nutrition, and population; and UNICEF focuses on its savvy country-level efforts to catalyse improvements in health. It is not only that member states and other non-state players can 'forum shop', take issues to another arena in order to get preferred

---

[16] D. John Shaw, *Global Food and Agricultural Institutions* (New York: Routledge, 2009).

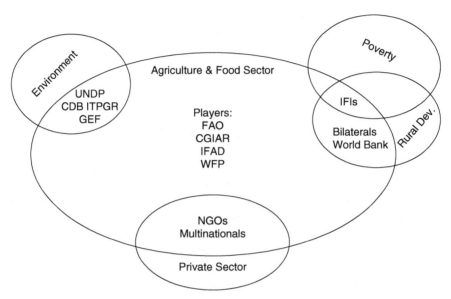

Figure 5.1. FAO's turf

Note:
CDB Convention on Biological Diversity
CGIAR Consultative Group on International Agricultural Research
GEF Global Environment Facility
IFAD International Fund for Agricultural Development
IFIs International Financial Institutions
ITPGRFA International Treaty on Plant Generic Resources for Food and Agriculture
UNDP United Nations Development Programme
WFP World Food Programme

Source: compiled by the authors.

actions, or sometimes react against programmes of particular IOs that they dislike. There is also the competition in interpreting any given issues by all involved: member states, NGOs, and IOs themselves. That is, as issues attract global attention, they are interpreted from multiple angles. Trademarks, for instance, were under the purview of WIPO; they are also considered as trade issues, discussed at the WTO, development issues under the purview of the UNDP and the World Bank, or/and health issues debated at the WHO. The global regulation of genetically modified foods was discussed at the WTO, OECD, FAO, and the Codex Alimentarius Commission.[17] The availability of the competing multilateral institutions covering similar ranges of issues not only affects where players can raise their interests, but can also define how issues are discussed and priorities set.

---

[17] Sebastiaan Princen, 'Governing through Multiple Forums: The Global Safety Regulation of Genetically Modified Crops and Foods', in Mathias Koenig-Archibugi and Michael Zurn (eds), *New Modes of Governance in the Global System* (Basingstoke: Palgrave Macmillan, 2006), 52–76.

A further striking feature of the international terrain is the emergence of many new organizations, groups and networks, with substantial interests and competence in areas covered in this study. Many NGOs, both non-profit and for profit, compete for the opportunity to voice their concerns in the international arena; many individuals live on the fringe of IOs, assessing, overseeing, criticizing, complaining, proposing, always believing they know best what the international community ought to be doing. These non-state players vary in size and capacity. Their desire to put issues to the IO agenda is sometimes designed to change domestic policies, what Keck and Sikkink call the 'boomerang effect'—'where governments are inaccessible or deaf to groups whose claims may nonetheless resonate elsewhere, international contacts can amplify the demands of domestic groups, pry open space for new issues, and then echo back to demands into the domestic arena'.[18] Their role in the agenda-setting process in IOs is as controversial as the issues themselves. In some IOs, member states would like to keep them at arm's length and ask the secretariat to do so. A few member states use NGOs to test the waters, as demands to expand the coverage are constantly made by these non-state players.

Agenda setting therefore is a political process taking place in this large complex environment, where member states, IO leaders, ICS, and a growing number of non-state for-profit and non-profit organizations interact in competing for their interests and their preferred policy agenda. The next subsections examine the role of each group of players in shaping the agenda in IOs.

Member States

States insist on their right to decide what IOs should or should not do collectively and what their priorities should be. When IOs were created, founding states had agreed on a set of missions that states saw at the time as crucial for collective and cooperative actions via IOs. Formal rules often also delineate who can nominally propose the agenda and in what manner. At the same time, all IOs nowadays assert in principle the mantra of member-driven organizations that member states should drive the agenda and decide the priorities of IOs' work.

In some IOs, the formal rules require member states to propose and decide the agenda, while in others it is the management led by the DG who proposes the agenda. If the question 'who sets the agenda' could be placed on a spectrum, the WTO occupies one end, where member states insist on their right and prerogative to propose anything that might be discussed among themselves. The IMF should occupy the other end of the spectrum, where it is

---

[18] Keck and Sikkink, *Activists beyond Borders*, 13.

always the management's agenda. Other IOs are along this spectrum with a general trend moving more towards the WTO. The actual process of agenda-setting nonetheless is always iterative, including at the WTO. Thus, strategies and tactics of all players—member states and the management—determine the process. The most effective leader in shaping the agenda is the one, as popularized by Nelson Mandela, who 'is like a shepherd. He stays behind the flock, letting the most nimble go out ahead, whereupon the others follow, not realizing that all along they are being directed from behind.'[19]

State representatives can take the leadership role if they have the determination, resources, and capacity to pursue the case and rally support both at home and in IOs. One example was the WHO's Alma-Ata Conference in September 1978, where primary health care was endorsed by member states. In the 1950s and 1960s, 'the first priority of WHO was the eradication of malaria and control of other diseases'—an agenda pushed by the US government and supported by West European countries. The Soviet delegation in the early 1970s proposed 'Basic Principles for the Development of Health Services'. Facing strong opposition and resistance from most member states and the secretariat and the reluctance of the DG, Dimitri Venediktov, the Soviet delegate to the WHO, in collaboration with the WHO director of Strengthening Health Systems, persistently pushed forward the agenda item at the EB in the 1970s in the politically hostile environment of the darkest days of the cold war. The reasons for the Soviet push for the agenda and the conference were suspected at the time to include: 'Fear of Chinese influence in the WHO; to prepare for the Olympics; Venediktov running for DG; to gain influence in the third world (pay for tickets).'[20] It was clear that, without the persistence and manœuvring of Venediktov, the Alma-Ata Conference could not have happened. He was the most influential person in bringing about the Alma-Ata Conference, which marked the beginning of a new international understanding of the real dimensions of health-care needs and enormous challenges associated with it; altered the WHO's focus on technical assistance and efforts at disease eradication; and opened up new prospects for international cooperation in health.[21]

A similar role was played by Argentina and Brazil to include development into the agenda at WIPO. IP issues were initially considered so technical and specific that few diplomats knew anything about them; nor did they care. Fifteen years after IP issues had been integrated into the trade negotiations at

---

[19] A quotation taken from Nelson Mandela's *Long Walk to Freedom* is widely used by journalists and scholars. It also has a connotation that let others take the credits of the work a leader has done.

[20] Socrates Litsios, 'The Long and Difficult Road to Alma-Ata: A Personal Reflection', *The Politics of the World Health Organization*, 32/4 (2002), 709–32.

[21] Dmitry Venediktov, 'Primary Health Care: Alma-Ata and After', *World Health Forum*, 19/1 (1998), 79–86.

the WTO, several IP-related issues, from access to medicine, traditional knowledge, and especially counterfeit products and piracy, had become so controversial that by the early 2000s they had become daily headlines. Meanwhile, a series of international events placed development on the agenda: the WTO launched the Doha 'Development' Round in 2001; the Earth Summit 2002 advocated sustainable development; and, in 2002, UN Secretary General commissioned the Millennium project, which led to the adoption of the Millennium Development Goals in 2005. Several countries decided to take the IP issues back to WIPO to redefine the IP issues with development in mind, because they had been frustrated with protracted trade negotiations at the WTO.

Taking advantage of the changing international environment, the delegations of Argentina and Brazil submitted an eight-page proposal to the WIPO General Assembly on behalf of a group of countries calling themselves 'Friends of Development' in August 2004, demanding development be put on the IP agenda. The proposal noted 'the need to integrate the development dimension into policy making on intellectual property protection' and called for, among other things, the establishment of a new subsidiary body within WIPO to examine technology transfer, a new treaty to promote access to the results of publicly funded research in developed countries, fair enforcement of IP rights, and more development-oriented technical cooperation and assistance. It took three years of bitter fighting within and outside WIPO for the initiative from a small group of member states to be endorsed at the WIPO General Assembly with forty-five recommendations, together known as a WIPO Development Agenda. The initiative inevitably met resistance and suspicion (as new issues tend to in all IOs) from some member states as well as some quarters of the WIPO secretariat, including many of its senior officials.[22]

During the process, the institution was sharply polarized, among member states, within the secretariat itself, and between some member states and segments of the secretariat. The division among member states was not a case of developed against developing countries. Some developed countries, such as Britain and Switzerland, had expressed their concerns of the potential division between developed and developing countries over IP protection since 1970 in the preparations for the establishment of WIPO.[23] After Brazil and

---

[22] For the controversies, see Neil Weinstock Netanel (ed.), *The Development Agenda: Global Intellectual Property and Developing Countries* (New York: Oxford University Press, 2009); Jeremy de Beer (ed.), *Implementing the WIPO Development Agenda* (Ottawa: Wilfrid Laurier University Press, 2009); Geoffrey Yu, 'The Structure and Process of Negotiations at the World Intellectual Property Organization', *Chicago-Kent Law* Review, 82/3 (2007), 1439–44; Coenraad Visser, 'The Policy-Making Dynamics in Intergovernmental Organizations', *Chicago-Kent Law Review*, 82/3 (2007), 1457–66.

[23] Debora J. Harbert, 'The World Intellectual Property Organization: Past Present and Future', *Journal of Copyright Society of the USA*, 54 (2006–7), 253–84; Henrique Choer Moraes

Argentina had tabled their proposal at the General Assembly at WIPO in 2004, Britain played a key role in bridging the developed countries and the Friends of Development by initiating a dialogue to build confidence. 'Several meetings and seminars took place outside WIPO with the participation of Heads of Delegations, IP delegates and experts to deal with the issue of IP and development.'[24] The three-year negotiations on the issue turned out to be difficult, hostile, and fraught with acrimony. The secretariat was deeply divided. Some senior officials at WIPO publicly viewed the initiative as a way to 'disrupt the status quo'.[25] The internal resistance to include 'development' into the WIPO agenda arose not only because of the complexity of so many technical issues involved, but also about who set the WIPO agenda. Historically, it had always been the management that proposed the agenda for member states to consider. The DG on behalf of the management 'sponsored treaty initiatives, produced treaty drafts and working papers, and drafted model laws either at the behest or closely aligned with the positions of the United States and Europe'—the largest users of the IP system so far.[26] As a 'conservative institution', without effective leadership, the institution became paralysed and dysfunctional. The battle eventually claimed the scalp of its DG, who agreed to resign before his term ended. The new DG was an advocate of the expanded agenda.

One controversial issue in the Doha Development trade negotiation was cotton. This time around it was the four West African countries, Benin, Burkina Faso, Chad, and Mali, which proposed 'the cotton initiative' to accelerate elimination of trade-distorting cotton subsidies and financial compensation for losses. These are four tiny economies with no particular clout in international relations or in the international economy. The key target was the cotton subsidy regime in the USA, China, and the EU. The proposal presented a complex trade and development challenge for the multilateral trade negotiations and international community; rich countries were no longer divided on the lines that had emerged during the Uruguay Round. 'Fairtrade plays a crucially important role in reminding us of the ethical dimension of trade, trying to ensure that trade genuinely benefits those, especially the world's poorest people, who participate in it,' stated the UK Secretary of State for Small Business. 'Cotton is at the heart of agricultural and economic development in many

---

and Otavio Brandelli, 'The Development Agenda at WIPO: Context and Origins', in Netanel (ed.), *The Development Agenda*, 33–49.

[24] Alberto J. Dumont and Ines Gabriela Fastame, 'World Intellectual Property Organization Development Agenda', *Journal of Generic Medicine*, 6/2 (2009), 101.

[25] Julia C. Morse and Robert O. Keohane, 'Contested Multilateralism', *Review of International Organizations*, 9/4 (2014), 386.

[26] Neil Weinstock Netanel, 'The WIPO Development Agenda and its Development: Policy Context', in Netanel (ed.), *The Development Agenda*, 9.

African countries.'[27] The proposal was eventually accepted and included in the negotiation agenda.[28] Bringing an issue to an agenda does not necessarily lead to a successful solution to the problem, but it is a necessary step to move an issue forward by drawing international attention. Increasingly, small countries, often with the support of one or two large ones, can set part of the agenda.

The above cases show that, to be able to make a difference in IO agenda-setting, member states have to care about issues enough to take the initiatives, have to know what they want, have to have the determination to fight the cause, and have to have the necessary resources and capacity to gain the support from a large number of member states and the support of the secretariat. In most cases and most of the time, most member states of IOs are *reactive* to the strategic directions, medium-term plans, and specific work programmes presented by the IO management. International organizations seldom rank high in government agendas, and representatives of most member states do not have the resources to drive an important, especially controversial, issue. This is the case in at least five of the six IOs. The comments that member states drive the agenda do not reflect their relatively reactive role. A chair of the FAO Programme Committee explained:

> The agenda-setting work is done at the Programme Committee where there is a lot of discussion and debate. There are twelve members plus the chair, two from each region. The rules require they be elected in individual capacity and speak in their individual capacities. Some are really good; they have shown a continued interest in the objectives and activities of the Organization, have participated in conference or council sessions and have special competence and experience in various fields of the organization's activities. Particularly, they are willing to do the homework and can bring in good ideas, while others are less so. But we work within the strategic framework and the medium-term plan and work on the work programme *proposed* by the DG.

In most cases, the DG and the management continue driving this iterative process even after the committee meeting. A state representative serving on the Programme Committee explained: 'after a discussion, the secretariat will take these various comments on board and produce a final draft agenda. Then we all feel a certain ownership to what is going to happen.' Another added: 'sometimes changes occur because this draft agenda goes for final approval by the DG, who decides that he would like to include some or another issue. When the programme goes to the council, as you can see, there is little discussion of it at all.'

---

[27] Vince Cable, 'Foreword', in Fairtrade Foundation, *The Great Cotton Stitch-Up* (November 2010).
[28] For the discussion on the cotton initiative, see WTO, *The Cotton Initiative*, and various documents at <https://www.wto.org/english/tratop_e/agric_e/negs_bkgrnd20_cotton_e.htm> (accessed 15 March 2015).

The reactive role of member states in agenda setting is in part due to the fact that 'the committee meets only twice a year for a week, and one day of that week is reserved for the joint meeting with the finance committee. Not all committee members are conscientious about the committee work and get information about what people [in their country or region] think about that,' explained a chair of the Programme Committee at the FAO. More importantly, countries could hardly agree on anything. 'You have a group of members who really want FAO to be much more of a global standard setting body, dealing with trade issues, food security, plant protection, etc., while others want to see FAO working on the ground, being operational, dealing with farmers in Africa, etc.' The Independent External Evaluation (IEE) of the FAO, funded by a group of rich countries, recommended the agenda of the FAO should be demand driven, 'instead of supply driven in terms of what the donors want' or what the secretariat would like to do. When many relatively poor countries want more technical assistance in the field and they would like to have more help in 'devising agricultural policy, supporting planning, drafting effective legislation, and creating national strategies to achieve rural development and hunger alleviation goals',[29] other member states ask, 'is this what the FAO should be doing?' Senior officials at the FAO agreed: 'we do not get strong direction from members', not only because of the disagreement of over 190 member states, but also because, with some many members, someone has to take the lead to propose a coherent work programme for the Programme Committee to work on.

Similar perspectives were proposed by both representatives and officials at the IMF, WIPO, WHO, and the World Bank: 'the agenda is always set and presented by the management at the board meeting'; 'we [African countries] find it extremely difficult as a group to keep up with what is going on let alone taking initiatives'. The ambassador of a large developing country explained:

> What happens is that the DG presents her agenda, her programmes; the secretariat prepares the papers, including those on strategic frameworks, annual plans and work programmes, sent to the missions. We look at them and put some comments and then send them to the capital with suggestions. If it is on technical issues, we simply ask for instructions. We depend on advice from the capital; there is a lot of toing and froing, sometimes until the time you enter the conference room. But the capital also realizes the expertise is over here, not there, especially with the secretariat. We also look at priorities of other countries in developing our responses.

---

[29] David Hallam, 'Turbulence and Reform at the United Nations Food and Agriculture Organization', in Patrick Weller and Xu Yi-chong (eds), *The Politics of International Organizations: Views from Insiders* (New York: Routledge, 2015), 187.

Agenda Setting

Member-driven agenda setting is further limited by internal disagreements within member states. This issue is discussed in several places in this book. The common assumption is that states always know what they want from IOs. In practice, countries often have varieties of views on a given issue—the technical people often do not agree with diplomats, or those in capitals with those serving as representatives in IOs. Taking states as single entities always leads to a flawed analysis of their participations in IOs. One former DDG explained to us:

> In dealing with member states, one often assumes that they know exactly what they wish to pursue in the organization. The reality is the contrary. State representatives may be talking a lot, but behind that veil of words, they can be so muddled about what they want out of that organization. Some of them have unclear positions, a reflection of internal national situations where the issue might be low priority for government, or different government agencies involved are not well coordinated.

Different expectations among agencies within countries create frustrations for those who work at IOs. At the General Assembly at the FAO and WHO, ministers tell the organization that it should focus on how to become a better normative agency for agriculture or health. Then their individual and collaborative evaluations of IOs not only assess the IOs according to different criteria but also demand actions that contradict what their ambassadors or ministers have said at the governing bodies in IOs.

For instance, in 2013, the British government organized a review of effectiveness of its foreign aid, including its voluntary contributions to IOs. The British government argued that 'when times are tight—as they are now—we have an increased responsibility to make sure we get the best value for every pound we spend on overseas aid'. Evaluation was about the aid delivery at country level, and it assessed how the country fieldwork was done in recipient countries. Seventeen donor countries had formed the Multilateral Organization Performance Assessment Network, a network 'with a common interest in assessing the organizational effectiveness of the major multilateral organizations they fund'.[30] This network's evaluation of the FAO in 2011 pointed out that 'the FAO needs to bridge the gap between strategic documents and programme implementation (e.g. gender mainstreaming, the environment, human-rights based approaches, and country programming)'.[31] None of these topics represents what the FAO was good at or what it was created for. More importantly, this was precisely what the IEE recommended that the FAO should avoid. As one senior official of an IO stated:

---

[30] Australia, Austria, Belgium, Canada, Denmark, Finland, France, Germany, Ireland, the Netherlands, Norway, Republic of Korea, Spain, Sweden, Switzerland, UK, and the USA.

[31] Multilateral Organization Performance Assessment Network, 'Food and Agriculture Organization (FAO) of the United Nations', volume I (December 2011), p. ix.

The General Assembly requires us play a normative role and specially tells us to 'do the standard setting'. Then the multilateral aid review evaluates us on a completely different set of criteria. Are there people who realize that this is contradictory? Yes. But the politics of keeping the aid budget going were behind the multilateral aid review. They could then say we have funded the ones that are good value for money. That helps protect the aid spending. It is, however, not exactly a great experience for us, but probably it is worth it.

This schizophrenia of member states in IOs sometimes makes it quite challenging for the DGs and their staff.

Heads of IOs

As often as not, initiatives at IOs come from the head of the organization. In some IOs, proposing agendas is part of their delegated responsibility. At the IMF and the World Bank, it has always been the case that 'the agenda is set by the management'. It is also the responsibility of the head of the IMF or the World Bank to 'sell' its agenda to the Board. Some had an easier time than others.[32] In other IOs, that responsibility is formally reserved to member states or an elected group of member states. Increasingly, even when the management is delegated by the Constitution or the Articles of Agreement to propose the strategic plans or work programmes, there is a lot of 'leading from behind work'. Member states need to believe they are in the driver's seat and have the ownership of the agenda for multilateral cooperation to succeed—'we initiated and led this "member-driven" reform process', explained a senior official at the WHO. However, not all heads of IOs are willing or capable of taking the lead in agenda setting.

According to the Constitution of the FAO, the DG of the FAO shall 'have full power and authority to direct the work of the Organization' and 'to formulate for consideration by the Conference and of the Council proposals for appropriate action in regard to matters coming before them' (Article VII, sections 4 and 5). Some DGs were more willing to exercise this power than others. By the 1990s, questions were raised about 'the lack of utility' of the power given to the DG, and, by 2005, the FAO Council decided to organize an IEE of FAO on, among other things, this specific question.[33] According to the IEE's report, the constitution provides a broad set of objectives for the organization to achieve. It 'requires FAO to be a global policy setter, facilitator,

---

[32] See, e.g., the discussion on organization restructuring under Wolfensohn in Zhang Shengman, *One Step at a Time* (先站住, 再站高) (Shanghai: Wenhui Press, 2006).

[33] Weitz, *Who Speaks for the Hungry?*, 6. FAO, 'Report of the Independent External Evaluation of the Food and Agriculture Organization of the United Nations', C2007/7A.1-Rev.1 (September 2007).

Agenda Setting

partner and coordinator, as well as a doer'. By the turn of the century, the FAO had lost its direction and become 'a facile excuse for doing nothing'.[34] This was because, to a large extent, the DG could not take the leadership in deciding the direction for the organization; the DG failed to propose 'bold options' for the organization; and the DG was unable to manage 'the priorities', explained ADG Louise Fresco, who resigned in 2006.[35]

While the DG at the FAO was criticized by the independent external review for not providing leadership, other senior officials differed: 'This DG brought the FAO a high profile when he initiated the World Food Summit in 1996', which eventually allowed the staff to pioneer the work on food security. Another official used the example of how the Voluntary Guidelines on the Responsible Governance of Tenure of Land, Fisheries, and Forests were developed to explain the dynamics of agenda-setting:

> The genesis of the initiative was that we raised an alarm when the world food price rose dramatically in 2005–8. The DG was pretty astute in spotting controversial things and asked us to set up an interdepartmental working group to look at the issue and decide whether we as the FAO should be doing anything about it. I then walked over each inch of this building [the FAO], trying to find people who were working in this area; no one was. There were people interested in land and land management, but they did not know investment. Those who knew investment did not know much about foreign direct investment. I started looking outside the FAO. We know agriculture issues, but not investment. UNCTAD at the time was working for the World Investment Report 2009, which would focus on agriculture and resources. They know investment, but not agriculture. We talked to a couple of World Bank people who were interested in the volatile food price too. The DG asked me to set up an interdepartmental working group to look at the issue. He gave us the task, but did not give us money. We talked to the Japanes,e who had invited me for several of their conferences. We then got $2 million from the Japanese and some from other donors too. We produced a number of studies on the topic from different angles and started the ball rolling. The DG took the issue to the United Nations General Assembly.

Whether DGs propose or support certain items on the agenda for the organization depends in part on the capacity of the staff to provide specific analyses to translate some vague visions and ideas to concrete and actionable plans. It also depends on the political skill DGs have to persuade member states to support them. As one senior official explains: 'This DG knew exactly what he wanted; unfortunately what he wanted was not always in agreement with what staff wanted or what some powerful member states

---

[34] FAO, 'Report of the Independent External Evaluation of the Food and Agriculture Organization of the United Nations', C2007/7A.1-Rev.1 (September 2007), 146.
[35] 'Resignation letter of Louise Fresco, ADG, FAO', 154 May 2006, at <http://www.theguardian.com/world/2006/may/14/foodanddrink> (accessed 15 March 2016).

wanted.' When DGs' agendas clash with both the staff and member states, it could create irrevocable animosity.

Similar responsibility of agenda setting is formally delegated to DGs at WIPO too. The Convention that established the WIPO specifically established an International Bureau as the secretariat of the organization, headed by the DG. The Convention clearly states: 'The Director General shall prepare programmes and budget and periodical reports on activities. He shall transmit them to the Governments of the interested States and to the competent organs of the Unions and the Organization' (Article 9, section 5). The DG also serves as *ex-officio* secretary to all the governing bodies of the WIPO—the General Assembly, Conference, and Coordination Committee—and any other committees and working groups. The governing bodies can 'discuss, approve and adopt' the direction, budget, and activities of the organization, but the initial power is vested in the hands of the DG and, by extension, the secretariat. Consequently, the DG and the International Bureau always play a significant role in shaping the direction of the organization by deciding the agenda of the organization.

In contrast, Article 28(g) of the Constitution of the WHO specifies that the EB will submit to the General Assembly 'for consideration and approval a general programme of work covering a specific period'—that is, the EB will decide whether the WHO should concentrate its work on 'maternal and child health' rather than 'research in the field of health'. Historically, however, it is the DG who shapes the direction of WHO work, as the *Lancet* comments: 'the job of WHO Director-General is as much about redefining the notion of health as it is about managing an international organization'.[36] How DGs define 'health' can frame the agenda and work programmes of the organization. Brundtland framed health as an economic issue with her acclaimed Commission on Macroeconomics and Health. Her successor, Dr Lee, saw health as a bundle of social determinants. For Margaret Chan, health is all about security: 'We are putting health on the security agenda because of the vulnerability due to new infections.'[37] By defining what health is all about, DGs can set the tone for programmes during their tenure. In addition, Article 34 of the WHO Constitution requires that 'the Director General shall prepare and submit to the Board the financial statements and budget estimates of the Organization'. By deciding the allocation of resources, DGs are able to shape the agenda and work programmes for the organization.

DGs can also use their position to facilitate, ignore, or frustrate the process when others try to bring issues on the agenda. Many have argued that WIPO missed an important opportunity when its DG, Arpad Bogsch, was asked to

---

[36] Hannah Brown, 'Profile: Margaret Chan: New is the Time for WHO to Achieve Results', *Lancet*, 369, 17 March 2007, p. 899.

[37] Brown, 'Profile: Margaret Chan'.

take on the issue of Trade-Related Aspects of Intellectual Property Rights (TRIPS) in the 1980s by developed countries, especially the United States at the initial stage. Bogsch was 'a lawyer, a very bright person, and a very clever person, but was useless in economics, useless, and he did not like the discipline'. When US IP-based industries 'displayed a significant catalytic and stimulative role in defining IP as a trade issue and in having US trade officials accept IP as part of their agenda',[38] 'Bogsch ignored it and kept doing his treaties on how to fill out trademark applications and so on; he missed the bigger picture of the growing economic importance of this IP issue.' Another senior official at WIPO added: 'it was early days of the knowledge economy; he missed this economic shift and did not quite understand what was happening. This happened even after WIPO was invited to be an observer at Uruguay Round trade negotiations over IP issues as Bogsch kept saying "what are they doing in my kingdom and they would not succeed".' When Bogsch dismissed the importance of IP as an emerging trade issue, WIPO missed the opportunity to take the lead in negotiating a global treaty. As leaders of IOs, DGs can also shape the agenda by actively engaging in bringing an issue to a global stage.

One recent controversy was whether it was the role of the World Bank to combat Ebola outbreaks in West Africa. Its president, Jim Kim, coming from a public-health background and with little understanding of banking or international finance, had always wanted to shape global health policies. Ebola outbreak presented him with an opportunity for the World Bank to get involved. He quickly committed US$400 million to fighting the epidemic, 'a quarter of which he pushed out in just nine days, [and] dispatched bank employees to afflicted west African countries'. He also contemplated including childhood stunting caused by malnutrition into the Bank lending programmes, arguing that 'we need to invest in grey-matter infrastructure; neuronal infrastructure is quite possibly going to be the most important infrastructure'.[39] Both met strong criticism from its current and former senior officials, who argued that the World Bank was not a humanitarian organization and fighting malnutrition or pandemics were not part of its development mandate. Of course, the president won the battle, with little internal support.

The ability of IO leaders to shape political agenda is subject to circumstances. Member states may not know exactly what they want, but their reactions cannot be ignored. Some heads of IOs can be quite skilful in 'convincing' member states that what they are proposing is what members really want. Agenda setting in a multilateral environment is 'opportunistic rather than designed', one DG explained patiently:

---

[38] Susan Sell, *Private Power, Public Law* (New York: Cambridge University Press, 2004), 90.
[39] Andrew Rice, 'How the World Bank's Biggest Critic Became its President', *Guardian*, 11 August 2016.

> In the best of all possible worlds, you would have a designed agenda. In the best of all possible worlds, you would sit everyone down around a table and discuss it. Now it is a multi-speed, multi-tiered world. You do multilaterally what you can do, rather than what you should necessarily do. Of course, you have got to be informed by the state of the world, have an idea of where you would like to go. You do not disclose it but you keep plugging away at certain messages and take small steps, hoping that you are going to be able to get an opportunity to push one through.

Various venues exist for the heads of IOs to engage in persuasion. One senior official at the IMF explained that, before management took matters to the board, it had already had extensive exchanges and decided on a view. The MD chairs the board meeting and informs the EDs about the agenda, policies, or actions to be needed. These are the formal meetings where the MD dominates in setting the agenda and deciding on the direction of actions.

> As you know we do not vote; so we meet again and again until we have at least the support of three-quarters of the EDs and often the rest would go along. As the MD chairs the meeting, EDs would be told 'I love your view, but I want your capital's view. This is not a seminar to exchange views. We need your decision, meaning your government's decision, in responding to my agenda.' At informal meetings, the MD and often the deputies would 'brief' EDs on where the institution is going and seek views from EDs on various matters, based on some of which, the MD would bring some of the issues back to the following board meetings. It is an iterative process but the MD is very much at the driver's seat.

Leaders of IOs need to choose their vehicles. Since the turn of the twenty-first century, it has become difficult for the international community to reach binding agreements. Yet, several IOs have pursued treaty negotiations, including the WHO, which had historically shunned them:

> One of the old arguments at WHO was that we did not need a treaty to make good public health. A treaty takes years; it is expensive; it is difficult; it is political, etc. In the past ten years, it turned out to be as difficult to negotiate a soft agreement, such as this global strategy of innovation, public health and intellectual property rights, or the pandemic influenza virus sharing. We did after all succeed in negotiating State and Community Tobacco Control. At the moment, we are not negotiating any treaties, but it can be a quite powerful instrument to pursue public health and to steer this organization.

So other strategies had to be adopted. 'With the general depressed view of capacity of the international community to agree on anything in town (Geneva),' one DG explained, 'we have to be skilful in what we want and how we pursue it.'

> We could reach this [limited] agreement at the time when other IOs are unable to do so because it is specific; it addressed a defined interest group. This is also important because we are at the stage of 'transition', where one system of power

relations is dead while a new one has not been born. So you have the emerging countries that are not ready to take responsibility. During this transition period, it is very difficult to get agreements on anything. When we have a specific subject matter with a defined set of interests and a defined set of beneficiaries, we then can work with them. This is how we succeeded this time.

While having some leeway, the heads of IOs have to be aware of the intricate politics underpinning the process of agenda setting. A western country proposed to a DG an African summit in order to persuade African countries to comply with some of its preferred policies. An eastern country wanted the DG to convene a summit in its country for a completely different matter. 'It was apparent that countries are plotting with me really for their own agendas and you can see quickly what each of those agendas is,' explained the DG.

Secretariat

In answering our question about who set the agenda, one DG simply said without any hesitation, 'me'. Of course, there are many qualifications of this 'me'. In a few cases, it is the ideas and vision of the DG that set the parameters for the agenda and work programme; in many others, 'me' is a collective effort of DG and the secretariat. In some IOs, the staff input is in the open, while in others it is more covert. Nonetheless, the role of the secretariat in agenda is crucial for all IOs, in part because the staff are the experts, know the subject matter, have the information, and have strong attachments to the organization. The way they work differs across IOs, depending on the nature of issues they manage as well as the culture of the organization.

At the IMF and the World Bank, their role in initiating and proposing agendas is seldom questioned. 'As the world has become more globalized,' explained one senior official at the IMF, 'it is impossible to conduct business without getting offices organized, including consulting ED offices, and developing a common view from the management, not two different views or positions.'

> Say, there is a crisis in country X, people working on the country would come and be part of the discussion. The idea is not to have a kitchen cabinet, but to have a process that is open where those who have ideas and solutions can put their views to the table. Then the management retreats to discuss which direction to go. That will involve the managing director, his or her office, three deputy managing directors, and the chief of staff who coordinates the management. The views each one brought on board initially may or may not be in conflict, and senior management people depend heavily on the technical work of its secretariat. Once they reach a decision, the final decision is the official position of the organization. We can have only one, not two, official position on a given country or an issue.

Within the IMF, the Department of Strategy, Policy, and Review coordinates with other departments to map out the work programmes for the management to make the final decision. 'This is the way for us to achieve consistency among countries and between countries and policy areas.'

In other IOs, the secretariat role in agenda setting may be hidden from outsiders. One long-serving senior official explained: 'Who sets an agenda? Member states, of course, but driven by our staff.' Their initiative is not only built on their expertise and information, but also driven by the lack of collective visions or even agreement of member states. Since 'we do not get strong direction from members', explained one senior official at the FAO, 'we have to take a proactive role in setting agendas'. Member states acknowledge it too. Commenting on how food security was placed on the FAO's agenda, one representative said:

> If we waited for one of our committee members to request a paper on food price volatility, we probably would just be ready to discuss it. But that would not have happened on time. The secretariat had access to and followed the market information, had analytical teams working on various related issues and expertise on the subject. When they came and talked to us, we all agreed it was an issue that needed attention.

At both the IMF and the World Bank, work programmes have always been developed by the 'management' and staff. For decades, their EDs have argued that they should be more 'strategic', and 'focus on strategic issues, rather than specific projects'. They have not wanted to change the practice. In discussing the agenda setting at the World Bank, Barnett and Finnemore explain it as a 'straightforward bureaucratic division of labour and the staff's expertise'—the staff propose the agenda at the Board and they 'rarely send proposals to the Board that they believe it will reject'.[40] Having the initiative to propose the agenda and work programmes does not mean there is no consultation with member states that would be affected. Indeed, prior consultation with concerned members and EDs is crucial, even at the IMF and the World Bank.

In terms of work programme development, one senior official who has worked at both the FAO and the World Bank explained the differences between the two:

> The Bank is a more flat institution than this one in Rome, which is quite hierarchical. But the job is what you make it to be, especially when you are in a management position. At the Bank, I put the programme together and take it to the board. I talked to the countries—both major donors and recipient ones—but not the President. You only got interference from the President's office or the vice president's (VP's) office if the Minister of Finance complains that you are doing

---

[40] Michael Barnett and Martha Finnemore, *Rules for the World* (Ithaca, NY: Cornell University Press, 2004), 50.

something that is upsetting them. Then you will have to explain. At the FAO, I ran my department and developed its programmes. In a way it is much easier to get support from member states, as the quality of country representation at this place is no comparison with that at the Bank.

Indeed, successful agenda setting at all IOs depends not only on the visions of DGs and/or the expertise and knowledge of the staff, but also, just as importantly, on their ability to persuade member states by presenting the issues and managing the process in such a way that member states seriously think this is their initiative and their agenda. One state representative explained:

> When there are many member states, there are a lot of different ideas about things. So when there is a degree of commonality, the secretariat follows that closely. When there is a lack of common understanding among the countries, or diverse ideas or ambiguities, it becomes a matter for the secretariat and the organization [management] to try and set a way forward. So it is kind of this idea of leading from the front, and leading from the back, like in any kind of leadership role. On some issues, I think member states can be quick and decisive, while, on other issues, the secretariat would say: 'well, you were not particularly clear on that so we are going to put this out there. What do you think of it?' When the secretariat leads, they often use formal and informal briefings to convey their ideas and proposals.

A senior official of another IO suggested that, if member states may decide on big issues, on others there is 'a process of serial ventriloquism' where staff suggest resolutions that can be adopted that advantage their interests.

At the WTO, member states insist they are the only ones who are allowed to propose any items for discussions. Even there, the process of agenda setting is interactive, as one chair of the WTO General Council noted:

> Yes, this is a member-driven organization; in other IOs, DGs and the secretariat have stronger roles than here and they can do things by themselves. Not here; ambassadors think they are the boss, and some of them even do not like the DG. As the chairman of the General Council, I meet him on a regular basis, on Tuesdays and in between. I also trust the director of the General Council and I use him as a sort of mirror. I do the same with Lamy. I talk through the issues with them and, in the end, it is up to me, right? The relationship is like the one between the minister and the head of department.

Another chair echoes the description: 'members come and tell me what they like to have on the agenda. I inform the secretariat and discuss what to do with it. There is a high degree of confidence between the secretariat and the chair. Otherwise, things would not work at multilateral organizations.' Chairs of committees can play a crucial role in agenda setting and agenda management. Successful ones tend to see agenda setting as a continuing process that is more than just setting agenda itself; issues are brought on board and deleted frequently. The advantage of the chair in managing the process is not only the formal authoritative position the person occupies, but more importantly the access to 'privileged information' that members might like to share with their peers, the brokerage role that comes with the job, the control of the procedure, and the room to manœuvre. They occupy important positions in shaping the agenda, but they never operate independently of the secretariat.

In other IOs where participation of members is less intensive, the DG and the secretariat basically decide the broad range of agenda and work programmes for the Council to approve. Occasionally, chairs of the Programme Committee can provide effective input in agenda setting, as they often know what some of their counterparts want in or out of the agenda. 'Sometimes, it becomes a bit of a tussle to see who can blink first and who can mount more pressure on the other,' explained one representative. The secretariat can play an honest broker role along with the chair of the committee. One of the latter commented:

> Generally, we can find *creative ambiguity* where everyone can read into the document what they think they meant and keep the debate down the road towards their direction. You have got a big idea and you want to push it onto the agenda. You do not just write a six-page position and announce it at the committee or the council meeting. It will never work. You have to get the secretariat on board, producing a lot of non-papers, having many non-meetings, and engaging in many non-debates. There is always a small group of active players. The group varies on issues—you may have some countries on budget matters, but different countries on technical issues. But, you must make people comfortable with the ideas before you propose them at the committee or council meetings. Otherwise, it is very difficult to get your ideas to fly. You need to understand the dynamics of how things work here; and, to make things happen, you also need a certain degree of discretion from the capital.

Senior officials across IOs have a common understanding. Increasingly, it has become important that DGs and the secretariat drive the agenda setting without being seen to do so: 'you do not necessarily say "we are in charge" or "we take the lead", but make sure that you write clear papers with clear ideas and clear narratives,' explained a senior official at the WHO secretariat. When and where the staff are given general directions, they will normally work within those parameters. Where they are not, or where problems emerge, they will take the initiative and develop proposals for the approval of the member states. It is important for member states to claim the ownership of the agendas and/or programmes, and retain their trust in the secretariat.

When trust of the secretariat is in short supply, it is difficult to set the agenda either by leading from behind or by attributing the ownership to member states. In 2008, upon taking office, Francis Gurry and the whole secretariat faced a serious challenge not only because some member states had felt that 'WIPO had failed to focus on its core activities of managing patent, trademark and copyright activities and had become distracted with promotion, grand gestures, and internal politics', but also because there were series of investigations of the use of WIPO funds and building contracts. One senior official at WIPO explained:

> We started off with quite a serious trust deficit between this organization and member states. A lot of members were not convinced the organization was an honest broker in the norm setting sphere, as there are intrinsic questions about intellectual property itself as a tool and about who is going to benefit from IP standards. Some developing countries became very distrustful of anything that smacked of harmonization of the intellectual property systems, and also because of the hostilities of some staff towards the issue of development and IP. We had to spend quite a bit of time just going out to win hearts and minds of these countries and to get them focused on the benefits they could draw from the system, not to get too sidetracked on the ideological issues.

Without that trust from member states, the secretariat could not take any initiatives in agenda setting. The secretariat at the FAO suffered from the similar 'very low levels of trust from member states and mutual misunderstanding between the two' in 2005–7; the entire dysfunctional organization had to 'be rescued'.

MULTIPLE PLAYERS, MULTIPLE VENUES

International arenas have become ever-more crowded as an increasing number of players demand a say on IO agenda setting and many more multilateral institutions exist where the players can pick and choose to compete for agenda, resources, and support of members. At some IOs, such as WIPO and the WHO, non-state players are formally recognized in the process of agenda setting, while, in others, such as the World Bank, their role remains to be consultative. Member states nowadays join forces with non-state players and take their issues to those multilateral arenas where they believe they would be able to protect and promote their interests most effectively or to avoid actions in other arenas.[41] One veteran WIPO official recounted this development:

> The most serious case of forum shopping that I lived through in my time was when they went *en masse* to WTO [GATT at the time], led by the developed countries, to start the TRIPS negotiations. This was because developed countries had become fed up with the fact that the WIPO treaties, good as they were in

---

[41] See, e.g., Marc L. Busch, 'Overlapping Institutions, Forum Shopping and Dispute Settlement in International Trade', *International Organization*, 61/4 (2007), 735–61; Alan O. Sykes, 'Transnational Forum Shopping as a Trade and Investment Issue', *Journal of Legal Studies*, 37/2 (2008), 339–78; Laurence R. Helfer, 'Regime Shifting: The TRIPS Agreement and New Dynamics of International Intellectual Property Law-Making', *Yale Journal of International Law*, 29 (2004), 1–84.

setting norms and standards, had no 'teeth' and therefore those countries not in compliance with the obligations could not be 'hauled over the coals'. Then there was talk in the late 1980s that WIPO would be reduced to a department of what would become WTO, running international facilitation of applications, and all norm-setting would move over to WTO. Once TRIPS agreements were reached, developed countries trooped back to WIPO to discuss and negotiate new technical treaties. Now the practice of forum shopping continues: whenever they [member states] are not happy with the way things are going on in one IO, they will reopen the issue at another IO, from WTO, back to WIPO, WHO, FAO, UNESCO, or even at the World Postal Union. Now we have to follow what is happening in seven or eight other multilateral institutions, trying to make sure that whatever WIPO does is in consonance with the development elsewhere.

By the time the issue of development was debated at WIPO, as discussed, there was 'considerable acrimony in tone and sometimes in substance because many came to this issue for the first time and were quite at a loss as to how it should be dealt with', explained the then DDG in charge of development issues, Geoffrey Yu.[42] The core of the debate, for some, was not only about 'development', but about where issues should be discussed—WIPO, the WTO, or the WHO. The inconsistency of member states across different international forums added more difficulties and confusion to negotiations. 'There are countries that say that some aspects of genetic resources should not be discussed at WTO because they are being discussed at WIPO and then the same countries, when they arrive at WIPO, say that the matter should not be discussed there as it is already being discussed at WTO. So things get all tied up in knots.'[43] For others, what paralysed the process of debate and WIPO as an institution was not the forum-shopping behaviour of some member states; rather it was the uncompromising resistance of some quarters of the secretariat, which was supposed to facilitate multilateral cooperation among member states and support the work on the principle of needs-driven, development-relevant issues that disproportionately affected developing countries.[44] After all, the first decade of the twenty-first century was the time when 'development' issues trumped many others in most multilateral institutions. The three-year negotiations on the issue of development turned out to be not only difficult but also fraught with hostility: when 'form replaces substance and language replaces content—I'm putting it mildly—there was a sense of frustration.'

---

[42] Geoffrey Yu, 'What WIPO Should Do Next', *Managing IP* (July/August 2008), 24.
[43] Geoffrey Yu, 'What WIPO Should Do Next', *Managing IP* (July–August 2008), 24.
[44] See the discussions in Jack Lerner, 'Intellectual Property and Development at WHO and WIPO', *American Journal of Law and Medicine*, 34 (2008), 257–77; Beer, *Implementing the WIPO Development Agenda*.

Forum-shopping is not restricted to WTO–WIPO–WHO. Everyone has to manage multiple players and multiple venues in an ever-more integrated world. One official explained philosophically:

> Geneva has many advantages and many disadvantages. The advantage of course is that everyone is here; so it is good to talk—theoretically you get a very fertile environment for policy discussion. The disadvantage of course is that you get linkages made and these linkages make it very difficult to have a high-integrity policymaking process. Human rights, for instance, have got nothing to do the issues down here, but some people whose country's behaviour on, say, sexual orientation or whatever it might be was criticized at the Human Rights Council, came here and blasted for no other reasons except that they wanted a place to express their views.

Being aware of the close links over issues among state representatives, the head of WIPO, the WHO, and the WTO initiated a trilateral cooperation on public health, IP, and trade. At the press conference on releasing the final report, 'Promoting Access to Medical Technology and Innovation', the three DGs clearly stated their institutional priorities:

> WHO DG, Margaret Chan, emphasized the importance of affordable medicine: Every country in the world is worried about spiralling health-care costs. Trade rules and the intellectual property regime could make prices artificially high and delay the market entry of more affordable generic products. All these policy spheres should operate in the public interest. As we all know, medical products differ in significant ways from other consumer goods. The international systems that govern intellectual property rights and trade have health-specific provisions.
>
> WIPO DG, Francis Gurry, focused on the IP protection to provide sufficient incentives for pharmaceutical industries: innovation and IP are essential components of an effective health policy. Without well-protected IP regimes, there will not be medical innovation or access to adequate medicines for all.
>
> 'Access to medicines requires the right mix of health policies, intellectual property rules and trade policy settings,' said WTO DG Pascal Lamy. 'And coherence is key to finding sustainable solutions. This is the spirit behind the joint study: to provide well-informed, comprehensive policy choices.'

When the three DGs initiated the trilateral cooperative process on access to medicine in 2010, they first set the boundary for discussion—access to medicine was not only about IP, health, or trade alone, but a combination of all—and they also identified the players who would participate in the debate and cooperation. In the following three years, various workshops, seminars, and high-level symposium were organized. According to one of the three DGs, most participants in the consultation process were 'technical' people; the DGs maintained their engagement with key member states on the political aspects

168   *The Working World of International Organizations*

of these issues, such as whether eventually it could be adopted as a report, a formal position, or even a treaty. It was quite clear who was in the driver's seat in the process. This does not mean those who drove the process decided on behalf of member states. It is only a way of managing the agenda and the process in a multilateral arena.

Some items got on the agenda at WIPO because other IOs invited WIPO to do so—on the issue of vaccine, for example:

> During the avian flu crisis, Indonesia provided the sample of virus to the WHO, of course, free of charge, with an understanding that the virus should be used for experimental research and eventually for the development of vaccine. What happened in the course of action was that WHO invited pharmaceutical companies to use the virus for developing a vaccine and vaccine was the product, on which pharmaceutical companies charged fees. So Indonesia argued that this virus was the origin of intellectual creation, so pharmaceutical companies would have to share the benefit of intellectual creation and intellectual property. Indonesia used as an argument of a genetic recourse field in biodiversity. Brazil argued that pharmaceutical companies came and took the soil away which contains lots of useful bacteria which were used to develop a new drug; so the pharmaceutical company should share the benefit as a result of this research and development work. This was the principle built in the convention of biodiversity. If soil and bacteria were regarded as a source of intellectual rights, why would not virus patent be? WHO asked WIPO to assist to enlighten WHO delegates, who are health people with little knowledge of IP. We then took it on. In so doing, we played an educational role.

An increasing number of non-state groups nowadays compete to get their desired issues on international agenda. This has had several significant impacts on IO operations. First is the way they try to influence some small developing countries. 'As many small states have only one or three people covering all IOs in Geneva, they become very vulnerable to NGOs coming and telling them: "here is one page that contains all you need to know about patent law harmonization and you do not have to read those three documents or those sixty-page documents". These become very susceptible because of lack of resources,' said one DG in Geneva, as noted in Chapter 2 on representation.

Second is the need to develop an elaborate process to manage an increasing number of participants. At WIPO, agenda items may come from special committees consisting of all member states who 'discuss and review existing international norms embodied in treaties that are administered' by WIPO— for example, on patent, trademarks, or copyrights. NGO and IGOs are invited to attend these special committee meetings, but 'do not have the capacity to make proposals; proposals can only come from governments. They are able to speak, and their views are often listened to very carefully, and often taken into account and responded to even, by the representatives of our member states.' They can 'circulate papers, but the papers would be circulated outside of the

Agenda Setting

meeting room, as opposed to member states that are able to circulate their proposals and their papers inside as conference room documents'.[45]

Similar development has taken place at the WHO. Take the EB meeting in January 2014 as an example: the meeting was expected to decide on the agenda for the coming World Health Assembly meeting in May 2014. Thirty-four board members came from the capitals, accompanied and supported by their compatriots from the missions in Geneva. The meeting itself had more than 800 participants, including representatives from member states and registered NGOs, both PINGOs and BINGOs. NGOs have to go through an accreditation process managed by the secretariat, and 'this is the only way for the system to work'. All—the members of the EB, member states and NGOs that had registered with the WHO—could speak. The meeting was supposed to last for five days, yet issues snowballed, starting out with unspecified financing, to the discussion on programmes and priority setting, to global health governance, including WHO's engagement with non-state actors, and eventually to the discussion on 'reforms for a healthy future'. Despite the efforts of the secretariat, there were sixty-seven items on its agenda (two more were added before the meeting even started, with seventeen resolutions that had to be discussed and voted on). Margaret Chan, DG of the WHO, commented: 'The heavy agenda...shows the diversity of [the] concerns and also some measures of confidence that the WHO is the right agency to address these concerns... but outstrips the capacity of the secretariat to prepare for this session and serve it well.' Even the chair of the EB, Jane Halton (Australia), warned members that the agenda was too crowded for the members to do a decent job. 'Many countries, EB members and non-EB members alike, said the excessive and growing volume of agenda items in governing bodies should be addressed.'[46]

The secretariat increasingly has to devote extensive resources simply to manage both the agenda-setting process and the size of the agenda. The participation of multiple players stretches the resources and the capacity of IOs. At several IOs, NGOs may not have the vote, but they can speak up at committee meetings and push member states to take on certain issues or shift issues from one IO to another. A WHO official noted,

> These changes have had consequences for the organization, cost wise but also resource wise in terms of supporting such an exclusive range of intergovernmental processes. This is the political reality about health and its policy dynamics. It is the countries that bring a trade issue into health, bring an IP issue into health; and bring agendas, such as human rights and development from other parts of the UN to WHO. These are fascinating challenges, but we are not designed to be so inclusive. We just have to reshape them in the process.

---

[45] Yu, 'The Structure and Process of Negotiations', 1448.
[46] Catherine Saez, 'WHO Board Tackles Reform, Engagement with Non-State Actors', *Intellectual Property Watch*, 24 January 2014.

CONCLUSION

Setting policy agendas is a creative task at IOs precisely because of the unclear and diverse demands from member states. Member states like to think they are in the driver's seat, driving the programmes and activities of IOs. The popular assumption is that agenda setting is power based—that is, the rich, large, and powerful states dominate the agenda setting. Political reality is much more complex. Powerful states can indeed be influential in setting the agenda where they have the determination and the cause. But more often the member states as a group find it easier to identify what they do not want than agree on what they do want. For instance, between the two types of responsibilities—normative and technical—members often cannot agree what they would like IOs to focus on. At the WHO, some countries want a focus on health, while others would like to see money and work go to diseases. At the FAO, there is disagreement not only on whether FAO should focus on normative or technical work, but also on whether it should be on food or agriculture, farm or fishery, forestry or soil. Some FAO members want it to be a global standard-setting body, dealing with trade issues, food security, plant protection; others want to see the FAO on the ground, being operational, dealing with farmers in Africa, etc. Some member states are riven by internal divisions between, say, the public health experts and foreign affairs diplomats, who often do not see eye to eye on certain issues.

The wide range of mandates and diverse demands open the space for the heads of IOs and the secretariat to take initiatives to which member states react. DGs and secretariat devise the work programmes and project descriptions and then receive the endorsement of members, as long as they fit within broadly agreed parameters. Detailed initiatives come from within; that is where the depth of knowledge, expertise, and information lies. The skill is presenting these programmes in a way that encourages member states to appreciate what is being done and accept ownership of the general direction and the particular proposals. It is quite consistent to argue that an agenda is both secretariat devised and member-state owned.

The advent of new players has added a further complication for all. Member states create new bodies and can then 'forum shop', deciding which arena is best suited for their particular purposes. In setting agenda, DGs and secretariats have an additional challenge: not only developing an agenda that member states accept but also persuading them that their IO is best placed to advance that cause.

The flexibility of agendas, the ability of all players to have a role in setting them, suggest it is simplistic to argue that agenda can ever come from one source or can even be isolated in one institution. Rather, IO leaders, member states, and secretariats must juggle opportunities, ambitions, and resources in an ever-changing environment.

6

Funding International Organizations

Accepted truisms are often hard to shake. Two common assumptions about international organizations (IOs) have continuing currency. First, like all organizations, IOs constantly seek to expand in size, activities, and thereby resources (human and financial); and, second, funding problems in IOs are the result of the unwillingness of the rich states to pay more. This chapter examines these two issues to challenge both assumptions. Organizations by nature have a tendency to expand; yet not everyone pursues mission creep to the same extent and with similar passion. More importantly, we need to ask who is behind mission creep, how it is pursued, and why. In some cases, the heads of IOs and the secretariats seize the opportunity and decide to set priorities and expand activities. They are at other times equally determined to restrain the ambitions of member states that seek to expand programmes, even while limiting funding. Second, the countries that contribute more to IOs are indeed more likely to demand accountability for their spending, but this demand cannot necessarily be interpreted as a reluctance to contribute or a demand for cutting. Behind these complexities is the politics of IOs, shaped by the dynamic relationship among the three groups of players in IOs—the head of the IO, the secretariat, and member states—and increasingly by non-state organizations, both large foundations and private for- and non-profit organizations. In general, all IOs have expanded their coverage and activities, and often their funding too, yet driven by different forces and for different reasons.

Several issues are at the core of the conflicts over how and how much to fund IOs:

1. There is an inherent conflict of demands of IO members: risings expectations for IOs to do more with selective willingness to finance some of them.

2. Those who benefit from IO activities are seldom those who have to pay; this is the nature of multilateral cooperation and creates an inevitable conflict of perspectives of member states.

3. As the sources of non-traditional players expand, member states grow increasingly uncomfortable and even suspicious.

4. The new players' capacity to shoulder financing and willingness to use their new-found muscle is perceived as a threat to the existing power structures at IOs.

An early study in 1976 identified six groups of players involved in the debates on funding and spending of IOs:

> government diplomats; government representatives, who are members of the parliamentary bodies of IGOs [intergovernmental organizations]; executive heads, who are elected to manage the administrative branch of the agency; members of the secretariat, who are international civil servants [ICS]; representatives of other international organizations, who may be viewed as interest group representatives; and experts, who are selected because of their technical expertise and serve in their personal capacity.[1]

The budget process involving these players at IOs followed a similar pattern to domestic budgets—that is, it was gradual and incremental; each budgetary exercise tended to be the same as the previous year.[2] In the following four decades, although funding to IOs was always a controversial issue for practitioners, very few studies were available on how such decisions were made: who were involved, who dominated the process, and why.

We now know that, in addition to the above-mentioned groups of players, a number of non-governmental organizations (NGOs), whether public or private, provide funding to IOs, and many, many more demand a say on who should pay for IO activities and where money should be allocated. We can also reasonably assume that there are competing demands among member states for the activities they would like IOs to adopt and how these activities should be funded; and there are differences of opinion between member states and the international bureaucracy. Then, the budget process at IOs is in essence about mobilization, negotiation, and compromise, and is to a large extent shaped by the internal coordination mechanisms, which vary across IOs.[3]

This chapter examines the internal competition and coordination in mobilizing resources from regular and extra-budgetary sources at the six IOs of this study. It argues that, while IOs may be players in international politics in their own right, they do not necessarily always seek an expansion of their budget actively; nor do states always hold back spending on a wide range of global issues. As the traditional assessed contribution from member states to IOs has been by and large fixed and the share of other sources has been

---

[1] Francis W. Hoole, Brian L. Job, and Harvey J. Tucker, 'Incremental Budgeting and International Organizations', *American Journal of Political Science*, 22/2 (1976), 275.
[2] See the analysis in Hoole, Job, and Tucker, 'Incremental Budgeting and International Organizations', 273–301.
[3] See the discussion in Ronny Patz and Klaus H. Goetz, 'Managing Budget Conflicts in International Organizations', paper presented at the Panel, 'Bureaucratic Perspectives on International Organizations',' ECPR General Conference, Montreal, 26–9 August 2015.

expanding, how to manage (*a*) the contribution from different parts of member states (assessed versus voluntary contribution), (*b*) the contribution of member states and non-state contributors, and (*c*) the participation of non-state bodies in IO activities that poses serious challenges for the head of IOs, the secretariat, and member states. Some IOs have increased their range of financial partners and levels of funding to support an expanding agenda without triggering serious political controversies, while others face perennial debates over sources of revenue and its allocation. These differences will be examined by analysing the role played by the head of IOs, the relationship between state representatives and the staff, and the dynamic process of budget and finance committees of all six IOs. We are particularly interested in the two descriptions of budget process provided by those we interviewed: managing the budget and deficit-driven budgeting. Why do IOs pursue their budgets so differently? How is the funding process decided across IOs?

TYPES OF IOs

All IOs receive financial contributions from their member states. The allocation of assessed contribution varies across IOs. At the Food and Agriculture Organization (FAO) and the World Health Organization (WHO), for instance, it is along the same line as the UN-assessed contribution. At the World Intellectual Property Organization (WIPO), assessment is based on the category a country belongs to, regardless of whether a state is only a member of WIPO without being a member of any treaties or all treaties. The assessed contribution at the International Monetary Fund (IMF) and the World Bank is based on the share of 'subscription' each member is allocated. The World Trade Organization (WTO) has its own trade-based formula (Table 6.1).

Our six IOs in this study can be separated into three groups, each involving different issues that affect the relationship among the players: (*a*) the two Bretton Woods institutions, where sources of funding are tied to voting power, (*b*) WIPO and the WTO, where revenue is not an issue but spending needs approval from member states, and (*c*) the FAO and the WHO, which are the two deficit spenders. Before we discuss them in separate groups, we need to highlight one issue: the large share of the US contribution to all IOs (with the exception of the WTO) is partially a historical development, as the USA controlled over two-thirds of the world's gold reserves when the Second World War ended. The USA was willing to take the lead in constructing a post-war world order, and the international community accepted its leadership role.[4] The downside of

---

[4] This is the topic well studied by scholars in international politics and international political economy. The 'embedded liberalism' presented by John Gerard Ruggie in his study of the

Table 6.1. Shares of contribution of fifteen large countries to various IOs, 2014/2015 (%)

Country	FAO	WHO	WIPO[a]	WTO	IMF[b]		World Bank	
					Contribution	Voting	Contribution	Voting
USA	22.00	22.00	6.48	11.31	17.68	16.74	16.91	16.0
Japan	10.83	10.83	6.48	4.49	6.56	6.23	7.82	7.42
Germany	7.14	7.14	6.48	8.15	6.12	5.81	4.56	4.34
France	5.59	5.59	6.48	3.96	4.51	4.29	4.27	4.07
UK	5.18	5.18	6.48	3.88	4.51	4.29	4.27	4.07
China	5.15	5.15	1.94	8.62	4.00	3.81	5.04	4.79
Italy	4.45	4.45	3.89	3.07	3.31	3.16	2.73	2.61
Canada	2.98	2.98	2.59	2.63	2.67	2.56	2.76	2.63
Spain	2.97	2.97	2.59	2.20	1.69	1.63	2.09	2.00
Brazil	2.93	2.93	0.52	1.28	1.78	1.72	1.98	1.90
Russia	2.44	2.44	2.59	2.24	2.50	2.39	2.94	2.80
Australia	2.07	2.07	3.89	1.39	1.36	1.31	1.49	1.44
South Korea	1.99	1.99	1.94	2.88	1.41	1.36	1.70	1.63
Mexico	1.84	1.84	1.94	1.74	1.52	1.47	1.0	0.97
Netherlands	1.65	1.65	3.89	2.98	2.17	2.08	1.97	1.89

[a] Member states' contribution at WIPO is allocated according to categories of countries. See the explanation in WIPO, 'Financial Regulations and Rules of the World Intellectual Property Organization (WIPO),' 30 September 2014. The specific data are based on the allocation in the 2014/15 budget. See 'WIPO Program and Budget for the 2014/25 Biennium,' approved by the Assemblies of the Member States of WIPO on 12 December 2013.

[b] The allocation of share of contribution and voting power at the IMF was decided following the governance reform in 2010, and the plan was finally approved by the US Congress in 2015. The distribution between the share of contribution and voting power at the World Bank was also the result of the reform when the Executive Board added one extra member from Africa in 2010.

the heavy reliance on the USA for IO finance was that, with the expansion of membership, funding became an instrument for the USA to resist or oppose demands from members.[5] The threat was quite effective until the early twenty-first century, when sources of financing multilateral actions were no longer restricted to states. The game of international politics has changed within IOs, because a wider variety of players can now make a difference in funding as well as in agenda setting in IOs. At the same time, the imbalance of assessed contribution to IOs among member states and the principle of one state one vote remain underlying problems besetting the financing of global governance.

Another point deserves attention. While historically the US government, on a few occasions, did withdraw, or threaten to withdraw, its funding or even membership to force IOs to reform or adopt policy changes, this has been overemphasized and overstated. The funding for IOs accounts for only about 3 per cent of the total foreign affairs budget in the USA.[6] Cutting the funding to IOs or threats of cutting funding to particular IOs always incur costs (not least because of the political capital required to undermine an IO) in materializing the threat. More often than not, the cost in political capital outweighs the potential success of the threat. The balance consequently tilts towards inaction and neglect rather than outright threat, as revealed in the following conversation between President Nixon (P) and Kissinger (K):

P: On this International Labour Organization (ILO) thing—the conference committee refused to appropriate...I do not think I should stick my neck out. What do you think? The organization is no good.

K: Yes.

P: Now we have the money and all that, but what do you think?

K: You'll get all the UN types after you... The only other possibility is to say perhaps they should go for this one more time but if there are no reforms, then you'll understand fully in a subsequent year...that they have not been put on notice.

P: I may just give a kick. What do you think?

K: That's a possibility. I just don't know at this time whether it's worth making waves in that direction.

P: Okay.[7]

---

post-war international trade and monetary regimes has been widely quoted and accepted. John Gerard Ruggie, 'International Regimes, Transactions, and Change', *International Organization*, 36/2 (1982), 379–415. See also, e.g., the arguments presented in John Gerard Ruggie (ed.), *Multilateralism Matters: The Theory and Praxis of an Institutional Form* (New York: Columbia University Press, 1993).

[5] Benn L. Bongang, *The United States and the United Nations: Congressional Funding and UN Reform* (New York: LFB Scholarly Publication, 2007).

[6] Susan B. Epstein, Alex Tiersky, and Marian L. Lawson, 'State, Foreign Operations, and Related Programs: FY2015 Budget and Appropriation', Congressional Research Service, 8 December 2014.

[7] Declassified 'Kissinger Telephone Conversations, 1969–1977', 3 August 1971.

The IMF and the World Bank: Self-Financing

The two Bretton Woods institutions, the IMF and the World Bank, in general do not have problems getting sufficient funding for their operations and programmes. This statement needs to be qualified, as the World Bank is a group of four institutions, the International Bank of Reconstruction and Development (IBRD), the International Development Agency (IDA), the International Finance Corporation (IFC), and the Multilateral Investment Guarantee Agency (MIGA); each has its own funding sources. MIGA is financially independent. The IFC was created to encourage public–private partnerships (PPP) through 'investing, advising and mobilizing capital from others'. Until very recently, this partnership operation triggered little controversy and concern.[8] Neither MIGA nor the IFC is part of this study. The IDA was created to provide loans to developing countries on concessional terms, which therefore needed to be backed by multilateral donors. Periodic replenishment of its funds has been a major political and diplomatic exercise for the international development community.

Since their creation, the IMF and the IBRD have been expected to operate as financial institutions. For both institutions, each member is assigned a 'quota' based broadly on its relative size in the world economy, which determines its maximum contribution to the financial resources of the IMF and the World Bank. At the IMF, members normally pay a quarter of their 'subscription' in gold or in other internationally accepted foreign currencies, with the rest paid in local currency. At the World Bank, member states are expected to contribute 2 per cent of their 'quota' in gold or in dollars (initially), and 18 per cent in their own currencies. The World Bank also raises funds at global financial markets by issuing AAA-rated bonds. It then lends these funds and the funds accumulated over time at higher interest rates through the IBRD. In addition, some forty donor countries contribute funds triennially for the low-interest loans and grants made through the IDA.[9] Even though the IMF is not primarily a lending institution, as is the IBRD, its lending to countries to manage their balance of payment problems operates on a commercial principle to maintain its financial viability. Thus the conversations at the IMF

---

[8] In 2012–15, a Chinese national, Jin-Yong Cai, was heading the IFC, during which period China pledged a large amount of funds for PPP projects and many IFC-supported projects went to Chinese companies too. Funding from China to various IOs in recent years has brought up a lot of ambivalent and uneasy feelings among traditional 'donor' countries. For the controversies at the IFC, see, Shawn Donnan, 'World Bank Hit by Executive Departures', *Financial Times*, 7 November 2015; Shawn Donnan, 'China Loses its Top Voice at the World Bank', *Financial Times*, 12 November 2015.

[9] Edward N. Mason and Robert E. Asher, *The World Bank since Bretton Woods* (Washington: Brookings Institute Press, 1973); Martin Ravallion, 'The World Bank: Why it Is Still Needed and why it Still Disappoints', *Journal of Economic Perspectives*, 30/1 (2016), 77–94.

and the World Bank ask how to generate more revenues from making more loans. One of Strauss-Kahn's main motivations in going after the job as the managing director (MD) of the IMF was to revive this institution by building 'a resource-efficient budgetary framework and a more sustainable income model'.[10] Such revenue-driven initiatives were criticized by those who argued that the interest charges on loans from the the IMF and the World Bank were the real reason many indebted poor countries have sunk into further debt holes.[11]

At both institutions, the debate over their finance is not on the spending side, rather on the revenue side—who should be allowed to contribute to what share of capital—because the contribution (subscription) is tied to voting power. Even though voting seldom takes place and consensus is the basic operational principle at both institutions, changing the allocation of quotas has been extremely difficult. Thus, it is not reluctance of members to contribute more to the revenue; rather it is the issue of whether and how shares of contributions should be changed. Following the two oil crises in the 1970s and early 1980s, the debate was whether Saudi Arabia could contribute more to the operational capital of the institutions; and, if so, to what extent the voting structure would change. At the beginning of the twenty-first century, the debate became whether and to what extent emerging economies should be allowed to contribute more to the IMF and the World Bank. The debate highlights the issues of a voice for new players rather than the problem of financing in these two institutions.[12]

The WTO and WIPO: Managing the Budget

Neither WIPO nor the WTO has financing problems, even though the management at both organizations has promised to follow the UN practice of zero nominal growth in terms of member contributions. The main issue involved in their budgeting processes is to ensure broad member support for their work programmes and corresponding spending. As one official explained: 'Our members have very limited argumentation to say that they want a lower

---

[10] Dominique Strauss-Kahn, 'My Vision for the IMF', *Wall Street Journal*, 21 September 2007.
[11] See, e.g., Tony Killick, *Aid and the Political Economy of Change* (London: Routledge, 1998); William Easterly, *The Whiteman's Burden* (New York: Penguin Press, 2006); Ngaire Woods, *The Globalizers: The IMF, the World Bank, and their Borrowers* (Ithaca, NY: Cornell University Press, 2006).
[12] See, e.g., Dries Lesage, Peter Debaere, Sacha Dierckx, and Mattias Vermeiren, 'IMF Reform after the Crisis', *International Politics*, 50/4 (2013), 553–78; Luc Hubloue and Orasa Vongthieres, 'Governance at Work at the International Monetary Fund,' in Patrick Weller and Xu Yi-chong (eds), *The Politics of International Organizations: Views from Insider* (New York: Routledge, 2015), 93–118.

budget; however, they have a big say in approving the budget. Can you see the difference? If they do not approve it, we do not have a budget or a work programme.' While the sources of revenue at the WTO and WIPO differ, how DGs manage the budgeting process at WIPO and the WTO is important to ensure such support.

The allocation of member contributions to the WTO does not follow the normal formula used at other UN agencies. Rather, it is based on a complex formula of the size of economy, the volume of trade, and other categories. The assessed contribution of Singapore to UN agencies, for instance, is 0.384 per cent, while its contribution to the WTO is 2.36 per cent. In contrast, the assessed contribution of the USA is 22 per cent at UN agencies, while its contribution to the WTO is 11.31 per cent. The sources of funding at the WTO are not tied to voting either, as the WTO operates on a consensus principle. On the spending side, WTO's requirements are precise, in that they largely cover the administrative costs of the secretariat that underpins the organization. The WTO does have technical assistance programmes financed by special grants from donor countries, but they are small in number and range.

At the WTO, member states seldom scrutinize the budget process carefully, as most consider it as the purview of the DG and do not want to interfere in decisions on where and how money is spent. One official in Pascal Lamy's *cabinet* explained:

> Pascal was the first Director General at the WTO ever to have gone to the budget committee to present his budget every two years. Normally DGs would send the DDG responsible for administration to the budget committee and tell member states that 'I want 100' and then you get 80. Lamy says that 'I want 80 because 80 is what I need; if I need more I will come back to you. If I have anything left, I will give it back to you.' The DG basically told the members that 'this is the budget that I need to run this house; I am serious about this. Don't negotiate with me.' It worked and members consistently accepted it.

To keep his promise, Lamy admitted that he 'had to exercise a lot of internal authority to do that'. Some members who were not happy with how Lamy handled the negotiations, but they were 'more supportive in terms of maintaining a very right ship fiscally'.

Meanwhile, when the management proposed spending cuts on staffing, member states were reluctant to go along, partly because the total budget of the WTO is minute in comparison with other IOs and with domestic spending on trade matters, and partly because ambassadors to the WTO work with the secretariat closely and appreciate the expertise and professionalism of the WTO staff. When Lamy, for instance, brought an outsider to head the Human Resources Department, who suggested that the 'inverted pyramid' within the WTO secretariat should be changed in part to control the spending, many members were reluctant to agree. They thought the high proportion of professionals at high ranks was needed, because the WTO wanted its staff to be the top experts. Take trade in services, for example: it covers many sectors, from financial, telecommunication, to transport services, and so on. The members argued that there was only one expert per sector, and 'you need one world class expert in that sector'. 'If the position is not high enough in rank, you cannot retain them in this competitive world.' 'Maintaining the high level of expertise in the technical work of the WTO should be the first priority.' The call to change the 'inverted pyramid' upset senior staff at the WTO even more. 'Putting HR on steroids and making it an instrument of control as opposed to being a back office supporting people's work can only harm this organization,' said one senior official. 'Our regular staff is only 700–800 people. You do not need to over-engineer HR and budgetary procedures to save money. You need to understand the functions the professionals serve here.' The resistance to change among senior staff then combined with the concern of many member states that, though accepting the matter was the DG's prerogative, they were not willing to sacrifice the expertise to save some money.[13]

WIPO does not have problems with revenues either, but for different reasons. WIPO 'earns its living with its work', according to the words of a former DDG. It makes its income by providing IP services. The income from processing international patent applications under the Patent Cooperation Treaty (PCT) alone often accounts for three-quarters of the revenue, in contrast to only 5–6 per cent from members' assessed contribution (Table 6.2).

Despite the minute share that assessed contributions make to the total budget, member states 'insist having a 100% control over its spending', said one senior official scornfully, while an ambassador stated cheerfully, as a matter of fact: 'that is because the governing control is still with the governments.' It is then up to the DG and the senior management to 'sell' their work programmes and budget to its members because, after all, WIPO is not a corporation but an IO. Members demand accountability, regardless of sources of revenue. The budget process has become a prolonged persuasion process, and it needs to cater to very different demands from those who have a lot of business with WIPO and those wishing to benefit from the WIPO's work. 'We are a public institution or an international organization combined with a big feature of corporate business,' commented one senior official at WIPO. 'We need to run this business well, but some of our members bring the UN politics here and treat this organization as a political football.' Member states have different preferences of what they would like WIPO to do and where they

---

[13] See, e.g., the debates at the WTO General Council's debates in WTO Committee on Budget, Finance, and Administration, 'Report of the Meeting Held on 3 March 2016' (WT/BFA/153) and 'Report of the Meeting Held on 14 April 2016' (WT/BFA/154), 14 April and 9 May 2016.

Table 6.2. WIPO income, 2004/2005 to 2014/2015

Income	2004/5	2006/7	2008/9	2010/11	2012/13	2014/15[a]
Sources of income (Swiss francs millions)						
Contributions	34.4	34.7	34.8	34.8	35.1	35.2
PCT	400.6	451.1	443.6	434.8	524.6	545.6
Madrid System	60.8	90.3	94.8	99.6	105.8	114.6
Hague System	5.0	5.0	5.4	5.9	6.2	8.6
Lisbon System	0.0	0.0	0.0	0.0	0.0	0.0
Rest[b]	21.8	28.1	28.7	17.7	11	9.3
Total	522.7	609.3	607.4	592.8	682.8	713.3
Share of income (%)						
Contributions	6.6	5.7	5.7	5.9	5.1	4.9
PCT	76.7	74	73	73.3	76.8	76.5
Madrid System	11.6	14.8	15.6	16.8	15.5	16.1
Hague System	1.0	0.8	0.9	1.0	0.9	1.2
Lisbon System	0.0	0.0	0.0	0.0	0.0	0.0
Rest[b]	4.2	4.6	4.7	3	1.6	1.3

[a] 2014/15 share of income estimated.
[b] Rest includes earnings from arbitration, publication, interest, and miscellaneous.
Note: PCT = Patent Cooperation Treaty.

Source: WIPO, 'Programme and Budget for the 2014/15 Biennium', approved by the Assembly of the Member States of WIPO, 12 December 2013.

would like spending to go; the consequence is a stand-off between those who are actively applying for patents, copyrights, and trademarks, and who thereby contribute most of WIPO's revenue, and the many developing countries who need assistance to be able to participate in the nineteen treaties covered by WIPO.

Behind this broad division is another layer of complexity. Over two-thirds of the income comes from users, who are represented by country IP officers; diplomats in Geneva from an overwhelming number of member states represent just 5–6 per cent of the assessed contributions. Some countries have better cooperation than others between the technical experts in ministries of industry or commerce, and the diplomats attending WIPO in Geneva, who are from the ministry of foreign affairs. Some countries deliberately present conflicting views at standing committees on what they would like WIPO to do in terms of programmes, which are different from the stances their diplomats have been fighting for at the Programme and Budget Committee.[14] Many meanwhile are not interested in, nor do they have the human resources to pay attention to, what WIPO is doing; they nonetheless have a say over the budget anyway.

---

[14] At WIPO, Standing Committees are ad hoc committees of *experts* established by a decision of the General Assembly for a given purpose, while the Programme and Budget Committee (with a membership of fifty-three) is one of the four permanent committees, often attended by diplomats in the local missions.

Their decisions may be shaped by the position taken by the grouping or influenced by some very active non-state players.

The management, however, does not want, nor can it afford, a few active players dominating the process. Therefore, in recent years, the management team at WIPO has developed an elaborate process to engage member states in its budget-making. The DG and his management team prepare the draft budget. Then, before the secretariat presented the work programmes and budget to the Programme and Budget Committee,

> our staff from the programme performance and budget division (often including the ADG in charge) would spend two weeks or so meeting each one of the regional groups to explain to them the budget we are presenting and how it came about, and also to get their feedback so that when we do go to the committee, we can say, 'we have already discussed this and have integrated your feedbacks already, can we move on?' We do want to make sure there is a level playing field in understanding the budget so that when we go to the committee, we focus on substance only, not on the mechanism of what this table means or why that figure is in this table. We try to get all the mechanics out of the way before the formal meetings.

As part of this engagement process, the DG organizes formal and informal (breakfast or dinner) sessions of small groups of ambassadors, explains the budget, and seeks their feedback. In 2010, the management also, for the first time, created a post of chief economist. 'He and his unit are to keep their finger on the pulse of the outside world and give us the level of confidence and assurance as to what we think the revenue stream is going to be and plan our spending accordingly.'

Getting support from member states is often not about substance alone:

> Language is important, and it can become a major hurdle. For instance, if certain members say they do not like the word 'harmonize', because it contradicts what is being discussed elsewhere within the organization, we will have a discussion on it. The whole exercise is to make sure that they [member states] feel that they own the document; otherwise we would fight forever. This is the 'pre-digestion'.

Member states do not hesitate to tell the secretariat what they do not like and what they would like to see in the budget. After each round of consultation, the secretariat would collate questions and feedback and post them on the intranet, while protecting the anonymity of the respondents, so that all members know what had been asked and what the concerns were. One senior official explained how they tried to set the terms of the discussion:

> The normal approach is that a budget is presented to member states and members discuss it. We did not do that. We presented them with a 'result-based budget, not a resource-based budget'. We are telling them what we are going to do *for them* in the next two years and how much the results will cost in

182   *The Working World of International Organizations*

> term of budget. Members wanted to talk about dollars and cents, questioning about 4 per cent or 3 per cent increase; 'why is it $100 million; can you bring it down to $90 million'. They like to talk about the budget; we focus on programmes. Our result-based budget is about what we have to do under the next biannual budget. We present them with the results, which cut across all of our areas. Each of these results has corresponding performance indicators. It is a steep learning curve for members.

After pre-meeting briefings and consultation, the secretariat prepared another draft budget for the Programme and Budget Committee.

> During the sessions of the Programme and Budget Committee meetings, every morning before meetings start, members meet in regional groups to develop a common position. Since there are 53 members in the committee, representing some 180 countries, meetings often give the floor to groups first. Each group would have a coordinator, speaking on behalf of the group. These are known as 'non-meetings', but they can become meetings because, at WIPO, this is a five-day process: the first four days are informal and the chair can declare the fifth day formal or if he feels there is a level of maturity in discussion on certain issues, he could announce the decisions then.

'We very very rarely go for a vote; we try to work on consensus,' we were told. At the end, 'it is so important that members see themselves *own* the document'.

Engaging members and encouraging their active participation are also necessary to secure their broad support for what the management seeks to achieve. The competing responsibilities and sources of revenue can create internal conflicts too, as some divisions are money-making units while others are spending units. It takes a great deal of internal coordination to balance the interests of the two demands. The senior management repeatedly told us that 'we need to take pro-active role in helping them (developing countries) build an infrastructure before we can deliver any services to these developing countries; this requires resources. This is also for our self-interest too, as a universal organization.'

The FAO and the WHO: Deficit-Driven IOs

In contrast to WIPO and the WTO, the narrative regarding funding between member states and the secretariat and among member states at the FAO and WHO is often on how to get as much financial support as possible from member states and from non-state actors who are interested in their causes. There is a disconnection between 'budgeting' and 'spending'. Internally, the management at WIPO and the WTO is expected to present a balanced budget for member states to approve. This is far from the case at the FAO and WHO. One senior official compared experiences at the WHO and WIPO:

At WHO, they present a budget based on the programmes they would like to have; it is aspirational; and they then worry about financing it. Here, at WIPO, we work at it the other way—we actually look at what our revenue is going to be and then we look at what we want to do and try to see how we build up our expenditure to correspond to the revenue that we know we will have. So we do not go towards a deficit financing.

A senior official at WHO confirmed the contrast: 'You have got to know at WHO, budgets tend to have very little relationship with actual levels of anticipated financing or expenditure.' One added: 'until 2011/12, our income exceeded expenditure, even though it was short of our budget'. Another further confirmed: 'at this institution budgets are aspirational: "wouldn't it be nice if..."? "If we are going to tackle disease X, what we need is a programme that will be operated in this number of countries and that would require this number of people and that amount of resources."'

This deficit-driven budgeting was the consequence in part of the broad mandate of the FAO and WHO and in part of the willingness of donor countries to fund specific programmes and/or specific countries. The main debates at the FAO and WHO, therefore, have always been about how they would be able to secure more resources to take on programmes that some members or some departments think they would like to do and should do; and not necessarily on how they would be funded or how they could balance their budget. With broadly defined mandates, funding at the FAO and WHO has been a steady source of friction between the management and the member states, but more often among member states themselves, even though neither IO really experienced serious funding problems until the 2000s and then for different reasons. The discussion of deficit-driven IOs has to be placed in this context.

Around the turn of the century, while the total funding of the WHO was still rising, the FAO started experiencing a steady decline. For decades, the UNDP had been a funding, rather than an operational, organization; the FAO was one of the largest recipients. 'When I joined the FAO at the end of the 1980s, money was pretty much provided,' explained a retired FAO official. 'We did not have to go and look for it. We had a big UNDP programme in those days, when the UNDP provided funding while we were doing the projects on its behalf.' Cross-IO funding was not unusual in those days. For instance, in 1970, extra-budgetary funds (EBFs) accounted for about 20 per cent of the total WHO expenditure, and over half of these funds came from other UN agencies. When FAO's EBFs from the UNDP dried up, initially member states made up some of the shortfall. The donors' contribution came with strings: donors were attracted to funding particular countries and regions and/or particular programmes according to their national aid policies. They then started cutting their voluntary contribution to the FAO, in part because of the shifting of domestic policies, but primarily because of their dissatisfaction with the DG at the FAO and its operations.

Between 1994/5 and 2004/5, the regular programme budget resources for technical work declined by 15 per cent. The decline in extra-budgetary resources over the period was 22 per cent, giving an overall decline of 19 per cent.[15] During the same period, the proportion of regular budget for the DG's office and the *cabinet* rose from 0.7 per cent in the mid-1990s to 1 per cent a decade later, and the share on administration went up from 15 per cent to 19.5 per cent respectively. Adding to the decline of cross-IO funding and the donors' contribution was the increase in arrears on payment of assessed contributions by dissatisfied member states. According to the initial arrangements, the FAO, like other UN special agencies, would get the majority of its funding from the assessed contribution of its member states, based primarily on their ability to pay. Most member states, therefore, as elsewhere in the UN system, pay less than 0.01 per cent of the budget; a small number of countries pay a lion's share (Table 6.3). For example, at the time of the creation of the FAO, six of the total forty-five member states contributed to over 65 per cent of the total budget. In 2016, the top six countries still contributed over 55.9 per cent of the FAO's total assessed contributions; the largest twenty-five contributors accounted for 88.35 per cent of the total FAO's regular programme budget. The remaining 11.65 per cent was paid by 169 countries, which controlled 87 per cent of the votes in electing the DGs and dominated the work programmes. A heavy dependence on a few countries' contributions to the regular budget made the FAO vulnerable. 'The level of arrears at year-end as a percentage of Regular Programme assessments was: 7 per cent, 8 per cent, 11 per cent and 11 per cent between 2001 and 2004, jumping to 25 per cent in 2005.'[16] Both developed and developing countries were in arrears. The four main contributors, which together accounted for 45.5 per cent of the total assessed contributions at the FAO—the USA, Brazil,

Table 6.3. Share of paid-up assessed contributions at the FAO, at 30 September, 2001–2006 (%)

Country	% of total assessed contribution	2001	2003	2003	2004	2005	2006
USA	22.00	0	0	0	0	0	0
Brazil	1.55	0	0	0	0	0	28
China	2.09	0	0	0	0	49	50
Japan	19.86	57	100	0	0	0	0

Source: 'Food and Agricultural Organization of the United Nations (FAO)', September 2007, C 2007/7A.1-Rev.1, p. 333.

---

[15] FAO, 'Report of the Independent External Evaluation of the Food and Agriculture Organization of the United Nations (FAO)', C2007/7A.1-Rev.1 (September 2007), 75–6.

[16] FAO, 'Report of the Independent External Evaluation of the Food and Agricultural Organization of the United Nations (FAO)' (September 2007), 331.

China, and Japan—paid on average only 12 per cent of their assessed contribution in 2001-6. By then, the 'financial situation of the FAO was dire', and the FAO depended on borrowing to meet its basic financial obligations.

The main reason for a rapidly dwindling funding at the FAO was that the principal funding contributors (of both assessed and voluntary contributions) lost interest in the institution as 'its DG had drifted to activities that would ensure re-election rather than concentrating on what member states really wanted from the organization.' As rich countries benefit little from the FAO anyway, keeping them interested in what the FAO does is important. IOs in general do not rank high in government policy of any country; agriculture ranks low too in government priority. Engaging member states thus is critical for the FAO to secure its assessed and voluntary contribution. For the FAO, the donor's contribution (voluntary contribution or trust funds) often comes from a government agency that is different from the funder of the FAO's regular programme or the home department of the representative to the FAO. Australia, for example, is represented at the FAO by officials from the Department of Agriculture and Resources, the assessed funding is part of the policy portfolio of the Department of Foreign Affairs, while voluntary contributions came from the Australian Agency for International Department, AusAid (formerly an independent agency and now part of the Department of Foreign Affairs). The priority of voluntary contributions was decided according to the foreign policy agenda, rather than the one set by the line department, Agriculture. A civil servant in the agriculture department explained:

> We need to do a lot of liaison work with foreign affairs and our aid agency, and all other agencies that might be interested in what we are doing. From our perspective, the FAO is an important organization because it is a standard setting body for food, agriculture, and trade. We need to make sure that we get the appropriation through the budget to pay our mandatory contribution to the FAO each year. Other agencies might make some voluntary payments to the FAO; they may also work with the FAO in particular countries, which we may not know about. So, the most we can do is to represent the country in Rome. Other political decisions always take the priority—foreign policy, election at home, outbreak of animal diseases, etc.

Governments of member states might not know that FAO resources were used to hold a regional conference in Niue (population of just 1,190 in 2014, with only chartered flights) so that the DG could secure thirteen votes in the Pacific. The DG might have been 'utterly energetic and devoted to' these small countries. When DGs and the management failed to engage with key contributing member states and especially when what the FAO did was seen only to ensure the re-election of the DG, key contributors to the FAO simply abandoned the organization until a group of Scandinavian countries decided to 'save' the organization by putting in money for an independent review of the FAO, 2005.

Internally, there were inevitable stresses.

> We cannot have enormous swings within the organization, because we have a staff complement which is stable; you can change the resources at the margin, but if you suddenly decide to cut your fisheries' work by 20 per cent and you have commitments to staff within that function, it is difficult to redeploy them on agriculture or something else. So we do not have that kind of swing.

This may be the political reality, but it is difficult to satisfy the demand of members when they lose interest in the organization or some of the issues. The other problem was that, even when the FAO was suffering from declining funding as the result of arrears and a reduced voluntary contribution, some departments within the FAO managed to receive a large amount of voluntary funding on specific issues, because some senior officials knew how to engage with individual countries. On food security, for instance:

> Yes, in the past three years, we have got a lot of resources to do a lot of work on this kind of politically hot issue. Member states love this because there are political implications for them. The moment food prices come down, which will happen at some point, and the issues of hunger and food security are no longer on the front of their agenda. I am afraid people will have to go.

Within the FAO, some divisions saw a significant increase in funding, while others suffered. In a period of fourteen years (1994/5–2006/7), the share of budget for transboundary plant pests, including locusts, increased by 102 per cent, while that for livestock (excluding animal health) declined by 40 per cent. The IEE concluded: 'it is difficult to gauge the extent to which these shifts align with indications of members' priorities, particularly in terms of orders of priorities'.[17] Yet, the report also noted that the FAO members were 'far less successful' in translating the FAO's purpose and broad goals 'into consensus on priorities, choices and decisions on what FAO can be expected to do—and not to do—with the resources at its disposal'.[18] The inconsistency between mandates, programmes and resources was one of the main reasons member states pushed the FAO for reform. Who is the FAO anyway?

Since 2010, the FAO, like many IOs, has adopted the so-called results-based budget. Yet, the trend of deficit-driven budget continued. That is, the DG proposed a medium-term strategic plan covering the issues of 'rising food demand, changing patterns of consumption, energy security and scarcity, food price increase and volatility, rural poverty, changing patterns of agricultural trade, growing impact of climate change on agriculture, and increased vulnerability to natural and human-made disasters', which were among a long list of

---

[17] FAO, Report of the Independent External Evaluation of the Food and Agricultural Organization of the United Nations (FAO)' (September 2007), 76.
[18] FAO, 'Report of the Independent External Evaluation of the Food and Agricultural Organization of the United Nations (FAO),' (September 2007), 72.

areas in the FAO's mandate. Based on this wide range of issues, the FAO then worked out a work programme for the approval of the Programme Committee and the Council, along with an 'aspirational' budget—that is, decide what you want to do first, and worry about how to fund it later. It projected, for instance, a total budget for 2016/17 of US$2.6 billion, of which 39 per cent would come from assessed contribution. The rest would be raised from various sources of voluntary contribution. 'Member states are fairly light on details,' an ambassador noted. 'What they are concerned with is the final budget figure for the biennium; once we are happy with it, we leave it to the DG to decide what departments get what share.'

Meanwhile, arrears remain a serious problem; FAO members paid only about 60 per cent of their assessed contribution in 2015/16.[19] This type of budgeting affects technical programmes in particular because nearly 100 per cent of the technical work is funded by voluntary contributions.

Funding at the WHO is probably the most analysed and discussed among all IOs,[20] partly because, as health costs everywhere are rising, demand for funding at the WHO has been rising too, and partly because, while sources of funding are expanding, new issues arise too. In general, 'funding of global health increased by sixfold between 1990 and 2008 when the global financial crisis broke out. The WHO's budget had not risen as fast as that of global health expenditure in general, but it too had a two-, or threefold increase. This increase was only in voluntary contribution, not the assessed contribution,' explained one senior official at the WHO. Another agreed: 'We did not have funding problems until 2011/12; the financing of the organization was up until then. The budget of the WHO nearly doubled from US$2.3 billion in 2000–1 to US$4.2 billion in 2008–9, US$4.5 billion in 2010–11.' Yet, lack of funding was a perennial topic for those working around the WHO,[21] and scholars whose research interest was on the WHO.[22] Internally, questions raised over

---

[19] FAO, 'The Director-General's Medium Term Plan 2014–17 (Reviewed) and Program of Work and Budget 2016–17', 2015/3, Rome (2015).

[20] In nearly all the studies on the WHO, financing is included. See, e.g., three Chatham House studies: Charles Clift, 'The Role of the World Health Organization in the International System', Centre on Global Health Security Working Group Papers, Chatham House (February 2013); Charles Clift, 'What's the World Health Organization for' (May 2014); and Charles Clift, 'Analysing Proposals for Reform of the Global Health Architecture' (August 2015); Nitsan Chorey, *The World Health Organization between North and South* (Ithaca, NY: Cornell University Press, 2012); Jeremy Youde, *Global Health Governance* (Cambridge: Polity, 2012).

[21] One good example is Fiona Godlee, an active contributor to *BMJ* in the 1990s. She wrote about the WHO's funding shortages that went back to the 1990s: 'The World Health Organization: WHO in Crisis' (series of eight articles), *BMJ* 309/6966 (1994), 1424–8, 1491–5, 1566–70, 1636–70, and 310 (1995), 110–12, 178–82, 389–93, 583–6; and 'WHO Reform and Global Health', *BMJ* 314/7091 (1997), 1359–60.

[22] See, e.g., Gill Walt, 'WHO under Stress', *Health Policy*, 24 (1993), 125–44; Bo Stenson and Goran Sterky, 'What Future WHO?' *Health Policy*, 28/3 (1994), 235–56; John W. Peabody, 'An Organizational Analysis of the World Health Organization: Narrowing the Gap between

the decades were not really about the adequate funding, but about the sources of funding and their allocations.

That EBFs were used to supplement the assessed contribution was the practice from the early days of the WHO. The Constitution of the WHO (Article 57) specifies that 'The Health Assembly or the Board acting on behalf of the Health Assembly may accept and administer gifts and bequests made to the organization provided that the conditions attached to such gifts or bequests are acceptable to the Health Assembly or the Board and are consistent with the objective and policies of the organization'. In the following decades, many decisions taken by the EB and the World Health Assembly expanded the scope and the sources of EBFs. In the first two decades of the WHO, most EBFs came from other UN agencies and accounted for about one-third of the total budget of the WHO. In 1970, for instance, the regular budget was US$75 million, while EBFs were US$25 million. In 1975, the EB organized a study on the use of EBFs to supplement regular funds. It concluded that: 'if WHO is to pursue its constitutional mission, it is evident that the upward trend in extra-budgetary resources must continue'.[23] EBFs then grew much faster than the assessed contribution from member states, and they, for the first time, exceeded the regular budget in the 1988–9 biennia, with EBFs reaching US$1 billion, while the regular budget was US$822 million.[24]

In the 1990s, the WHO experienced some similar problems as the FAO—dissatisfaction of member states, conflicts between some member states and the DG, and increased shares of unpaid assessed contribution. The WHO's success in its polio and smallpox eradication programmes could not reduce the resentment of many in rich countries for its DG's neglect on HIV/AIDS.[25] Clashes between Nakajima and Jonathan Mann, the head of the WHO's Global Programme on AIDS, resulted in the resignation of Mann in 1990. This clash was never forgotten or forgiven by some major contributors, such as the United States. Indeed, global expenditure on AIDS did not change at all in the first half of the 1990s. A group of developed countries took the issues to the United Nations in 1993, even if few believed that any actions would be taken. While 'the WHO continued to maintain that the new programme

---

Promise and Performance', *Social Science & Medicine*, 40/6 (1995), 31–40; J. Patrick Vaughan, Sigrun Mogedal, Stein-Erik Kruse, Kelley Lee, Gill Walt, and Koen de Wilde, 'Financing the World Health Organization: The Global Importance of Extra-budgetary Funds', *Health Policy*, 35 (1996), 229–45.

[23] Quoted from Vaughan et al., 'Financing the World Health Organization', 231.

[24] Gian Luca Burci and Claude-Henri Vignes, *World Health Organization* (The Hague: Kluwer Law International, 2004), 202–9.

[25] In 1988, the World Health Assembly adopted the Global Polio Eradication Initiative. At the time polio was widespread in developing countries, and there were over 350,000 cases each year. The number of cases reduced to 784 by 2003 after twenty million volunteers and US$3 billion were devoted to the programme. See the discussion in Jeffrey D. Sachs, *The End of Poverty* (New York: Penguin Books, 2005).

would be administered and located in the WHO,' major donors, such as the Danish government, USAID, and the UK Department for International Development (DFID) had little confidence in the WHO to put the efforts together. Thus emerged the UNAIDS.[26]

What brought the WHO to its so-called crisis in the mid-1990s was more the discontent and neglect of its member states than their financial contribution. Rich countries were dissatisfied with its operation; so were many developing countries. For instance, while the amount spent on the World Health Assembly and the EB went up 33–35 per cent in the WHO budget for 1992/3, the amount spent on countries' health programmes fell by over 10 per cent. 'Simultaneously, though there was no cutback in headquarters spending (budget and finance office itself being several millions overspent), allocation to the WHO's six regions were reduced by some 10 per cent from the sum originally budgeted.'[27] Some forty countries, rich and poor, had failed for at least two years at the time to pay membership contributions. The WHO had depended on 'borrowing' to finance its operation—'a situation that cannot be allowed to continue', announced the US representative to the WHO, Nell Boyer, even though the USA was one of the countries in arrears. For the American government, it was not the money, because its total assessed contribution to the WHO was smaller than the smallest unit at the National Health Institute. Nakajima's 'inability to rise to the epidemic fast and effectively led to UNAIDS, the Global Fund, and [other] initiatives created to tackle what a more effective Director-General could have led from WHO'.[28]

In the mid-1990s, the morale at the WHO had dropped to a historic low, and the institution was plagued by political tension and accusations of poor management. Changing the leadership to Gro Harlem Brundtland as DG (1998–2003) made an impact on the willingness of member states and non-state players to finance the causes of the WHO. Her first official act was to introduce new financial disclosure rules requiring all senior staff to submit forms detailing financial interests, patents, and positions held in the public sector. To assist her restructuring of the organization, the Rockefeller Foundation, a long-standing supporter of the WHO, immediately pledged US$2.5 million to establish the Global Health Leadership Fund under the WHO.[29] In addition to the internal organizational restructure, Brundtland proposed the WHO should 'reach out to others—UN agencies, the multilateral development banks and the International Monetary Fund (IMF), NGOs and the private

---

[26] UNAIDS, *UNAIDS: The First 10 Years, 1996–2006* (Geneva: UNAIDS, 2008), 27.
[27] Alan McGregor, 'WHO again under Fire from External Auditor', *Lancet*, 343/8908 (1994), 1278–9.
[28] Stephen Pincock, 'Hiroshi Nakajima', *Lancet*, 381 (2013), 1178.
[29] Alan Dove, 'Brundtland Takes Charge and Restructures the WHO', *Nature Medicine*, 4 (1998), 992.

sector (including a WHO-industry roundtable)' and form 'a stronger partnership with member states'.[30]

For Brundtland, the WHO had clearly failed to explain itself to its member states and to the world as a whole.[31] When she took the health issues to the world stage and particularly engaged 'whole governments of member states', including presidents, prime ministers, and ministers of finance,[32] serious money came in to supplement the frozen assessed contributions in supporting global health issues. By the turn of the century, a series of funding agencies had been created 'outside' but in partnership with the WHO: the Global Alliance for Vaccines and Immunisation (GAVI, in 2000), Stop TB Partnership (in 2001), and the Global Funds to Fight AIDS, Tuberculosis and Malaria (the Global Fund, in 2002). By taking health issues to the global stage, Brundtland led the WHO to 'refashion itself as the coordinator, strategic planner, and leader of the global health initiatives'.[33] EBFs, funding from both member states and non-state players, grew much faster than before, while the assessed contribution was frozen.

Developments during the Brundtland era show, if nothing else, the willingness of member states and other non-state players to invest in health. Yet, when the management fails to engage with member states and is ineffective in getting their support, states have a tendency to abandon IOs and take their issues elsewhere. While global health in general benefited from the rising spending from various sources—states, private, and non-profit foundations, several new issues came to the fore: the sustainability and predictability of these 'voluntary contributions' and, more importantly, the need to align priorities agreed upon at the WHO governing bodies and the sources of funding.[34] Many had pointed out that a steady increase in the proportion of EBFs as a total budget would not be a problem if they, as the constitution states, 'are consistent with the objective and policies of the organization'. A senior WHO official commented:

> Everybody is obsessed with core versus non-core funding. That is the whole argument in the rest of the United Nations. As the core funding is diminishing and tied funding of one kind or another is increasing, the constant refrain coming out of New York is 'we need more core funding; we must persuade donors to give more core funding'. We have not completely given up the hope that member

---

[30] Clift, 'The Role of the World Health Organization in the International System', 39.

[31] Antony Robbins, 'Brundtland's World Health Organization: A Test Case for United Nations Reform', *Public Health Report*, 114/1 (1999), 30–9.

[32] Robbins, 'Brundtland's World Health Organization', 34.

[33] Theodore M. Brown, Marcos Cueto, and Elizabeth Fee, 'The World Health Organization and the Transition from "International" to "Global" Public Health', *American Journal of Public Health*, 96/1 (2006), 62–72.

[34] See the discussion in Rebecca Dodd and Christopher Lane, 'Improving the Long-Term Sustainability of Health Aid', *Health Policy and Planning*, 25/5 (2010), 363–71.

states would increase their assessed contributions to IOs. Yet we are saying, it would be nice to have more flexible funding, and there needs to be a closer alignment between agenda priorities and funding.

Indeed, this was the position taken when Margaret Chan, soon after getting elected as the WHO DG, stated: 'people always say we don't have enough money; we don't have enough this, that, and the other. Yes, resources are important, but we also have to ask ourselves should we be doing so many things.'[35] It is the organizational culture of the WHO to budget for what it thinks the global health will need. It is not only donors, state or non-state, who would like to contribute to the WHO, but those 'able' individuals and departments within the WHO who raise funds from various sources. One senior official provided an analogy:

> Running the WHO looked more and more like running a university. Deans are no longer relevant, as professors are able to build their empires with their own funding sources. If a professor is a very good fund raiser and can create an empire, it is not just an academic empire; it is a financial empire. So you had a situation where the World Health Assembly approved 23 per cent of the budget, said how this 23 per cent would be used by appropriation and noted the other 77 per cent. Then some departments managed to raise 60 per cent of that estimate and some managed to raise only 30 per cent. The whole budget became a purely aspirational exercise without the slightest relevance. Financing became a major force of incoherence...Entropy in physics is that you have to invest energy for order. That is the reason we identified financing as the major problem in the current reform.

The new initiatives since 2010 are designed to solve these problems.

MANAGING VOLUNTARY CONTRIBUTIONS TO IO FINANCE

All IOs receive voluntary contributions from state and non-state donors. Some are 'tied', so that they can be used only for specific programmes, projects, or countries. Some go to a pool managed by IOs. Some countries are both donors and recipients, when their voluntary contribution is used to fund IO programmes or projects in their own country by taking advantage of the technical expertise IOs can offer. Regardless of the sources of voluntary contributions, they need to be aligned with the IO mandate as well as the strategic directions member states have endorsed. This balance is managed better in some IOs

---

[35] Hannah Brown, 'Profile: Margaret Chan: New is the Time for WHO to Achieve Results', *Lancet*, 369/17 (March 2007), 899.

than in others. For instance, the Energy Sector Management Assistance Programme (ESMAP) administered by the World Bank operates entirely on voluntary contributions from member states (also known as the trust funds).

WIPO may be one of the better-funded IOs with its 'independent' sources of income; it also receives a large amount of voluntary contributions for its technical assistance and development programmes. One official explained: 'as the UN has a large development agenda, so do we, and we have to fulfil our obligation while running the business.' Another added quickly:

> I have got big technical assistance programmes, but I do not have to go out and solicit funds from donors, as some other IOs do. They are in-house funded and also funded with trust funds. The Japanese government, for instance, has a significant fund in trust with us for many technical assistance activities in the Asian region, which have extended to Africa and some other countries. The Korean government has a very sizeable fund with us too. In fact, the funds in trust from Japan and South Korea are larger than the regular budget of the Asian Bureau to fund those technical assistance programmes in developing countries. Why—the Koreans are very keen to share their experience, and they feel that they were a developing country not long ago and they are so passionate and eager to share their experience. Of course, there may be a 'feel-good' factor about it. These are funds with no strings attached. I think maybe one could say these are the countries that are very strong in IP; they file a lot of patents and trademarks with us. So I suppose it makes sense that they would like all countries with the infrastructure to support and respect intellectual property systems. It is also in their interest not to have a system where counterfeits are rampant; piracy is rampant; and there is no protection whatsoever for IP.

Technical assistance projects at the IMF and WTO are funded by voluntary contributions from member states too. They seldom become politically controversial, primarily because they are targeted and small. The World Bank each year has received a substantial amount of trust funds from its member states; indeed, trust funds have become 'a significant pillar of the global aid architecture, used to address limitations in bilateral aid and fill perceived gaps in the operations of existing multilateral institutions'.[36] While there are some 200 donors to the World Bank trust funds, member states remain the main donors. In the first decade of the twent-first century, ten traditional donor governments accounted for about two-thirds of the total contributions, with the USA and UK accounting for over a quarter of the total contribution. 'Our trust funds are always from members of the Bank,' discussed a vice president (VP) at the World Bank:

---

[36] World Bank Independent Evaluation Group, *Trust Fund Support for Development* (Washington: World Bank, 2011), p. v.

They give us the money to do projects because they feel comfortable with the work that we do and they also know the money will be handled reasonably. If we make a mistake and find out about it, we are more than honourable in sending the money back. I find a little disingenuous that countries that are telling us not to expend our regular budget are coming to us with trust funds, saying, 'Would you do this for us with this amount of money?' To me, this is a little too cute. I would much prefer the board sat down as a group, telling us: 'Right, we would like to increase our contribution to the Bank and we would like the Bank to do this or that with the resources.' Then we both can be held accountable; both have some explanation to do; and also strategies and resources can be matched. Now, the board does not do this. So I have told the donor countries, there is no free ride and their resources have to be integrated into our country strategies.

Aligning what donors want their entrusted funds to do with the broader strategies agreed upon by all members has not been easy for some IOs, where the issue often divides member states and creates rifts within IOs themselves. While understanding the desire of donor countries to have tied voluntary contributions to IOs, the IO management and staff prefer to receive voluntary contribution in a more flexible manner. 'I think it is inevitable that countries have their specific projects or countries they want us to work at.' When donor countries 'come to us with funds and projects because they do not have the capacity to do the work themselves, we do charge them 13 per cent overhead costs'. Sometimes the request can be quite complicated, as the department of a donor country that allocates trust funds decides to contribute precisely because it wants to reduce transaction costs and prefers IOs not to charge overhead fees, while the department that sends officials representing the country to the IO insists that the assessed contribution for regular work programmes should not be used to 'subsidize' the work funded by the voluntary contribution.

Some developing countries have established their own unique unilateral trust funds—funds contributed by a country to be used in its own country. For instance, countries such as Brazil, Columbia, Chad, India, Mexico, and Nigeria provided the FAO with voluntary contributions, sometimes in kind, for the FAO staff to carry out certain projects and activities in their own countries. On the one hand, such unilateral trust funds do help engage these countries in their own development processes, as they can benefit from the technical expertise while fully funding a programme themselves. On the other hand, such funds also raise the issue whether they are funding the programmes and projects in line with the broader mandate of the IO and/or whether these programmes and projects are the priorities of the IO.

That is the reason that the secretariat prefers donor countries to make a contribution to a multi-donor trust fund established at the level of the organizational strategic objectives, rather than the traditional project- or country-specific tied contribution. One of the recommendations made by the IEE for the FAO was to 'turn down donors if they are asking us to do things that are not in our strategic plan', one senior official explained:

> Of course, we can nudge members, pointing out 'this is where we really need the money', and some members actually said yes because they supported our strategic programmes and wanted to fund them. Sweden is a good example: it wants to lower its transaction costs for its development assistance; so it is quite happy to say to us: 'We like the strategic framework; we want to support the objectives on food security and gender and we will just contribute x amount towards the achievement of the targets as measured by the indicators and the strategic framework.' Yet, I still do not have any cases where we really turned down a donor.

Voluntary contributions to the WHO raise similar challenges: how to ensure that voluntary funding provided by member states can fit into the strategies of the organization and that donors do not take a free ride:

> Of the voluntary contributions, the largest part are highly specified not just for a topic but often for a country, a particular staff, a part of a programme. So when we first come to a point where there really is a deficit, there remain parts of the organization that are relatively well financed and others that are not. Yet, the capacity to move money from one part to another is extremely limited. So within the WHO, you have feast and famine. This is not the slightest bit unusual to anyone who has run a ministry of health in a developing country, or any country.

An increase in the share of voluntary contributions in the total operational budget has changed the internal operation of the WHO under the broad umbrella of global health, and altered the relationship among member states, between member states and the secretariat, and between the WHO and the broader international health community. By 2010, there were eight partnerships formed by the WHO, 'with serious amounts of dosh involved'. These partnerships raised some serious questions about multilateralism, governance of global funds for health, and the accountability of the WHO. The WHO's normative role is a highly sensitive intergovernmental issue. Did an expansion of these partnerships encroach on the WHO's normative role? Did the staff that joined the partnerships have the right of returning to the WHO? If the partnership collapsed, or if the partnership ran out of money, did the WHO have an obligation to bail it out, and, if so, was it the first priority or the last on the list? Were they too big or too important to fail for the WHO? Or what would it mean to the WHO if the Gates Foundation suddenly did not think that a particular disease or issue was important any more and stopped funding it?

Managing extra-budgetary sources of funding is a challenge for the WHO management, not only about its work programmes, its priorities, and human resources. One senior official explains:

> We hosted the global fund for AIDs, TB, and malaria. We were very instrumental in its creation. We helped UNICEF and others get GAVI off the ground.

Meanwhile, we created a lot of governance headaches for ourselves and our staff working in the field.

Another senior official at the WHO with detailed knowledge of country operations explained:

> The flow of resources for actual operations in countries is not coming primarily from the WHO. It comes from multiple sources: in AIDs and malaria, it comes from the Global Fund; in vaccinations, it comes from GAVI; huge amounts come through the World Bank and regional development bank funds for health; and many important flows of resources from the bilateral arrangements.

These partnerships are fairly long-standing fixtures; some are quite successful and some of the relationships work extremely well. Even well-run ones tend to be fragmented. Others can be problematic, because they are not getting the resources that they need. It is an interesting quirk, added another official. 'It is not uncommon in some of these multilateral organizations to have this kind of dual governance. Some of our country staff find it very difficult, because when someone pitches up with a business card of the partnership and someone pitches up with one from the WHO, are they different or are they the same? Who do you listen to; who pulls whose strings, etc. It does raise accountability issues.' 'That is what we are doing now by bringing member states and those interested in the health issues together to have this financing dialogue. We do not know how it will turn out, but we do want a shift in thinking.'

In January 2010, the WHO DG initiated a finance reform dialogue by organizing a meeting, 'Future Financing of the WHO'. The DG invited to the meeting

> many traditional donors, such as the UK, the USA and the EU, as well as some other countries, such as Brazil. She included some health attachés working in missions, some academics, and some from donor countries. She also appointed a special envoy on the future of financing of the organization. The meeting was initially about the shortage of funding, but soon became more about the 25–75 split between member contributions and the voluntary contribution, and the growing mandate.

Distrust was apparent at the meeting over the H1N1 vaccination issue. As one delegate said at the meeting: 'The WHO was going through an identity crisis.' People were asking: 'What is the role of WHO within this new architecture of global heath actors?'

Quickly, the process changed to proposing a more accountable and iterative process between the secretariat and member states. The DG was asked to develop a 'member-driven' process. She wanted to develop an integrated budget, so the World Health Assembly would no longer just approve the 25 per cent expenditure of assessed contributions but would agree to the broader strategy of approving a budget that incorporated all income and programmes. This process started internally before the initiative was taken to the members. After working out a draft budget, the DG presented a first version of that budget to the six regional committees; the six regions provided their feedback. Then, based on the feedback, the DG directed the secretariat to prepare another version integrating the bottom-up feedback and top-down vision of the DG, especially on the global health goods. This version of the budget would then be discussed at the EB, and the final budget would be discussed, debated, and decided at the World Health Assembly. As one senior official working closely to the process noted: 'The penholder of the budget process remains the director general.'

The main idea behind the finance reform was not only about the amount of contributions member states are willing to provide to global health, but, more importantly, to develop a process whereby member states could get engaged, put forward their demands, and make compromises and balances, before an integrated budget could be developed for which member states could claim the ownership. The amount of the resources IOs receive from member states and other organizations is important for the smooth operation of an organization. It is important for an IO to have a predictable and flexible budget that the DG and the secretariat can work with to meet the expectation of member states and collective objectives embedded in a strategic framework and/or a medium-term plan.

'When member states like the strategic plan, they are more willing to put resources in to implement these plans,' observed an official. For member states, however, this requires coordination among different parts of the government—the line ministry (whether agriculture, health, or intellectual property), the agency in charge of development assistance (donors of the trust funds), and the finance department. Internal coordination often turns out to be difficult. For decades, the United States argued that UN agencies needed to reform their bloated bureaucracies and control their spending. Yet the USA itself is also the largest donor of a wide range of extra-budgetary funding in most IOs. Consequently, in the budget-making process of a given IO, the US representative and many alike insist on one position, while the USAID or US Exim Bank, or other agencies, contributing voluntary resources for this or that course, can take different positions. 'Can you believe that the US government was asking us how much it gave us as trust funds,' a senior official at the WHO asked us rhetorically.

EXTERNAL NON-GOVERNMENT FUNDING

Even though EBFs have been part of the funding arrangements for some IOs since the very beginning, particularly in the FAO, the WHO, and the World

Bank, they have become controversial in recent decades because a large amount of funds are from non-state organizations. Some are large foundations; some are profit-making organizations; others may represent a pool of resources from a wide range of small organizations. When EBFs from the Gates Foundation to the WHO (US$568 million) nearly reached the level of the combined assessed and voluntary contributions of the largest contributor, the United States (US$615 million), in 2012/13, it alarmed many who asked who really set the agenda at the WHO.[37]

While many accept that sources of funding beyond the assessed contributions to IOs are critical for the international community to manage some collective problems, whether health, nutrition, environmental protection, or development in general, other scholars have argued that EBFs are 'undercutting the collective decision making that is central to multilateral governance';[38] or are 'corroding elements of international organizations that are crucial to their capacity to facilitate cooperation'.[39] Often these arguments are made without distinguishing between EBFs from governments, global foundations, or private profit-making institutions. Within IOs, however, the distinction is emphasized by donors and recipients. Non-government sources bring controversy with their funds.

In 2002, the WHO formally distinguished Public Interest NGOs (PINGOs) from Business Interest NGOs (BINGOs).[40] The UN Standing Committee on Nutrition repeated the distinction in 2004.[41] BINGOs are organizations that are funded to serve for-profit enterprises or advocate their interests, and include associations and charitable foundations that are separate legal entities with an arm's-length relationship to the for-profit enterprises that provide their funding. Such organizations may or may not be registered as non-profit, with or without charitable status, and may or may not express an explicit public purpose. Despite these formal definitions of PINGOs and BINGOs, working with them at IOs is difficult and sometimes can be quite controversial. Often PINGOs and BINGOs do not agree on much, while neither agrees with the WHO or member states: 'member states disagree with us [the WHO secretariat] in failing to distinguish between PINGOs and BINGOs.' How to manage the participation in IO activities by the so-called civil society is a difficult issue because of these criss-cross disagreements.

---

[37] Clift, 'What's the World Health Organization For?', 28. See also the discussion in Chorev, *The World Health Organization between North and South*.
[38] Erin R. Graham, 'Money and Multilateralism: How Funding Rules Constitute IO Governance', *International Theory*, 7/1 (2015), 162.
[39] Devi Sridhar and Ngaire Woods, 'Trojan Multilateralism: Global Cooperation in Health', *Global Policy*, 4/4 (2013), 329.
[40] WHO, *Understanding Civil Society: Issues for WHO* (Geneva: WHO, 2002).
[41] UN System, Standing Committee on Nutrition, *SCN Private Sector Engagement Report* (Geneva: SCN, 2004).

In April 2011, for instance, the WHO organized the first global ministerial conference on health lifestyles and non-communicable diseases control in Moscow. The conference dedicated one day to discuss the role of multiple stakeholders. An official said:

> The conference went well until then. Then people got a bit anxious about it when we brought it into the domain of governance of the organization and coordination of global health more generally. There was quite a strong feeling with civil society groups; they were the NGOs that populated our meetings. They hated the fact that non-government organizations could only come from a purely public interest point of view: Oxfam, Save the Children Fund, and the likes. These civil society groups included, for instance, trade associations and patient groups—patient groups are the usual Trojan horse for industry... these 'civil society' groups included not only pharmaceutical ones, but increasingly the food and alcohol, tobacco industry, and many other front organizations that deliberately undermined our work such as tobacco control. Concerns about conflicts of interest and the relationship with private sectors were raised by member states and public interest foundations.

The term 'civil society' is used in WIPO, however, to distinguish those for-profit NGOs. One former DDG identified the complications:

> There are the NGOs primarily from business sectors which are predominantly multinationals, while there are the civil society NGOs, representing the so-called consumers and the public in favour of the diffusion of knowledge and information preferably free of charge. The irony is that most of the latter organizations originate in the developed countries, although they often claim to speak for developing countries. Who gave them the mandate? It is not clear at all to whom and how they in turn are accountable.

Similar civil society NGOs at the World Bank are simply called 'Northern NGOs'. Many of them are known as 'campaign NGOs, as distinct from those with programmes in the field [and] their whole reason for existence is to be implacable... if they stop denouncing big organizations, nobody will send them cash or quote them in newspapers anymore'. These campaign NGOs also differ from PINGOs, such as Oxfam or Save the Children Fund, as they 'do not have an off switch' and have no intention of working with IOs.[42] 'These NGOs were able to exert considerable political pressure on large shareholders, especially at the time of various IDA replenishments.'[43]

At the WHO, to be able to attend meetings of governing bodies and to speak, NGOs need to have 'official relationships' formally recognized by the WHO through an accreditation process.

---

[42] Sebastian Mallaby, *The World's Banker* (New York: Penguin Book, 2004), 277.
[43] Shahis Javed Burki, 'World Bank Operations: Some Impressions and Lessons', in Indermit S. Gill and Todd Pugatch (eds), *At the Frontlines of Development* (Washington: World Bank, 2005), 143.

What happens is that one NGO in official relationship now sometimes registers 80 or even 100 participants. The place down the road, for instance, the Ecumenical Centre, Christian Medical something or another, usually acts as the Trojan Horse. It puts something up on the web and says anyone who wants to come to the World Health Assembly meetings under our flag, just sign up here. That is how we could get some 900 participants for our board meeting. It gives some players more voice than they deserve.

If these civil society NGOs are controversial, those for-profit NGOs, or BINGOs, are more so. They are able to bring funding to IOs, and, as one senior official dealing them explains: 'They then legitimately would like to know what they are funding and how others are funding the organization and its programmes. Some of them even tell us, "we are giving these funds to you because it is voluntary to do what we want you to do. If you want to satisfy everyone, then jack up the membership fees."' Member states in general are suspicious of all types of non-state organizations as they insist 'it is unacceptable to agree with anything that impinges on the purely intergovernmental nature of policymaking within the organization'. Some senior officials at IOs are equally cautious about receiving funding from BINGOs. One regional VP at the World Bank explained: 'our trust funds primarily come from member states with the exception of health, where we do get funding from the Bill and Melinda Gates Foundation'. When funding is provided by private for-profit organizations, it comes in as a public–private partnership. In 2002–10, that accounted for about 4 per cent of the total trust funds at the World Bank.[44]

While the issue whether BINGOs are shaping the agenda at the WHO is highly debated, the contribution from the for-profit private sector (BINGOs) accounted for 1 per cent of the total voluntary contribution in 2011/12, 2 per cent for 2014/15. Thus, some argue that the impact of BINGOs on the WHO was overemphasized.[45] Member states remain the largest contributors to voluntary contributions (Table 6.4). The imbalance therefore is (*a*) the voluntary contribution accounted for 80 per cent of the total revenue, while the assessed contribution was 20 per cent; meanwhile, 78 per cent of the assessed contribution was allocated towards salary payments, while only 22 per cent went to WHO programmes; and (*b*) the top ten member states contributed 71 per cent of the programme budget and 44 per cent of the voluntary contribution.[46]

To avoid the problem of 'who pays the piper calls the tune', some non-OECD countries started calling for an increase to the assessed contribution. 'We cannot be dependent on just ten donors, because, if one of them goes

---

[44] World Bank Independent Evaluation Group, *Trust Fund Support for Development*, 15.
[45] Clift, 'What's the World Health Organization For?', 28–9.
[46] WHO, 'WHO Programmatic and Financial Report for 2014–2015, Including Financial Statements for 2015', A69/45, 29 April 2016, pp. 22–3.

Table 6.4. Voluntary contribution to the WHO, by source, 2011/2012 to 2014/2015 (%)

Sources	2011/12	2014/15
Member states	53	53
UN and IOs	22	24
Foundations	19	13[a]
NGOs and other institutions	5	8
Private sectors (BINGOs)	1	2

[a] The reduced share of voluntary contribution from foundations was due to a reduction in certain contributions to the Global Polio Eradication Initiative.

Source: WHO Programmatic and Financial Report for 2014/15, Including Financial Statements for 2015, A69/45, 29 April 2016, pp. 22–3.

badly, we have a problem,' said one state representative. 'By now we have even had countries like China call publicly at the Executive Board that we have to consider increasing assessed contributions,' said another senior official at the WHO. 'It is still a taboo, but the initiative has to come from member states.'

At the WHO, when members raised concerns about the influence of non-state players, the DG directed the secretariat to study the issue. 'We worked out several concept papers on the WHO's engagement with non-state actors, private sector NGOs, philanthropic foundations, and academic institutions. We consulted member states. Then we wrote a policy paper on the issue. When we took the policy paper to the World Health Assembly, member states said that they were not ready to discuss the issue,' explained a senior official. It is understandable because, first, the line between PINGOs and BINGOs is not always clear. There are clear BINGOs, such as the International Federation of Pharmaceutical Manufacturers, or the International Food and Beverage Alliance. There are also ones with 'hidden front group'. Take the International Alliance of Patients' Association as an example; some of its members 'are totally grass-root' organizations, while others are '100 per cent pharma-industry funded'.

Second, the issue of conflict of interest is much more complex for institutions than for individuals. For board members of any institutions, public or private alike,

> if you are a board member, you cannot hold shares in this or that company. In contrast, as the WHO has a combination of huge normative and operative mandates, it is very difficult to create firewalls. That is, if you are a purely normative institution, you have no voluntary contributions, and everything you do is funded. If you are a pure operator, you do not care if you have plenty of funding coming from anywhere.

Some member states were wary about the WHO receiving large amounts of funding from non-state players, PINGOs as well as BINGOs, because the WHO had a record of 'being infiltrated' by the tobacco industry in the

1990s, when 'tobacco companies ran more or less a secret service kind of activity, such as paying scientists to speak against our agenda, or paying some to come and serve in our expert groups'.

> In 2013, in a speech, the current DG said that we have clear evidence that big alcohol, big soda, big food are using the same strategies as we know from big tobacco. The Executive Board called for an emergency meeting the very next day under the pressure of the biggest companies of the world. We [the secretariat] received so many phone calls, asking whether the DG's talk was a declaration of war. The trickiness is that with tobacco we had total non-engagement. With food and pharmaceuticals, it is impossible not to engage. If we want to have a Stop TB programme, you have got to vaccinate. If you vaccinate, you have got to deal with pharmaceutical industries. How can we fight obesity if we cannot speak with the top people in food industry on reducing salt or sugar? How can we avoid being influenced when we engage with them? What money can we accept; what not? The contribution from BINGOs currently is small, but it is an issue we have to discuss.

This is the political reality many IOs face. The WHO management suggested the business of financing the organization be separated from the business of agenda setting, which is the prerogative of member states. The line is never easy to draw. When a large amount of money was given to infectious diseases, the work programme would inevitably tilt towards infectious diseases unless member states decide to refuse to accept the funding. Many did not see this as an option, as, under the existing arrangements, these funds are at least under some scrutiny from a multilateral institution. Meanwhile, some PINGOs and BINGOs 'can be quite pushy in pressing member states to advance their causes'. 'Now we have had some pro-NGO states that were fed up with some NGOs and wanted us not to deal with them at all.' This is the challenge faced not only by the secretariat at the WHO but by its counterparts in most IOs—who should be included in consultation, whose funding could IOs accept, and on what conditions? Accountability issues have become ever more complex. There is no end of the debate yet.

CONCLUSION

There is a need to redefine the debate about the funding of IOs. It is usually expressed as a shortage of funds. We have argued it is more a question of priorities and conditions, or, as a senior official at the WHO described it, the alignment between the willingness of donors to pay and the strategic plans member states can agree upon.

The IMF and the World Bank generate most of their funds through lending. For them, trust funds constitute only a small part of their income; rarely do they become controversial. The WTO is small and uses its funds effectively to run its secretariat, with limited trust funds for its programmes of technical assistance. WIPO generates its income by providing IP services to cover nearly all its costs; assessed contributions make up around 5 per cent of its income. The challenge for its management is to convince its member states that they are in 'control' and persuade member states to approve its work programme.

The two institutions with the real challenges are the FAO and WHO, whose budgets tend to be aspirational, rather than managerial. Assessed contributions now constitute only a small percentage of their income. Member states, especially a dozen rich countries, have been willing to contribute and even to increase their contribution to the programmes and activities at the FAO and WHO, but they are willing to do so on their terms. This may not be the issue of lack of trust, even though many have argued that member states do not trust IOs to 'spend their money'; rather it is because voluntary contributions are preferred by governments, both because they are easier to justify to their own electorates and because they are flexible under changing domestic pressures.

DGs at both organizations have been trying to convince donor countries to place their voluntary contributions in a common pool of core contributions without conditions attached. This remains a serious challenge for both organizations. Heavy reliance on voluntary contributions challenges the management in terms of planning for programmes, not only because some areas are better able to attract funding than others, but also because of the unpredictability of the sources of funding. It also challenges the management in terms of managing its human resources. Even if rhetorically the IOs talk of refusing offers if the funding does not fit their priorities, there is little evidence that they have turned any down.

The second issue is the sources of voluntary contribution from non-government agencies. Those from large foundations, such as the Global Fund, the Gates Foundation, and so on, are now greater than those of some large member donor countries. This raises the concern that IOs might become hostages to the fortunes of private organizations—what would happen if the private partner suddenly withdraws funding—and the concern about the priority and stability of funding. The concerns are nonetheless accepted as a political reality. Both the FAO and the WHO have continued encouraging them to make contributions to their causes. What makes member states nervous is the contribution from profit-making organizations, whether they are from pharmaceutical industries or food and beverage industries, or from some NGOs, religious or not; would these organizations undermine the member states' ability to set the agenda and oversee the expenditure of IOs where they should be the master?

Neither issue is likely to be resolved quickly. They both go the core of the IOs' funding challenges if they are to maximize their ability to deliver the diverse ambitions some member states and ICS want them to achieve in a climate of stalled contributions and expanding philanthropy.

7

Location

International organizations (IOs) have a membership of over 150 states, spread around the globe. All have a substantial core of staff in their headquarters (HQ), but the issue of where their staff should be located is always a potentially divisive one, especially for those IOs that need to deliver direct services to the poor and the needy. The questions of location invariably touch on other contested issues that are fundamental to both the philosophy and the practices of IOs. They often act as proxies for divisions within IOs and thus provide another perspective on some of those ideas that are at the core of these IOs and have been encountered in different guises in earlier chapters.

This chapter first identifies the two groups of IOs among those we study—those that are centralized and those that are dispersed. It then explores the dilemmas raised by issues of location and centralization. These can be summarized as:

1. the constant interplay required to balance geographical representation and subject specialization;
2. the need to identify priorities: the balance between normative standard-setting and service delivery and support to member states;
3. the affect that location has on the levels of discretion and lines of accountability by considering what issues or decisions should be delegated away from head office, to country offices and which should be maintained in the centre; decentralization creates networks in member states that can cut across any established chain of command as officers in the field interact with local governments, with non-governmental organizations (NGOs), and with other IOs;
4. the nature and culture of an IO's staffing and management, especially in cases where service in the regions or country offices is seen as an essential part of the careers of its staff; there is often talk of 'One Bank' or 'One WHO', questioning whether, and how, local staff employed in country offices should be part of one IO or part of a two-tier system where international and local staff have different terms of employment and different career prospects.

204   *The Working World of International Organizations*

The first two are issues of organizational design, and are often at the centre of reorganizations when a new head seeks to change the way an IO operates. The second two are issues of management, determining within an IO who should have what responsibility for what decisions and how power and authority should be distributed among the key players.

LOCATION OF STAFF: HOW AND WHY IOs DIFFER

The six IOs in this study vary dramatically in their geographical distribution of staff, and fit into two categories. Three are essentially based in HQ. Three have extensive, sometimes historically powerful, regional and country networks. In the first three, staff go 'on mission' in the field when services and support are required. In the other three, a large proportion of their staff can be located in the field.

The World Trade Organization (WTO) is primarily a forum where members must work together in order to negotiate on various trade and trade-related issues, or resolve their differences over these issues. Most members have ambassadors in Geneva accredited to the WTO. The director general (DG) and the secretariat are based in the one building, recently extended so that it could bring all the staff under the one roof; their role is to assist, even guide, the members in their work; they deal with the ambassadors in Geneva, who in turn seek instructions from politicians in capitals. Given that the WTO works by consensus, concerned countries must have their presence in the room. That requires attendance in Geneva. 'Since 2005 we've moved around from a very narrow agenda of trade negotiations, enforcing rules and consultation—a place where members consult in order to make the rules work properly and make the multilateral trading system work properly,' explains one senior WTO official. 'Pascal Lamy has taken on that this organization should do more on technical assistance and more specifically capacity-building to help developing countries build the capacity to trade, such as training custom officers, or providing advice on standards or rules.' Such a function is carried out either in Geneva or in the field, when the secretariat would send its staff on missions to advise and assist; there is no continuing need for their presence in the country. 'Whether that's really a core responsibility of this organization I question, but nevertheless that's what he wants us to do so we're doing that.' All IOs nowadays have a function of providing technical assistance to members that are in need. It is a matter of balancing it with other priorities.

The World Intellectual Property Organization (WIPO) is almost entirely based in Geneva too, both in its activities and in its staffing. This is primarily because WIPO was established to support various treaties before it was established as an international organization. It processes registration of patents, copyrights, trademarks, and all other activities related to intellectual property (IP). Meanwhile, as an IO, its member states have demanded support too, especially with the adoption of development agenda. Such assistance and support are often offered in Geneva and occasionally in regions or countries when a very few staff are sent on missions to explain and support the understanding of IP regimes and help countries wishing to establish IP offices. In so doing, they sometimes had a catalytic effect. IP is often not a central issue in governments; responsibility may be scattered across departments, all with slightly different interests. Occasionally those concerned with IP within a government met for the first time when they gathered to listen to the presentations from WIPO, and as a consequence it became potentially possible to develop a coherent response. More often it remained true that individual member states did not really know what they wanted. Different departments, for all of whom IP is a secondary issue, have divergent opinions and demands. They often do not have the time or expertise to develop a nationally consistent stance at WIPO, even assuming they could agree, thus leaving WIPO staff a degree of discretion as to how to make it work.[1]

Recently, WIPO has begun to open a number of small external offices: initially in Singapore (2005) and Tokyo (2006), then in Buenos Aires in 2009 (where the regional director (RD) was the just defeated candidate for the top job), and in Moscow and Beijing in 2014. According to the WIPO DG, Francis Gurry: 'WIPO's network of external offices forms an integral part of the organization designed to bring our services and cooperation closer to our member states, our stakeholders and our partners.'[2] The purpose of the offices is to act as a link to the local IP community. Decisions and programmes are made in Geneva; WIPO seeks to develop a network of consistent support and services in relation to its treaties and consistent IP practices across countries. That is a challenge, as there is deep-seated suspicion among developing members that 'harmonization' really means dictation by the United States and developed countries. There may be an increasing need for enhanced engagement of WIPO with its member states and stakeholders on the ground, but an international regime needs common ground. There is thus no requirement for local representatives and local variations.

The third centralized IO in this study is the International Monetary Fund (IMF). While all its staff are located in Washington, they work closely with national governments represented by officials from the ministry of finance or

---

[1] Geoffrey Yu, 'The World Intellectual Property Organization: A Comment', in Patrick Weller and Xu Yi-chong (eds), *The Politics of International Organizations: Views from Insiders* (New York: Routledge, 2015).

[2] Francis Gurry on External Offices, see <http://www.wipo.int/about-wipo/en/offices/> (accessed 10 March 2015).

the central bank, or through the office of executive directors (EDs), mainly out of HQ. IMF staff visit capitals regularly when a country's monetary policy is under review and sometimes for intense sessions when there is a crisis or a need for assistance. There is, however, no arrangement that requires IMF staff to be located in capitals, and the distance, both geographically and intellectually, from the client protects the authors of reports from the potential pressures that might accrue from day-to-day contacts in the national capital. It is expected that these processes will ensure consistency of proposals across its member states. An official argued:

> We are very headquarters-based as opposed to the World Bank. The reason is that, for us, learning comes from observing what is happening in our member countries. I do not think we can bring anything to Australia that Australia does not know... What we can bring is that different countries in similar situations have different challenges that lead to results not on their own radar... That kind of knowledge is generated more when you are together. To engage in the field, you do not have to live in the field. That is critical.

There are substantial policy reasons for maintaining the majority of their staff at the WTO, WIPO, and IMF in HQ. The subject areas draw the need for expertise and consistency, and hence missions are the best use of resources. None of them delivers specialized services that require constant attendance and oversight. These practices have led to charges that officials who fly in tend to propose 'one-size-for-all' solutions and lack of sensitivity to local conditions. Yet, similar charges were made on those decentralized IOs too.[3]

The other three IOs provide a dramatic contrast, with their staff far more dispersed.

The World Bank has changed its approach since the mid-1990s. Location has been one of the indications of a permanent tension between geography and content. It raises the question: is the comparative advantage that the Bank holds based on technical knowledge or good connections with clients? The issue was always whether one or the other should be master or, at the least, how they should best cooperate. By the mid-1990s, the World Bank remained 'a highly centralized institution not only in its headquarters operations but also with respect to overseas activities. All stages of the project cycle are managed from Washington, and field operations are carried on by short-term missions.'[4] A number of experiments where staff were located in regional offices were in place, but they were seldom regarded as a success. There were problems in determining how much discretion should be granted to the decentralized staff and what kind of expertise they could maintain in the

---

[3] Ngaire Wood, *The Globalizers: The IMF, the World Bank and their Borrowers* (Ithaca, NY: Cornell University Press, 2006).

[4] Edward S. Mason and Robert E. Asher, *The World Bank since Bretton Woods* (Washington: Brookings Institution Press, 1973), 741.

field. Significant changes were adopted in the first term of James Wolfensohn as the president and completed by his second term (1995–2005). Country offices were gradually established and formally institutionalized, staffed with permanent Bank employees. Country directors (CDs) were located in the capitals, with only a few exceptions. Each country office included a number of international civil servants with required expertise and others who were locally recruited, often highly qualified but employed to work from the local workforce in the country. In a matrix structure, CDs had the budget and the networks had the staff. CDs contracted staff, who then worked in the country offices delivering projects. The system 'nicely combined country responsiveness with technical expertise', explained one former vice president (VP) of the World Bank. 'After all, decentralization is in our DNA in terms of what we do and our success depends on our interaction with client governments.'[5]

The Food and Agriculture Organization (FAO) provides an example of the changing pressures. When the United Nations Development Programme (UNDP) funded many of its field programmes, its staff were located in country offices. When that funding dried up in the 1990s, the number of international professional officers in country offices was reduced. The management determined that more staff would again be posted to the field. By the end of 2014, the FAO had representation in over 120 countries. It delivers a series of programmes to individual countries through its five regional offices, eleven subregional offices, seventy-four fully fledged country offices, eight offices with technical officers, and thirty-six countries covered through multiple accreditations.[6] Each has to be customized to the local conditions and delivered with the cooperation of local departments of agriculture. Currently, only 53 per cent of the FAO's staff are based in Rome; the others are spread around the globe, often in remote rural areas overseeing projects. Even that number is, according to José Graziano, the FAO DG, too high. He had won his first election with a commitment to push further decentralization.

What difference do the decisions to decentralize the FAO make? The FAO has undertaken a number of evaluations of the benefits of country representation, but a report that reviewed those evaluations decided that the findings were inconclusive in terms of benefits of decentralization. What matters rather was 'the competence of the FAO representative and the quality and timeliness of the technical cooperation that the country office can channel to the hosting

---

[5] For the reorganization on decentralization under James Wolfensohn, see Sebastian Mallaby, *The World's Banker* (New York: Penguin Books, 2004); Zhang, Shengman, *One Step at a Time* (Shanghai: Wenhui Press, 2006); Xu Yi-chong and Weller, *Inside the World Bank* (New York: Palgrave Macmillan, 2009), esp. ch. 5, pp. 105–32.

[6] See FAO, 'Programme Implementation Report 2014–15', C2017/8 (2016), 75–6. See also David Hallam, 'Turbulence and Reform in the United Nations Food and Agricultural Organization', in Weller and Xu (eds), *The Politics of International Organization*, 194.

member, regardless of the source'.[7] The report states that there are no organizational models guaranteed to work. 'The main finding across the regions was that "there were no equals". The choice of location for regional and country offices, the mandate of each office, the structure of regional or subregional, all differed.' Analysis did not 'allow identifying a "good structure" let alone a "best one"'.[8] Local conditions and staff competence were crucial in each case. So there was no evidential basis for decentralization; the case was political, even ideological. Yet, the push for the further establishment of country representation continues, not only from those members who see the value of operations on their turf, but particularly from the DG.

The World Health Organization (WHO) was always decentralized in both its structure and the location of its staff. There are two distinct issues: one is the legal independence of the regional offices; the second is what happens when WHO international staff go into the field and what levels of discretion are delegated to them. The WHO operates like a federal system; the RD is directly elected by the member states in the region, and each region has its own staff. The independence and capacity vary significantly across the six regions. This arrangement was entrenched because the Pan-American World Health Organization (PAHO), created in 1902, long preceded the WHO. PAHO 'wears two institutional hats'—as the specialized health agency for the Inter-American system and as regional office for the WHO. It has over 500 staff and generates much of its own funding, independent of the WHO. This 'federalist' structure has been a constant challenge for DGs and HQs. Over the decades, some DGs have tried to weld them into a team; some talk to them individually; and a few even try to ignore them. There is a tension built into the legal structure of the WHO as a world (and now even global) health organization. In addition, its HQ staff are located worldwide too. They deliver programmes across the globe, work with local staff on elimination of communicable diseases, and provide developing countries with assistance and advice on non-communicable diseases and even health systems. A field presence is crucial, but managing decentralized activities and dispersed staff is a challenge.

So, unlike the World Bank and the FAO, there is never a question of whether the WHO will be decentralized. Its history and constitution determine that it is. The fear is always that the WHO will disintegrate, as one official described it, into a Balkanized organization with six mini-WHOs. Thus, amid continuing demands for decentralization, there is a case for a strong centre. Not every function can be decentralized; legal advice has to be consistent across the organization, and these core staff activities are retained in Geneva.

---

[7] OECD and FAO, *Synthesis of the Evaluation of FAO's Regional and Subregional Offices* (Rome: FAO, 2013), 16.

[8] OECD and FAO, *Synthesis of the Evaluation of FAO's Regional and Subregional Offices*, 14–15.

There is a continuing debate to determine what needs to be organization-wide and what should be local. It can be encapsulated in the dilemma posed by a senior official: 'When the DG speaks, does she actually speak with the authority of the organization or the authority of Geneva? It depends on the specific issues.'

Where the IO staff work obviously makes a difference to the staff themselves: the degree to which all staff work on similar terms, with comparable career prospects. But the decisions relate to far more than that. Location affects the relationships between the players. In central offices, member states, represented by either EDs or diplomats, interact most regularly with their counterparts and with the secretariat. It can become an enclosed world in Geneva, Rome, or Washington.

For staff working in the field, the world looks different. The range of contacts within a national bureaucracy and with NGOs is much more extensive, constant, and immediate. Knowledge of the impact of projects is first hand. Feedback is continuous. And supervision, in contrast, tends to be more distant. One World Bank country director asserted it was preferable to have at least two oceans between him and his VP. For many international staff, being in the field was the very essence of the job. At HQ, 'there were too many meetings, too many regulations, and too much politics', one explained. In the field they could appreciate far better what they could achieve. Some officers from the FAO spent their first twenty years in the field, and many WHO officers have never worked anywhere else; they 'belong' to the regional office. However much those international staff enjoy working in the field, close to the people they help, they all face practical issues of promotions or children's education, which often bring them back reluctantly to HQ.

To understand the different relationships these centrally located or field-based international staff have with member states and heads of IOs, we need to appreciate different perspectives and often motivations. At HQ, the broad policy issues, the debates on normative and operational work, or the standing of the organization may all be important indicators of the health and vibrancy of the IO. In the field, it is about programmes for fisheries, vaccinations, microfinancing, or family planning; these can alter local conditions and require officers to deal directly with clients who will benefit. At HQ, international staff can draw substantial professional help from their peers, while in the field they can be quite lonely. The interaction between the two levels may be limited, especially at the bottom, where the focus is all on the project, and a change of the head of an IO or senior management team may not be seen as consequential. Yet, both matter for the viability of the organization, for the member states as clients, and for the officials for whom this is their daily round.

In sum, there is a considerable variation between IOs, from the highly centralized with all staff based at HQ, to circumstances where many of the staff permanently work in regions or national offices. Our task here is to ask how these different arrangements affect the relationships of the key players and shape their capacity to influence decisions in different IOs. We concentrate in the remainder of this chapter on the three IOs where location of staff is a continuing issue.

PRINCIPLES AND DILEMMAS

Choices about location touch on a number of fundamental issues about the nature of the IOs: the assumptions that underpin IO activities and the way it relates to its clients; lines of accountability in theory and practice; levels of responsiveness and the informal processes that determine who maintains the crucial knowledge of what member countries want or need. In particular, issues about location identify the divisions within groups of participants: state members hold diverging views about the role of IOs in capitals; staff deal with ministers and bureaucrats directly, rather than through EDs. What is significant to the staff of IOs in the capitals looks different from the traditional HQ perspective.

Balancing Geographical Representation and Subject Specialization

Questions about location raise issues about the organizing principles for IOs: representation versus specialization. Both are needed for IOs to be able to pursue their missions effectively. Yet, it is always a challenge to balance them.

Since the mid-1990s, the World Bank has shifted from centralization to decentralization. The organizational structure set up in 1952 divided the Bank among the project departments, responsible for appraising and supervising particular loans, and the area departments, responsible for country lending policies. In much of its first forty years, the project departments held sway, determining Bank standards to be adopted and implemented across all countries. Engineers played a substantial role as they oversaw the road, ports, dam, and electricity projects. Then, there were powerful regional VPs, who might be Washington-based, but with empires including the sectoral disciplines needed to develop country programmes and specific projects. In the 1980s, complaints grew that the six regional VPs became too strong, with constant references to their fiefdoms (or silos, depending on the perspective). These debates were as much about power as they were about practice: who was to be in the lead in determining relations with clients? Often reorganization was sought by new presidents upon taking office to adjust that balance when they used strategic reform as a means of breaking up these established empires.

James Wolfensohn, as part of his Strategic Compact, introduced a matrix management scheme in 1997. Network directors (based on the old project departments) managed human resources to ensure cadres of staff had the necessary skills and professional qualities. These network directors then contracted out their professionals to the country directors, who were responsible for delivering projects as part of the country strategies for which CDs had responsibility.[9] At the same time the World Bank decided to move most CDs to the national capitals, giving them regular and direct access to the client countries.

Locating CDs and staff in capitals changed the way that the relationship with member states was developed. As one CD said: 'When you are in the field, you have a very different perspective from when you work on mission and when you tend to have preconceived ideas.' The traditional Bank perspective became softened by a greater appreciation of what the client country wanted and needed. Initiatives came through CDs, who developed Country Strategies with client members that were then approved by the bank board. CDs could then 'purchase' services from networks as CDs controlled the budget, although many of the network staff were thereafter located in the national capitals too. It was a complex arrangement that sought to balance the different demands, but it left CDs as the principal intermediaries between the Bank and the clients. They were responsible for developing new proposals (often with the government), and for managing their progress through the Bank's channels to gain the EB's approval. The CDs' positions, particularly in large countries such as China, Indonesia, and Brazil, all of which had big programmes, were eagerly sought. The system worked for two decades, by which time around 40 per cent of the Bank staff were located in the field.[10]

After he had been appointed as the president in 2012, Jim Kim sought to reorganize the World Bank by giving more weight to the international, rather than country, perspectives. He created Global Practice Cross Cutting Solutions divisions and recruited most directors from outside. CDs were kept on location. His decision to reorganize the Bank generated a highly contested internal battle. One group wanted to continue the current practices, with the substantial authority located with the regional VPs and CDs; the other argued that the World Bank was 'losing its expertise due to decentralization' and had lost its cutting edge as an innovative thinker. The push came from those in the sectors who wanted more control over resources, which, they argued, should

---

[9] For the matrix system, see World Bank Independent Evaluation Group, *The Matrix System at Work: An Evaluation of the World Bank's Organizational Effectiveness* (Washington: World Bank, April 2012).

[10] On the issue of decentralization at the World Bank during the Wolfensohn era, see Xu and Weller, *Inside the World Bank*, esp. ch. 5.

be concentrated in Washington to develop international solutions. Sadly, the principal advocates in both camps were pushed out and left the Bank. Jim Kim then went cool on the demands for global solutions, as 'half the global practice super directors he hired left'. The sector divisions reverted to their earlier network titles of Human Development, Sustainable Development, and Equitable Growth and Institutions, with a single managing director overseeing their activities—the same organizational structure under Lewis T. Preston (1991–5). The responsibility for coordinating the parts lies with the Operations Policy and Country Services division, sometimes referred to as the World Bank's plumber, which ensures all run smoothly. Where the key weight resides—with regional or network VPS—is disputed and, more importantly, the return to the old organizational structure did not change fundamentally the already decentralized structure. In 2010, 90 per cent of CDs and country managers, and 38 per cent of staff, were in the field; by 2016, the figures were 96 per cent and 40 per cent respectively.[11]

The World Bank's experience emphasizes that decisions about the location of staff and responsibilities have important implications; it requires a balance between competing demands, although there can be no perfect solution. Its success depends on both sides having something to offer: the CD knowing what programmes are needed and proper for the country and the networks having the skills to deliver them. That was not true everywhere.

In the FAO, an official with experience in the field as a country representative in a large developing state argued that, in a declining organization, if too much were decentralized, little would happen. When asked if normative work should be done in the field, another FAO official responded:

> Most of us would say no. We think it makes sense to decentralize operational issues, to get decisions on operations that affect a project or a programme in a country and decentralize those. Certainly, sitting in the country where I represent the FAO, I was a strong proponent of a business model where I did not have technical staff in the country beyond specific project staff, but I could dial them up in Rome when I needed them.
>
> If someone had to say to me, 'Okay, in the next five years we need to post staff to your office, do you need a fisheries, a forestry, whatever, what do you want?' I would not be able to do it. I would get it wrong at least 80 per cent of the time, because you really just cannot predict what it might be. You simply cannot have all of them. Even if you have a fisheries person, the probability is that it is fisheries versus agriculture, or that it is shrimps versus tilapia. You cannot get it right. So for me, in a country office, I was much more comfortable knowing that there were 500 to 1,000 people in HQ with expertise that we can draw on and, if I planned it properly, I could get them.

[11] World Bank, *Annual Report* (Washington, 2016).

This debate is more than about normative work versus assistance work, areas versus expertise, or even resources. Another senior official at the FAO identified the dilemma:

> As I say, many of us feel that that is the way it should be [with expertise in Rome]. Many of the OECD countries feel that. G77 countries are a little different. For a small country in Africa, the opportunity to have a bigger FAO office somehow has a certain status; it carries a certain manana with it. So sometimes these decisions are supported not for the right reasons.

If the reasons for creating country offices were more about politics than programme logics or assistance delivery, those considerations became even more significant when the DG had to consider which (if any) should be closed.

> One of the findings of the Independent External Evaluation (IEE) of the FAO, which was confirmed by the Immediate Plan of Action (IPA) for the FAO's renewal, was not to change the balance of resources between HQ and the regions until we had sorted out this rationalization of the country offices, which is highly political. Basically, the DG is saying: 'I am not going to be the one who closes the country offices; member states have to tell me which offices to close.' Eight criteria were specified in the IPA and, if you apply those criteria, you close almost every office. It is just bouncing back and forth.

Not much happened. As an evaluation noted: 'no FAO office was ever closed down'.[12] Country offices are seen as a benefit, and DGs, particularly those who value the support (and votes too) of individual countries, are unlikely to start upsetting member states by removing their offices. Indeed, at the FAO, the decision on where activities should take place altered the relationship between regions, countries, and HQ. A senior official at FAO notes:

> After the independent evaluation of FAO, the regional conferences have become more of a decision-making, rather than a body where you were historically making recommendations to the FAO Council or the FAO Conference. The offices at the FAO HQ are supposed to be involved in country programming and assisting governments.

Letting regional and country offices dominate decision-making always has its downsides, not only because of the risk of inconsistency in policies of any one IO, but also because of the risk of 'political patronage' in regional or country offices. As one senior academic noted about the WHO's Regional Office for Africa: people at this regional office 'are very, very frightened to say anything that might be critical of government... they essentially are subservient to governments. That is part of what they are supposed to do, but... regional

---

[12] OECD and FAO, 'Synthesis of the Evaluation of FAO's Regional and Subregional Offices', 6.

offices can be dominated by political patronage, which seriously undermines their capacity to enact, let alone to lead, collective health action.'[13]

The political dynamics at the WHO create its own tensions. On the one hand is DG Brundtland's adamant statement: 'the WHO will never be a field agency, with large numbers of its personnel working in member countries.' She wanted the WHO to be an organization able to 'give the best advice, develop and support the best policies, and stimulate the best research'.[14] On the other hand, the WHO is a federation in effect, if not in theory. RDs, elected by countries in a region, do own their accountability and loyalty to the member states in the region. Their direct election also gives them a degree of independence from WHO HQ, and provides a unique internal dynamic within the WHO system. An assistant director general (ADG) in Geneva made the point: 'When we are in a meeting with RDs, they clearly outrank us ADGs. Now some ADGs might question that, but I never would. They are elected to serve a constituency while I am a senior international bureaucrat.' That has implications for the way that the whole organization is managed. That is, the elected status of RDs requires DGs to develop strategies that recognize their semi-independence, but also the need for a unified organization. There is no one correct way to manage the relationships between RDs and DGs at HQ. An ADG explained: 'Dr Lee did not want to engage with the RDs as a group; he would talk to them one on one.' Dr Brundtland was reportedly saying: 'I don't want to deal with RDs and I want to go past them.' In 2006, Margaret Chan's transition team was handed an unpublished document, entitled 'Competent People, Incompetent Organization', warning that the 'WHO had lost its sense of unity [and] the goals of headquarters are not aligned with those of the Regional Offices'.[15] Others argued that some of the WHO's serious failures 'can be traced to...its governance structure'. 'There are serious tensions between the WHO headquarters and its six regional offices. The DG does not have authority over the regions. As long as regional directors are elected by countries rather than the DG, the global capacity to collect information and do things is breeched.'[16] Instead of ignoring them or bypassing the RDs, Margaret Chan, according to one of the ADGs, adopted 'more collaborative strategies, completely opposite to what Dr Lee or Dr Brundtland had done'.

> I have seen this DG [Chan] personally work with the RDs as peers. She is *primus inter pares* but she is not a different category or person. They are all elected; she was elected to make sure that they work together. She sees it more as a republic

---

[13] Quoted from Udani Samarasekera, 'WHO AFRO: Looking for a Leader,' *Lancet*, 382/14 (2013), 1974.
[14] Quoted in Anthony Robbins, 'Brundtland's World Health Organization: A Test Case for United Nations Reform', *Public Health Reports*, 114/1 (1999), 35.
[15] Richard Horton, 'Offline: Can WHO Survive?', *Lancet*, 380 (2012), 1457.
[16] Quoted from Udani Samarasekera, 'WHO: 60 Years On', *Lancet*, 371 (2008), 1151–2.

than as a monarchy and certainly more than a presidential system and has a great respect for and recognition of the role of these RDs. She gets it in a way that, coming from a regional office background, I have not seen very many people get it. Everybody speaks, talks the talk; she actually walks it. She will not commit the organization without their agreement on something.

The so-called global policy group, consisting of the DG and the six RDs, meets regularly with only the seven of them, to work out common positions, common strategies. It 'really is a serious attempt to look at corporate issues as one group'. According to another senior official:

> Dr Chan said, the only way we are going to make sense of this organization is to work hard on these relationships because it is a question of building trust. She engages with them very heavily and intensely as a way of trying to create more alignment. I think it is much more effective than Dr Lee's one-on-one relationship. This is where I can say it has worked. The relationship with regions is much stronger. It does not necessarily mean it is any easier, but it is much stronger than it was in the past.

The push to give precedence to regional demands with its changing dynamics can be seen elsewhere too. Traditionally, some IOs are seen as presidential, with considerable authority in the hands of the head of the organization, certainly insofar as the management of the secretariat. That assumes that all staff are, at least nominally, their subordinates who can be shuffled across the IO's divisions and even their multiple locations. One way to remove VPs at the World Bank was to offer them a demotion to CD in an obscure post like central Asia. Defeated opponents in a leadership ballot can be posted to a newly created post on another continent, as occurred in WIPO. FAO directors can be shifted against their wishes to distant country offices too.

Location as Proxy for Identifying Priorities and Roles

A second parallel dilemma seeks to identify an appropriate balance between the roles IOs should fulfil. This is a perennial issue for all IOs, especially the FAO and the WHO for this study—whether IOs should be predominantly normative agencies, setting standards, developing guidelines, and providing information that can be used by governments and agencies when implementing their own programmes, or whether they should also be involved in implementing programmes themselves. We are concerned here with the part of the debate that is tied to the issue of decentralization. If an IO is seen as an organization with its primary role as providing assistance to member states, then regional and country offices not only are necessary but also need to be close to people who receive assistance. If IOs should focus on standard-setting and norm creation, concentrated expertise is essential.

The core is a substantive debate on the appropriate role of, for instance, the FAO, of which decentralization is an outcome. If the FAO is to be a standard-setting organization, then regional and country offices are not an essential component needed to achieve its principal purposes; much of the work can, and should, be achieved in Rome, where the deep expertise resides. If the FAO's purpose is to deliver technical support, apply expertise, and assist national governments develop policies for their particular needs in the field, then decentralization becomes essential for its success.

Developed member states often think the emphasis is on the wrong roles. A capital-based official in a developed member state commented:

> Our view is that the FAO needs to focus its effort on what it's really good at. They happen to be things that align with our objectives, which are all around the standards-setting work and the scientific knowledge base, and becoming a knowledge-based organization. We acknowledge that it has got some advantage in on-the-ground implementation, but our own view is that we should be only doing that where the implementation is consistent with the objectives of the overall organization, instead of what it has ended up. That is, stuff going on all over the place that has not a lot of bearing to the central purpose of the organization. So we're not supportive of a broadly dispersed, segregated bottom-up organic FAO. We're interested in a centrally driven but de-centrally implemented FAO.

If that statement identified the differences of opinion about the broad purpose, there was also an issue of whether the FAO had the capacity to provide consistent services on the ground in multiple locations at the same time as it developed its critical knowledge base. A senior official commented:

> The donor countries... are concerned that by decentralizing you lose the critical mass in headquarters. If you've got a much bigger organization, then fine, you can do it. But with the way the organization has shrunk over the last few years, maybe you can't.
>
> The idea of decentralization is that you have these teams of technical expertise in the regions, with a vet and a policy guy and a market guy and whatever. In fact you're going to have one vet covering the whole of Africa. That's just window dressing, that's not real decentralization. So there is some scepticism on the part of some members.
>
> Politically it's very attractive. And it's half responding to some of the criticisms that have been made by the Department for International Development, UK (DFID) and the Australian Evaluation about country-level delivery. But just moving one person out to a regional office doesn't necessarily do much for country-level delivery. If you took a hundred out, then what would they deliver, because there would be nothing being produced in Rome: no global public goods, no nothing. So it's a difficult balance; probably you need a bigger organization to actually achieve the kind of things that are being asked.

The member states are well aware of the tensions. An ambassador to the FAO from a developed country noted: 'Decentralization in itself is not a goal; it is not an objective. It is a measure, a means to achieve better delivery of normative goals to the field.'

At the WHO, one official with experience at both field and HQ commented:

> Geneva is the site or the locale for the development of norms, standards, policies of global nature. The staff report on experiences; they are placed to generate the knowledge derived from lessons from stocktaking of policies, strategies, programs, the repository of global knowledge generation, applied knowledge for public health action, producing public goods.

It is very important to understand 'the dual nature of what WHO does for the collective interest in public health for all member states and for what it does for each member state in terms of technical cooperation', he continued. 'Unless one understands this duality, and the way in which you have to combine it, you don't get the nature of this specialized organization.'

The tensions are exacerbated by the suspicion between the different groups of member states who fear that the one group is trying to dictate to others. In the WHO an official explained the challenges for the secretariat when it sought to promote reform of the the WHO's financial management.

> There is concern, particularly among developing countries, when they see the donors, the OECD countries, being incredibly enthusiastic about reform, crawling all over it. They see reform as the WHO withdrawing more into its normative upstream policy-type role, and perhaps decreasing direct levels of country support. And so we want to make sure that their interests are not ignored. There is very little trust between member states... I think there is a high degree of trust of the secretariat to go in the right direction, but the trust between them at this stage is limited big time.

DISCRETION, DELEGATION, AND ACCOUNTABILITY

The value of working in the field depends on the degree of discretion that field staff have. If an IO wants to remain centralized, to ensure that there is a coherent set of policies and a unified way of doing things across countries, discretion then is limited and field staff will have little ability to adjust programmes for local conditions or to adapt to client needs. If an IO agrees to delegate much of the detail, then similar programmes will differ from client to client. A key question is the impact of the arrangements on the way that the staff and others perceive their roles and their relationships. Two issues are intertwined: the quality of the staff in the regions and the preparedness of HQ to delegate to country offices.

The different perspective of officials in capitals was epitomized by the comment of a World Bank CD in a very different time zone from Washington: 'During the day I lobby my country on behalf of the Bank. At night I lobby the Bank on behalf of my country.' Location changes the balance between responsiveness to member states acting in this instance as clients, and accountability to superiors in the hierarchy.

The differences in responsiveness could be shaped by a number of factors: the distance from head office, the immediacy of connections with the client country, and the links with the local authority, which often lead to requests for assistance that would not otherwise have occurred. More important, location changes actual lines of accountability, even if formal ones are nominally unaffected.

Changing Hierarchies

IOs have tended to be hierarchical, with lines of authority from the DG or the president through management. Staff in HQs respond to member states, but, except in a few cases where they are acting as secretaries to members' committees, it is an indirect process. When the staff are based in capitals, the dynamics change. The formal superiors are a long way away, often divided by time zones as well as by distance. The clients are along the road, in contact as often as they like, immediately accessible for crisis or lunch.

A former CD explained: 'In the field, the accountabilities seemed so much clearer, and the feedback loop was so much shorter. There was no comparison in terms of job satisfaction and effectiveness... they know we are here, so they will ring us up and ask for advice.'[17] Others had different ways of expressing their relationships with HQ and client countries:

> In Washington I work for an organization. Here I work for a client.[18]

> China's Minister of Finance during most of the 1990s said to me when I took over the management of the China department: 'I have been told that more than 100 professionals work for you in your department. I want to say to you they also work for me—for the Chinese authorities. We should take joint responsibility for their work programme.' And he did.[19]

During a global financial crisis, a CD could be in contact with the Minister for Finance or the departmental head on a daily basis, or more often. The contacts in the capitals are with people far senior to the middle-ranking ambassadors or

---

[17] Basil Kavaksky, 'Pictures and Lessons of Development Practice', in Indermit S. Gill and Todd Pugatch (eds), *At the Frontlines of Development* (Washington: World Bank, 2005), 42.

[18] Cited in Xu and Weller, *Inside the World Bank*, 118.

[19] Shahid Javed Burki, 'World Bank Operations: Some Impressions and Lessons', in Gill and Pugatch (eds), *At the Frontlines of Development*, 132.

EDs attached to the IOs and allow a constant and direct input into national policies, for which there is no equivalent from Geneva or Washington.

Country Ownership

An important element in that change comes as a consequence of the growing weight given to the idea of 'country ownership'. An FAO official noted:

> The country offices are assuming much greater responsibility both in an administrative sense with a higher level of delegation of authority and spending, but also in the use of what we call the country programming framework. So the idea is that what the organization does should be a combination of a discussion between the organization and the member government in the country to establish priorities that are bottom up, coupled with governing bodies and other secretariat decisions coming down.

The more operational the activities are, the greater is the need to understand local conditions and to gain local support. The WHO has a number of large field programmes, both its own and those funded by the various partnerships it has entered. Speaking from experience in the field, a senior WHO official commented:

> To be able to manage a joint programme about work, we cannot dictate and it has got to be agreed. It just makes more sense anyway, and we did provide an opportunity for everybody to share experience. What I found is, if you are a regional office, you usually want to know what works, or won't work, in another region, or what Geneva thinks, so you have got to set up mechanisms to facilitate.
>
> I think Geneva's role is to facilitate that cross-regional interchange of experience. Now a lot of people think Geneva's role is to tell regions what to do. That is where we run into major problems, and it is a culture I am not used to. I came here and set up a programme and I came from the regions. I found a group of people here in Geneva. I had all the people I had worked with in the regions and they were the ones who I needed with me, not the ones in Geneva. So I just set up a mechanism to make that work.

When the World Bank shifted more senior staff to the field, it changed the dynamics of the organization. A CD commended:

> Decentralization forced the Bank to give far more responsibility to the country director, even though the pre-1997 system ostensibly integrated both the program and sector functions under the country director. Being on the spot enables the country director to identify demand and needs as they arise and to organize responses to them.[20]

---

[20] Kavaksky, 'Pictures and Lessons of Development Practice', 42.

There was consequently greater discretion for staff in the field.

In some views this decentralization liberated the CDs and gave them greater scope to be innovative. Various CDs appreciated working in the field and discussed their scope for action: 'The CD is the best job in the Bank and the best CD jobs are in the field;' 'when you as the CD have the confidence of the VP, you have room to manœuvre and thus the CDs are crucial players at the Bank'; or 'the notion that we as CDs are dictated to from Washington is crazy; the Bank needs a massive engagement in the field'.

In the FAO, distance also reduces the burden that comes with any oversight by, and involvement with, HQ. An FAO official noted:

> We do have quite a measure of independence and, of course, we're just that physical distance away from headquarters and a lot of the day-to-day nonsense that is associated with the headquarters of any organization, not just the FAO; it's just a fact of life.

There are, of course, necessary conditions for that scope: the relations with the supervising VP/ADG are important, even while some did not want too close a relationship: 'The role of the VP is to help an autonomous CD to get his way in Washington; we don't need him in the field.' Most appreciated was the closeness to clients and the ability to identify the problems and impacts of programmes and projects more readily.

Delegation to Country Offices

The dispersal of decision-making was intended, in theory at least. One long-serving FAO officer in Rome spent his first twenty years in the field. He recalled:

> When I started there were no country offices for the FAO. We maybe had a senior adviser sitting in the UNDP office, and it was more of a case of you working directly with the whole UN family. Then the country offices started to be created; so then you have a separate identity. When I was in the field (and that was up to 1995), the regional offices were quite weak. I never dealt with the regional office. I always dealt directly with HQ.

Jacques Diouf, as FAO DG, wanted to reinvigorate the country offices. 'He started creating subregional offices, so quite a few positions were moved out to the field. That was at a time when development assistance was changing and projects were having fewer and fewer international staff and so the capacity to support those was being shifted, through regular staff, to the field.' Of course, the quality of local country directors matters too. An FAO officer with experience of other IOs compared the differential impact of the FAO and the World Bank: 'I feel the [FAO] field offices are very weak, so I feel that some are good, but the majority are weak and they don't have the same impact. In any case, the FAO can never have the same weight as the World Bank in countries.' A review of programme implementation in 2014–15 identified continuing problems in the running of offices away from Rome. While it took the policy of 'delegating responsibility and authority to decentralized offices' as given, it argued that the calibre and quality of its field officers remained problematic. The review questioned whether FAO local offices were observing corporate standards and argued that 'too many projects were in need of management intervention, because of slow rate of spend, over-expenditure, overdue closure reports, or outstanding actions to administratively close a project'. It suggested 'improving the calibre of FAO representatives' in the field, 'strengthening the internal control of decentralized offices', and 'further refining the selection process'.[21]

In the past, appointments to CD positions had indeed been almost fortuitous, as patterns change:

> The process of appointment of the FAO representatives at country level has changed. There was a long period where external people were brought in as representatives, very often individuals who had served in member governments at a fairly senior level. The difficulty that was discovered was that these individuals didn't understand the organization; much of the work is operational, so there was a very steep learning curve. Probably about five years ago there was a move towards using the FAO's own staff resources as representatives, and that's continuing now. It's not an exclusive policy, but the lion's share of appointees now has FAO experience. The process was quite serendipitous. I happened to be talking to a colleague who was a director from a large country. We were talking about something and he said to me you wouldn't want to go to—as the FAO rep, would you? I said I could. He said: 'tell me tomorrow morning if you're interested'. Then it went to the DG and the DG said yes. I went very quickly.

So the pendulum swings between giving priority for local connections and an appreciation of the cultures and mores of the IO.

An ambassador to the FAO from a developed country noted the concerns of some member states:

> You have to have really good people on the ground. This has not always been the case; it has to be professional people recruited on merit and promoted on merit. I mean this may sound basic to you, but I can assure you that it's not... I'm sure if you have an under-represented country there will always be people there that can do the job perfectly, but maybe not the President's cousin or something like that. Also they need to be very, very competent and they need to have the skills for accountability, as well as the technical skills. So these are the kinds of things that we tell the organization, this is what you should be doing. How do we know that they've done it? They will report back to us on all the different items.

---

[21] FAO, 'Programme Implementation Report 2014–15', 75–6.

Local relations differ from one IO to another too. Organizational reputations vary. One official noted: 'It is amazing. When on a mission for FAO, the way I am treated is so different from the way when I went on mission from the Bank. They like me much more, but I am the same person.' He accepted that, although the FAO could bring deep specialist knowledge in precise areas, it could never compete with the World Bank in the range of knowledge and resources that it could access. Reluctantly he concluded: 'I feel we can be a supporting role in the set-up but we will always be a very small player.'

The functions of CDs will be managerial (running the office), operational (overseeing the project delivery), diplomatic/representational (interacting with government), and often educational (explaining the IO's role to the broader community). The diplomatic function becomes particularly significant when the DG visits the country or expresses an interest in a country or a project. IO leaders rightly regard the interaction with national leaders as the most important part of their task. Diouf, the FAO's DG, was constantly on the road, visiting member states, listening to requests. Wolfensohn saw himself as the personification of the Bank and his presence as a means of getting things done. He would travel and talk, hoping to achieve progress in his persona as an international diplomat. The arrival of the president was an important event for any CD, an opportunity both to present a case for his or her projects and to be noticed by the top management. It could also be stressful, meeting the president's expectations, responding to his or her sudden quirks, and ensuring that both visitors and national hosts achieved what they wanted out of the meetings (not always possible or even explicit).[22]

One FAO country representative explained that part of the job:

> You have to set up a series of meetings and the DG will typically prefer to meet with ministers and want to meet with more than just the Minister of Agriculture. The Minister of Agriculture will always, out of courtesy, take a meeting. [The DG may want to see] the Minister of the Environment, the Minister of Forests, because the FAO's mandate covers more than purely the agricultural mandate. We would need to arrange for the press [coverage]. Very often we have to manage that in the sense of [identifying] what are the issues that they're really going to want to talk about. It's a lot of work; it's very intense. Typically he stays three or four days; you are at his shoulder all the time, and are judged by how many doors you open.

At country level the local staff have the contacts, the history, and an overview of programmes; no one at HQ is likely to know the details. Whether the country's ambassadors do might depend on their experience and links. Missions to a country, or the country expert based in HQ, do not have the same flexibility, either in determining when the visits are convenient for the clients or in getting access to the right people. Constant presence makes the links grow stronger.

---

[22] See also the discussion in Sebastian Mallaby, *The World's Banker*.

Networks

The staff can also build networks at local level with their counterparts in other IOs. As noted earlier, FAO staff who were in the field for twenty years in the 1980s and 1990s recall that they had far more contact with the representatives of other IOs in the country than they did with their superiors in Rome; in those days they bypassed any regional offices. Tighter controls and more formal lines of accountability were gradually increased as the local management presence grew; staff reflected ruefully on the decline of their autonomy. Sometimes, however, these local networks were vital. The World Bank office in Indonesia convened meetings of donors in the aftermath of the tsunami in order to increase the effectiveness of aid. The WHO was the lead IO in developing a response to the Ebola outbreak in West Africa. Collaboration on the ground is an essential step that allows both quick and responsive coordinated actions.

The additional pressure in the FAO is now on the regional ADG:

> In the regional office, the regional representative used to be responsible for managing the countries in terms of the country offices, managing the relationships with governments in the region, and dealing with regional issues. They are still responsible for those offices; now they have got a mixture of responsibilities in a technical sense as well as responsibilities in an operational and political sense. In Rome, it's primarily technical and internal politics. As an ADG, it's your political antennae; it's clearing a press release; it's dealing with something that's happening in the organization and just saying 'hang on, how's this going to play out'.

The consequence of considerable discretion is that the public get muddled images. An experienced CD at the World Bank summarized the contradiction: 'The [World] Bank...has a somewhat schizophrenic quality, with marked rhetorical focus on decentralization, a reality that most day-to-day decisions in practice are made by operational staff, and a mystique of centralized and often rigid decision-making.'[23] The central officers may wish they had as much control as public legend attributes to them.

MANAGING A SINGLE INSTITUTION: STAFF CAREER PLANNING

IOs often have a rhetoric that stresses their 'oneness', the assertion that they are single institutions. Those working in the field and those at HQ are seen as one unified body. International staff in the field and local staff are meant to be

---

[23] Katherine Marshall, *The World Bank* (London, Routledge, 2008), 72.

integrated. The 1997 World Bank's reorganization espoused 'One Bank, One Staff; or, as Brundtland expressed it, there was 'one WHO, not seven'.

It is never that easy. Inevitably in large organizations different practices and traditions develop, whether between the centre and the periphery or even between regions themselves. One opinion of a former VP at the World Bank may be idiosyncratic but it makes the point:

> Each region adopts a certain culture that essentially derives from its clients, so, if you take the Middle East, relations between staff are full of intrigue, mutual suspicion, high degree of incompetence; you know masquerading as a sense of knowing everything. The Middle East is generally quite disgruntled as a group of staff and I think that it is, pound for pound, not particularly high performing. In Asia Pacific, on the other hand, you have some of the best clients in the Bank, so you have a funny mixture of things. You have some very high-end technical and economic bank staff, because that is what the countries require, so you get some exceptionally good work. There is also some degree of complacency in the Asia Pacific, because the clients are generally so good that they pick up on a lot of mistakes that staff make. That does not happen in Africa.

Developing a 'single' IO, therefore, covers two issues: the management of the careers of international staff who spend time in the field and their integration (or not) back to HQ and, second, the integration of locally employed staff in the organization.

Working in the field is what many international staff want to do. They appreciate the direct daily links with clients, their immersion in local problems, and the ability to identify their impact as it happens. Understanding what happens on the ground can make staff more sensitive to the political pressures on member states. Occasional missions, they argue, are no substitute for daily contact. Not being in HQ had one perceived advantage too: 'we are not caught up in bureaucracy and meetings, nor suffer from the bureaucracy.' They find the field challenging and the return to HQ an 'emotional letdown'; in country offices they were big fish, but they become small when back in the larger pond. But working in the field creates its own issues for international staff in terms of their own careers and their personal life. Managers become concerned that international civil servants (ICS) in the field get out of touch with developments and too narrow in their perspectives.

Integrating those international staff coming back from the field can be difficult. After the World Bank reorganization under Wolfensohn, official Bank policy required that staff rotate every three and no more than five years. A lead economist, or a sector director, in a region at HQ can easily be shifted to the same position in another region. The same principle is applied to those on a lower rank of bureaucracies. If staff rotate, they get to know the Bank better. But in practice this turned out to be quite difficult at the end of the 1990s and early 2000s. Those international staff who went to work in the field were entitled to have a similar promotion to those who stayed at HQ. The staff often felt that 'they were out of sight, out of mind when promotion came along'. This was not an exaggeration, according to a former VP:

> At senior management meetings when VPs, regional as well as sector, decided personnel matters, a few VPs pushed hard to get their own people promoted in other regions or sectors whether they had knowledge or not. Those who worked in the field were forgotten. This left some returned CDs hanging. So one day, at such a meeting, MD Shengman, intervened. They created a roster system and we had to take the integrating of returned international staff as a priority.

This was easier to say than do. Some senior international staff accepted going to the field, but their spouse might not be able to go, owing to either family or career reasons; others went to the field, but had to return because of either children's education or familial problems. Some were left hanging, without proper positions for them to return to. They were effectively 'parked' as senior advisers in a regional VP's office. Practices for reintegration varied from time to time. One CD noted:

> It took longer than I or [the regional VP] or anyone expected it would and partly that is the way the market system works in the World Bank. At that particular time, there was a preference for everybody at director level having to apply for their next job rather than doing a managed transfer. These things come and go over time and nowadays again we have gone back to the system where there are more managed transfers so that if somebody comes back from a job and there is nothing wrong with their work, they shouldn't have to hang around for almost a year which is what I had to do and that is not considered normal or useful.

One issue was that promises made on one occasion might not still be relevant when the opportunity came to access them. When one officer was persuaded to take a distant appointment as CD:

> Wolfensen was still around, and he and Shangman said: 'look, there won't be any problem when you get back, don't worry, there will be a good job for you and we understand you need to be in Washington for a while'. When I got back of course they had gone and that [promise] didn't mean anything any longer. It wasn't an institutional commitment in any way that held up, so I was surprised. I couldn't get a director-level job in Washington and for that reason by around the middle of the year I started to apply for jobs in the field because I began to be concerned that I might otherwise be made redundant. That is just a personal thing and I fell within a particular period where a lot of things came unglued.

In 1998, about one-tenth of the Bank staff was in the field; by 2005, the share had reached 25 per cent, and in 2015 it was over 40 per cent. Ensuring careers and family needs was essential for a successful decentralization programme.

The potential problem of reintegration was one reason many people at the FAO resisted the call to go to the field when Graziano became DG. Career-planning in these decentralized IOs by and large is left to the individual. A job for an international civil servant in the field may have a nominal tenure of five years in the country, but then they are left to decide what is next. One country representative said he had to compete for a job to come back to Rome. 'It would be understood that probably after five years or so there would be a discussion about where I might have gone next in terms of a country.' In the end he took the initiative: 'there was a position open here and I competed for it and won it'.

He added that there were a number of limitations on where he could seek to go.

> Language is the barrier more than anything else. So probably not in the rotation that you've just described, but certainly Asia to Africa with English-speaking countries is altogether possible. Going into Latin America, unless you go to the Caribbean, where English is fine, then you need Spanish. So your ability to move depends on your language capability.

Career-planning requires a central capacity. If regional offices have extensive autonomy, the centre may not have the ability to develop a satisfactory scheme. In the WHO, the effective powers of the DG over staff are less absolute than the formal documents suggest:

> The senior management positions in the regional office will be discussed with the DG; it doesn't mean she has the right to appoint anybody and doesn't mean she has the right to have a say. The degree of consensus depends on the region. Some regions are very unilateralist, others much less so. In some regions the deputy has been selected among existing staff of senior staff in the regional office, in other regions the newly incoming RD has brought in his or her own people, so it is not consistent.

Of course, in the WHO, a larger proportion of staff in regional and country offices have no desire to be appointed to Geneva. They are local appointees who expect to remain in the region.

The second issue is how to manage the locally appointed staff in the country and regional offices. Their numbers are increasing; they are often as well qualified as international staff. Some come from universities in developed countries that could not offer nearly as attractive pay and conditions, but either do not want to be transferred elsewhere or under the terms of employment cannot be. The inevitable problem is that two classes of employees develop: the international staff who come and go, the local staff who, as one put it, 'have to live with the consequences long after they [international staff] have gone'.[24] They may be well connected with local elites, even involved in local politics; they provide the institutional memory for the CDs. But their experience is limited usually to a single country, or at least a single region, and

---

[24] Xu and Weller, *Inside the World Bank*, 115.

they see the problem through a different lens. Some tensions are inevitable, even if we were told that local staff will seldom challenge the conclusions of their senior international colleagues because they depend so much on their continued employment.

The World Bank's significant reform 'One Bank, One Staff' programme was controversial at the time when it was introduced. The issue of whether locally appointed staff can shift to international status remains open. They can in theory, a few do, but most do not. All IOs are appointing more locally situated staff, but each IO has its own approach to determining their standing in their structures.

CONCLUSION

Distance and location challenge easy assumptions about control and agency in IOs. They are factors in creating the incoherence that is part of any international organization. The existence of regional and country offices provides a series of perspectives that divide both member states and staff. They fundamentally affect the traditional notions of control by member states interacting with one another and with the heads of IOs and staff at the IOs' HQs.

Some member states, often the wealthier donors, question whether IOs should be into too much bottom-up project delivery, rather than normative standard-setting. The very activity of country offices is regarded with a degree of scepticism. The creation of country offices is determined more by politics, and sometimes electioneering, than by any set of criteria, and that will continue. The consequences are different, often fractured, lines of accountability.

Country officers feel that they are far more responsive to clients than their HQ colleagues. They deal with the senior ministers and officials in the client government on a regular basis. Their contacts there are invariably more senior than the EDs or ambassadors appointed at the HQs of IOs to provide the daily oversight of those organizations; their standing as representatives of the IOs on the spot gives them significance in seeking to ensure country ownership of any plans. Identification with the country can occur when officers are appointed from HQ for a length of time, as with the World Bank. It is far more apparent when the staff are locally appointed, or, as in the case of the WHO's RDs, locally elected. Many of the staff working for the WHO or FAO spend their whole career in the field; some may never have visited HQs in Rome or Geneva. The arguments about oversight from there are far beyond their concern; the country is their point of reference.

The more that officers identify with their country, the more they consider that each programme has to be shaped for local conditions and that the one-size-fits-all notions cannot work. They encourage and assist the local community to propose and develop projects and programmes that meet their needs. Their initiative to do so is recognized and often applauded. The more decentralized the IOs are, the less detailed control and oversight the centre, with increasingly fewer staff, can apply over what they do. The more offices there are, the greater the discretion that will, inevitably, be delegated for routines and daily interaction. Many CDs consider they have the scope to initiate, and they will seek assistance from their ADG or VP only when they need the particular support at country or organizational level that only VPs can deliver. Dealing directly with governments and meeting their needs provide a degree of gratification that many IOs' staff desire; that is why they are there.

If the member states, as principals, cannot direct and oversee IOs in one place, the IOs themselves, this time as principals, and even with administrative authority, cannot oversee in detail what is done in their name in the regions and countries. There are a series of cascading relationships where each delegate has a degree of freedom of action that is far greater than the officers in centralized IOs such as the IMF, WTO, and WIPO will ever have. It is not coincidental that these IOs are considered to be much tighter hierarchies. Location has made it so. The centre may seek cohesion and coherence, but in a widely dispersed community of offices that is beyond their practical reach they must live with difference and ambiguity.

8

Conclusion

Authority, Capacity, Legitimacy

An official experienced in both national and international bureaucracies neatly identified the problems in defining influence in international organizations (IOs); he stressed the unreal expectations of many of the participants.

> Incoherence remains the norm. Strangely enough, people in the secretariat make the wrong assumption of coherence of member states, and the member states make the wrong assumption of coherence in the secretariat. When someone at the secretariat tells me that 'the UK government said...', does this refer to the person in the mission, or the Department of Health? Is this the individual's position or the position taken by the parliament. I know enough about how government works to ask the questions. When member states tell me, 'Oh, the secretariat said...', was it from the regional office, the regional director's office, or the DG's office here? Incoherence is applied to private sectors too. Can you imagine that not long ago the Bill and Melinda Gates Foundation did not even know how much it gave to the WHO?

His insights—that incoherence is a natural state for IOs that are disrupted by different perspectives; that there is a constant struggle on both sides to try to understand the position of others and a desire to find some level of consistency; and that inconsistency is an organizational norm, not cynical hypocrisy—reflect the working world of IOs we have tried to present in this book.

This conclusion has three purposes: (1) to illustrate how using public policy and institutional approaches and questions helps us understand the working world of IOs; (2) to show how the insights can add to and amend the literature currently available on IOs and suggest that some of the current conclusions oversimplify the dilemmas IOs face; and (3) to suggest that influence in IOs requires a combination of authority, capacity, and legitimacy, which, in most cases, rely on the input of different participants. We contend that interpreting IOs through a public policy prism provides a more nuanced picture, with the additional benefit that it is one that practitioners might recognize and whose lessons they might appreciate.

PUBLIC POLICY AND INSTITUTIONAL APPROACHES

We suggested in Chapter 1 a number of characteristics that could be derived from public policy and institutional approaches. Key insights from those literatures propose those involved in decisions can be assumed (1) to act rationally, (2) to operate within the formal rules and framework, (3) to work through a network of informal rules, traditions, practices, expectations, norms, and culture, and (4) to make progress through processes of political persuasion. We did not try to impose these concepts on each chapter of the analysis, but they provided the general framework of assumptions that guided our explorations. We can illustrate here how those concepts help to shape our interpretation of IOs, drawing together the evidence we have sought to lay out in the previous chapters.

Rationality. Institutional approaches to interpreting organizations assume that actors behave rationally. Whose rationality should be considered? How participants act and react depends on how they assess their interests at stake and the situations they face. We have shown that IOs are not unitary bodies with a single view. Not only will member states, leaders, and staff perceive problems differently, but also within each group of them there will be a series of competing rationalities that underpin action and determine choices.

Member states have diverse interests and levels of commitment. The structure of IOs provides opportunities for the powerful and the weak to participate. The large and powerful members may have the greatest potential, as they have more resources (political, human, and financial), but whether that potential is realized depends on whether they are interested in a particular case, or indeed with any of the issues a given IO might manage. Even when they are interested, there is no guarantee they will always get what they want, because procedures encourage participation, not domination. There are other rifts that shape members' rational responses. Donors and recipient member states want very different criteria applied to proposals. Small states with few resources may want support and advice that is regarded as unnecessary by others.

The heads of IOs also face choices that will differ by the institution and circumstance. We have illustrated the pressures of election, the contradictory demands placed on them by member states, and the subtle requirements that they lead without leading. Their formal position seldom defines their available levers of influence. The lack of a job description means that they must calculate how to make advances; they cannot read off a response from a set of defined rules or allocated authorities.

The staff in the secretariat represent a wide variety of programmes and interests. Their rational responses are concerned with obtaining the support and resources needed to deliver the programmes that are often designed without much input from governing bodies. It is too easy to become blinkered in considering the pressures they face. IOs are more than just the politics of central offices. IOs are necessarily responsible for multiple activities in a wide variety of places. What the Food and Agriculture Organization (FAO) does in Africa, the World Intellectual Property Organization (WIPO) in Asia, or the World Health Organization (WHO) in the Pacific are significant for those regions. The client countries there often welcome the direct and practical assistance that can be provided. At a regional and country level, there are daily interactions with government and non-government officials, trying to settle a variety of pressing issues. For those clients, for better or worse, these services in the field *are* the FAO or the WHO or the World Bank. In the assessment of IOs, and in the battles to determine the locus of influence, these local, often beneficial, services are too often overlooked. Daily interactions occur as projects are developed and delivered. As we have commented elsewhere, in IOs that have strong local presence and activities, the whole is often less than the sum of its parts.

This study shows that, to understand the working of IOs, we need to focus on the key players and their 'rationalities'. In most instances, there is not a single uncontested view about the preferable definition of the problems; nor are there often obvious answers. How responses are worked out depends on how participants act and interact with one another. Their rationality is identified through puzzling and choosing, as all the participants assess the circumstances and conclude what they should or can do, within the framework created by the formal rules and by the expectations and culture that shapes the IO.

The formal rules and framework. Formal rules and machinery shape the choices people make, but by themselves can do more than provide an initial framework. All IOs have a past. The founding agreements that established them reflect the constellation of powers at a given time—in the case of many IOs, the post-war dominance of the victorious powers. The IOs have a formal structure based on an agreement made between the original members. Like national constitutions, they can be hard to change: hard but not impossible. The creation of WIPO to consolidate the management of a collection of intellectual property (IP) treaties; the transformation of the General Agreement on Tariffs and Trade (GATT) into the World Trade Organization (WTO); these illustrate what can be achieved where there is consensus and drive. But such incidences are rare. More often, as the difficulties in changing the voting powers in the International Monetary Fund (IMF) illustrate, it is hard to persuade some member states to give up privileges that reflected past glories in order better to represent the new power alignments.

IOs have a present and a future. History may shape their approaches and the levels of trust they engender. They have to adjust to live within those frameworks. Missions have to be explored to discover how widely 'implied powers' can be stretched. Voting patterns are taken into account as decisions are made. The challenge is how to fit new initiatives within the existing formal networks. At the same time, member states have to consider the impact that, for better or worse, their decisions may have on the future of the organizations.

Informal rules, traditions, practices, expectations, norms, and culture. An appreciation of the constantly evolving practices of IOs is necessary if we are to understand how they work. Decisions are made within the formal rules, but they can be guided by a network of informal rules, traditions, expectations, and norms, often subsumed in the idea of established practice. The original decision at the World Bank that the Executive Board would consider only papers forwarded by the president became the convention that underpinned the president's power. The request by the WHO member states that the director general (DG) develop member-driven processes for determining the budget is another example of how formal powers can be ceded.

We have shown that IOs seldom work the way that the formal rules suggest. That is neither surprising nor necessarily a matter for concern. However, the reliance of IOs on developed norms, traditions, and practices means that, inevitably, almost everything can be contested: the approach of state members, the levels of delegation or discretion granted to the secretariat, the election and influence of the head of IOs. Even what may appear anodyne and uncontroversial—the seating at a conference table, the circulation of an agenda, the writing of the minutes of a meeting—can become a contested issue because of past events and (sometimes imprecise) memories.

Decisions depend on the ability of participants to analyse a situation, appreciate the options, understand the rules and expectations, and finesse the other participants. The outcomes will be contingent because opposition may be unpredictable, caused by an unfortunate choice of words, or by a decision to object in one IO forum as a result of a setback in another, or because some skilled diplomats choose one forum over another to exercise their wiles.

Political persuasion. IOs are run primarily by persuasion. All those meetings, all those members, all those programmes: to get anything done, as we have shown, a wide range of people with different interests has to be persuaded that there are benefits and advantages. Member states cannot command one another. Leaders cannot direct member states, and secretariats have such a range of knowledge and skills that they need to be brought into discussions. Effectively no governing body votes on anything that matters because there are no sanctions that can be applied without the initial consent to participate in an agreed regime. At the WTO, 'nothing is agreed until everything is agreed' is a trade axiom that brings everyone onside before a negotiation is complete.

In other IOs there may at times be a lack of enthusiasm or interest that acts as a hindrance to progress.

A strategy of interpreting IOs as institutions works because IOs can be understood only if they are seen as a set of *relationships* within organizational structures, norms, and practices. Those relationships have been the focus of our analysis. If we conclude that, at different times, each of the three principal players—the member states, the heads of the IOs, and the secretariat—may initiate, develop, and support proposals, then an emphasis on the relationship between them is essential. The IOs cannot work without the input of, and initiatives from, all three, depending on the occasion.

By asking how the IOs work as institutions, with formal rules, informal practices, traditions, and cultures, we were able to move away from formal lines of authority and easy assumptions that IOs should work the way the original founders initially anticipated and the all too common complaints of critics who often assert that IOs should do better or be more energetic, with little regard to the realistic possibility for achievement. Our approach allowed us to probe behind the rhetoric of 'member-driven' organizations and ask who could drive what. It was by no means always the members. They sometimes do, and almost always pretend to, but participants at all levels, when out of the public arena, have a far more realistic view of what actually occurs. Most of them are aware of their limitations and the reliance they have on the others who contribute to final decisions.

Asking the public policy questions of 'who decides what' provided a more complex picture too. We did not assume that practice followed formal authority but sought to plumb the distribution of expertise and knowledge, and the consequential levels of interdependence. The way in which problems were solved, from the institutional to the local, depends on a range of influences. The crucial decisions may be made long before the authorization is sought and given. Who puzzles about problems and where they stand in the hierarchy, and where they work geographically, will depend on the issue.

These questions do not allow neat answers or firm conclusions about the location of authority or the differential influence of, for instance, the secretariats across organizations. The conclusions can only be more tentative and contingent. But then, that is our understanding of how these organizations work. We can describe the modes of operation, the circumstances in which different players get involved. We cannot predict particular events, but then, as those actually involved in making the decisions often insist, nor can they. Reality is messy.

Perhaps in drawing those conclusions we were conscious of the exhortation of our interviewees who asked us to tell it as it is, not as how some observers thought it should be. IOs have many advocates who see them as beneficial solutions to international dilemmas and then rue the fact that they too frequently fall far short of that ideal. We were asked to understand them as institutions that sometimes deliver significant benefits, yet, even when they do not live up to lofty aspirations, are still important to understand in their own terms.

UNDERSTANDING INTERNATIONAL ORGANIZATIONS

If the purpose of a study is to understand the workings of IOs, we suggest our insights, based on institutional and public policy approaches, may have some implications for, or provide amendments or additions to, the mainstream literature on IOs.

First, the old-styled functional approach to IOs, looking at their formal constitutions and agreements, may be mostly outdated. There are studies that ask what we can learn from the original negotiations and form of IOs,[1] and others that propose revision to those original documents, often proposing a new mode of formal member-state representation.[2] Those original constitutions or articles of agreements may provide a starting point or a framework for understanding the IOs, but the changes have been so extensive, as we have documented, that the founding authors might be aghast at the interpretation now put on their words. Most analysts will agree that the powers allocated have inevitably been changed by time; for example, as stated earlier, the comparative influence exerted by the secretariat is much greater than that initially incorporated in agreements, which observers have described as 'trivial'.[3] To understand the workings of IOs we need to combine an appreciation of the formal and informal rules. We also need to appreciate that these are constantly contested and evolving. IOs of 2017 are the lineal descendants of the original bodies but have mutated. Many of the certainties of the 1970s and even the 1990s have disappeared as new forces emerge and new interests dictate the agenda. So, too, the IOs of 2040 will be shaped by history but will be different bodies where the allocation of influence and the capacity to make progress will depend on events as yet unforeseen. Charting that change is surely the most significant challenge that faces scholars of IOs today.

Second, our findings raise questions about any interpretation that regards state sovereignty as the fount of initiative and change. As an example let us

---

[1] See, e.g., Barbara Koremenos, Charles Lipson, and Duncan Snidal, 'The Rational Design of International Institutions', *International Organization*, 55/4 (2001), 761–99.

[2] See, e.g., Colin I. Bradford Jr and Johannes F. Linn (eds), *Global Governance Reform: Breaking the Stalemate* (Washington: Brookings Institution Press, 2007).

[3] Kenneth W. Abbott and Duncan Snidal, 'Why States Act through Formal International Organizations', *Journal of Conflict Resolution*, 42/1 (1998), 9.

repeat the claim of Lisa Martin: 'IOs gain autonomy as a result of intentional state decisions, not through a careless process driven by staff.'[4] In one sense that may always be true, in that authorization of initiatives requires the support of member states in executive boards, health assemblies, or other governing bodies. That is a very low threshold to define as intentional state actions. We have illustrated where IO leaders have developed initiatives themselves, as seen, for instance, in Wolfensohn's Strategic Initiative, or Diouf's World Summit on Food Security, or where the head of the IO and staff have developed proposals at the request of member states but have been left to design the details that are presented in almost final form after extensive internal negotiation.

Our evidence challenges the extent of 'intentional state actions'. Sometimes member states are uninterested or ill informed; sometimes they do not have the resources or the skills to develop initiatives and have to rely on an IO's staff. Where member states lose interest in the proceedings of an IO, they may leave it to wither, because trying to abolish it would use too much political capital. In those cases, any new initiative must come from the leader or staff. In local sites in the field, other member states often can have little idea what is occurring between staff and the client state. State sovereignty may explain some of the initiatives, and some of the grander public stances; it cannot explain the myriad of other decisions that are made. There is a danger of developing two categories of decisions: those that are important and are made by member states, and those that are routine and made by staff, when the only definition of 'important' is whatever the member states chose to decide. The arguments for state sovereignty need to be made more sensitive to the actual workings of the IOs and to the different levels of decisions that are made.

Third, we suggest that our findings show some serious limitations of the principal–agent analysis in explaining IO operations. By definition, IOs have multiple principals. Studies have also shown that each member state is also a system of multiple principals. It is difficult to see how the principal–agent analysis can help explain an authoritative decision of an IO, unless the analysis is based on the assumption that a single member state makes all authoritative decisions on behalf of an IO.[5] Our study clearly shows that even the richest, largest, and most powerful members do not single-handedly 'make' an IO take certain actions. IOs have multiple principals with no common view on what they want done, or sometimes whether they want the IO to flourish at all. The failure to complete the Doha negotiations and the successful adoption of

---

[4] Lisa Martin, 'Distribution, Information and Delegation to International Organizations', in Darren G. Hawkins et al. (eds), *Delegation and Agency in International Organizations* (New York: Cambridge University Press, 2006), 141.

[5] Mona M. Lyne, Daniel L. Nielson, and Michael J. Tierney, 'Who Delegates: Alternative Models of Principals in Development Aid', in Hawkins et al. (eds), *Delegation and Agency in International Organizations*, 41–76.

tobacco control by the WHO are both examples of the diversity of opinion and complex negotiations among members. Even where some actions were deliberately limited in scope to provide some chance of agreement, such as the WIPO treaty to assist the blind, the proposals were still contested, as member states could not agree initially on details.

If the principals are divided, then the idea that they can direct their agents in clear and unequivocal terms is untenable. Time and resources ensure that even resident executive boards are primarily reactive; the more distant oversight by local diplomats or capital-based staff is even more dependent on the proposals presented to them from leaders and secretariats. Nor can these state representatives in IO governing bodies develop and apply criteria that control the actions of agents. Often, indeed, the secretariat (often seen as the agent) will have a better knowledge of what each of the principals thinks than the principals do of each other.

There are two additional complications. In any IO, there are sets of cascading principals and agents, each relationship providing opportunity for shirking and slippage. Member-state representatives are agents of their capitals and principals for IOs' leaders. Leaders are agents of member-state representatives and act as principals in relations with staff; within secretariats there are additional cascading sets of relationships. Geography and epistemic communities add to the kaleidoscopic relationships that defy close supervision.

Further, IOs have become part of international and national networks; they cooperate with one another, coordinate activities, and share information. On occasion, they issue joint reports. It is primarily leaders and staff who coordinate these activities. The more integrated their actions, the less control that nominal masters can apply and the less useful principal–agent analysis is in understanding the 'what and how' of IO activity, except for a few carefully defined cases.

Fourth, we suggest our findings ask more of the lines of enquiry that have recently explored the influence of secretariats when we stress the multiple interest and contested procedures within IOs. Secretariats have received more attention, particularly by Chwieroth on the IMF and Barnett and Finnemore more generally.[6] The work of the latter takes the bureaucratic characteristics of IOs seriously; they argue that, contrary to the image of IOs as forces for good, bureaucratic behaviour can make them dysfunctional and self-serving. Of course they can, but they need not do so. In the face of divided instructions, they must sometimes use initiative based on expertise and experience. Bureaucracies are necessary for IOs to have any effect, but they also will seldom be unitary, whether on objectives, on tactics, or on judging the competence of

---

[6] Jeffrey M. Chwieroth, *Capital Ideas: The IMF and the Rise of Financial Liberalization* (Princeton: Princeton University Press, 2010); Michael Barnett and Martha Finnemore, *Rules for the World* (Ithaca, NY: Cornell University Press, 2004).

their managers. Yet often analysts assume they are, if only for the sake of simplicity of argument; it can be a device for testing a proposition.[7]

Nor can their behaviour be assumed from some common feature such as their country of origin or their formal education. It is naive to make assumptions about how any participant will act on the basis of some common criterion.[8] All ICS are required to sign a commitment that they will act without favour to their country of origin. Most obey that exhortation; there is no credible case that they are all agents of those governments. However, their socialization after decades in an IO may still leave them deeply divided on the strategy or objectives their organization should pursue. The World Bank staff contest the president's strategies. WIPO is divided on support for management. The FAO is organized in silos. The WHO is fragmented by regions. These staff characteristics cannot be ignored. Our findings suggest that any explanation of IOs needs a finely defined understanding of the interpretations and traditions that IO secretariats adopt.

AUTHORITY, CAPACITY, AND LEGITIMACY

Even given this uncertainty, we were able to chart both within and across IOs considerable variations in influence. Our initial intention was to identify the opportunities the key IO players (member-state representatives, IO leaders, and international civil servants (ICS) in the secretariats) have to shape the activities of IOs. Here we suggest that a way of combining these insights is to ask what each brings to the table. We need to appreciate organizational authority, capacity, and legitimacy.

Organizational Authority

Formal *authority* remains with the member states that created IOs to manage areas of collaborative policy. The initial negotiations were undertaken primarily by a few powerful states. The governing arrangements were designed to take account of those interests. In some cases the balance was achieved by weighted voting with members maintaining a continuing presence in a standing Executive

---

[7] Note: Lisa Martin did admit that IOs are more complicated than she suggested: 'management and staff are not the unitary actor I represent it as here' (Lisa Martin, 'Agency and Delegation in IMF Conditionality', paper for the Utah Conference on Delegation to International Organizations, 2002, p. 5).

[8] See, e.g., Michal Parizek, 'Control, Soft Information, and the Politics of International Organizations Staff,' *Review of International Organizations* (2017); online first <https://link.springer.com/article/10.1007/s11558-016-9252-1> (accessed 1 January 2016).

Board. In others the original terms of agreement established a more hands-off oversight, through diplomatic missions combined with participation of capital-based experts at appropriate times, usually once or twice a year. That may have been seen as adequate when the membership was small, when the range of activities was constrained, and when there was some common agreement on the IO's mission and the purpose of the enterprise.

Those foundation moments were a long time ago. To assess the exercise of member states' authority, it is no longer enough to ask what the original intentions were; rather, it is necessary to ask how, as conditions change, the accepted practices have been altered. The increasing diversity of member states, the expansion of the mission of organizations (whether a consequence of greater demands from member states or of bureaucratic empire-building), the growing number of activist delegations pursuing more divergent objectives, and the rapidly enabling technology have all made the oversight practices of the 1950s and 1960s antiquated. The means through which the member states' authority is applied has evolved, even if often without any alterations in the formal rules.

At the World Bank, it was quickly established that all proposals that the Executive Board (EB) would consider would come through the president; the EB's scrutiny became a reactive process of oversight: by no means unimportant but responding to proposals developed by the president and the secretariat. At the IMF, the USA could exert influence in chosen instances but could not use that influence too readily without depleting the political capital that would be required.[9] At the WHO, the EB mutated from a group of people appointed nominally for their personal standing and expertise to the delegates of member states. WIPO shifted from being seen as an institution that reflected the demands of the IP industry in advanced countries to one that put weight behind a development agenda. As GATT was transformed into the WTO, a small dominant group in the former was replaced in part by a multiplicity of regional and economic groupings that sought representation in any formal negotiations.

The expansion of member states brought different understandings of the roles that IOs should play. Systems based on decisions by consensus made it hard to develop any agreement on what should be done. It was easier to agree to disagree than to decide. Groupings of smaller or weaker member states combined to use their weight of numbers and provided evidence of 'the strength of the weak'.[10] Multiple members with differing perspectives have made multilateral cooperation much harder, whether it is about negotiating treaties, agreements, or annual work programmes, or about how to finance IO activities and what types of work IOs should do.

---

[9] Randall W. Stone, *Controlling Institutions: International Organizations and the Global Economy* (New York: Cambridge University Press, 2011).

[10] Peter Katzenstein, *Small States in World Markets* (Ithaca, NY: Cornell University Press, 1985).

Even if there is no argument about the authority of member states in theory—the mantra 'member driven' has become ubiquitous, even if all too often remaining a myth—some of that authority, where it cannot be effectively asserted, has leeched away. When member states lack the desire or the ability to push an agenda, others will fill the void, to the extent that they are allowed. In the WHO, member states wanted a member-driven financial reform process but asked the DG to develop one, which she did with the assistance of the secretariat (the irony of this often escapes member states). As a matter of necessity, new and sometimes wealthy entities such as the Global Alliance for Vaccines and Immunizations (GAVI) or the Gates Foundations set their tents at the WHO, where authority was shared among stakeholders. In the FAO, member states tried, but were unable, to develop a response to the external review on behalf of the organization and independently of the secretariat. They did not have the expertise or resources and had to ask for help. Whether the power is formally delegated, or ceded as a matter of practicality, some of the capacity to shape interventions has indeed been transferred. Projects are managed through organizational routines that sort, analyse, and propose along established practices. When activities are operationally and geographically diverse, that capacity to direct is often missing. Authority provided as *ex post* approval may be cursory.

In part that is a comment on the comparative capacity of the governing bodies. The ability of member states to provide oversight is patchy. Large states have a considerable ability when their local presence is combined with the expertise based in national capitals and where they make a commitment. An alliance of member states can always prevent something from happening, even if they cannot guarantee to gain support for what they want to do. Smaller countries with multiple IOs to oversee find it much harder. In Geneva, there is a shortage of time, with a need to cover a range of IOs, some of which seem to be more relevant to the people back home. They do what they can. For the Bretton Woods institutions, EDs hold dual loyalties, to the countries they represent as well as to the institution itself.

So there is, for instance, debate about the form and circumstances in which the secretariat should be given discretion. Stone sees no problem at all in the IMF; he argues that the consensus among members and staff about market-oriented reforms means that 'the fund's principals can safely delegate substantial operational autonomy and substantive authority. In ordinary times the United States and the other share-holders have no compelling interest in intervening in the details of conditionality, and the fund creates policies autonomously.'[11] The IMF staff will still argue about the form and size of interventions, but their remit is narrower than those of other IOs, and the

---

[11] Stone, *Controlling Institutions*, 25–6.

degree of common culture and expertise within the organization will limit the parameters for choice.

In those other IOs, where the range of activities is broader, and more staff are involved, and where the diversity of opinions and options is much greater, no such comfortable conclusion is possible. There is little consensus, whether among member states or staff. The secretariat may be required to find solutions, because the member states cannot agree on what they want, and often do not have the expertise or knowledge. The traditional authority is diluted by differences of opinion, by differences in resources, and by different levels of interest among members. Sometimes, if members cannot get their way, they may prefer that nothing happens. Obstruction and gridlock may be policy choices. Where authority is fragmented, it is easier to construct a coalition of negatives. When consensus is required, one determined member state can hold up progress.

Organizational Capacity

The core of the *capacity* lies in the secretariats. Their formal power may be scant; their potential to influence is ever present. IO secretariats cannot force member states to do something they object to (hence the often-cited gridlock), but if there is scope for mediation the leaders and staff should know how to do it. At the World Bank, the FAO, and the WHO, staff will develop projects with clients, without the need to ask for prior approval from the councils or EBs that provide their final endorsement to work plans but not the details. At the WTO, the original self-described 'member-driven organization', the secretariat can provide careful and well-timed contributions to nudge member states along. When common ground exists, particularly in a crisis, IOs can move fast because of these permanent staff with their expertise, institutional memory, and experience working across various parts of the organization. IMF staff could quickly provide advice where financial crises demanded a response. The WHO's officers were soon on the ground to combat Ebola, although whether they were there fast enough became a later point of dispute.

ICS have the traditional benefits that can accrue to career bureaucrats everywhere. They have continuity, specialized expertise, knowledge of the ways of their institution, and comparative security of tenure. If the capacity of the secretariat is based on its bureaucratic characteristics, then of course the consequences can be dysfunctional too. IOs can fragment into siloes of expertise: fisheries at the FAO, services at the WTO, patents at WIPO, where the interests become narrow and the focus is out of sync with the institutions as a whole. ICS can become imbued with a culture that is inward looking, conservative, and self-protective. The knowledge that they will probably outlast state representatives and/or the head of IOs can give them a sense of self-importance—'we run the world trade system,' said one WTO director—that, even when expressed whimsically, is not justified.

Their possible influence will differ from institution to institution and from time to time. In almost all the main respects, ICS have the advantage: they have greater depth of expertise than most member-state delegations, and more time to dedicate to the topic. The discretion they can use will depend on the perceived importance of the topic at the time, the point in the electoral cycle, the relationship between ICS and key delegates with whom they may work to get items or projects onto the agenda. The variables that might affect the interaction of member states and staff are so diverse, both within and between institutions, that for any particular case it becomes difficult to predict who or what will be the decisive factor. It depends on the history of the topic and the relationships between the key players at the different levels.

IOs must be responsive to member states; they are not, cannot be, directly accountable to non-governmental organizations (NGOs). Criticisms from NGOs about the democratic accountability of IOs are often rejected by member states, who see the activities of NGOs as either self-promotion or ideological. Who do they represent, they ask? The NGOs may have some good ideas that can be considered, but their accountability is often questioned by member states too. Thus, members frequently want to leave the problems of dealing with them to the secretariats.

Constructive roles played by both member states and secretariats are a necessary condition for the effective working of an IO. Often there is a deep chasm between them, a suspicion from member states that secretariats are ignoring the wishes of the member states (in principal–agent terms 'shirking') and pursuing their own preferences and interests in preference to those of the members (slippage). The *cri de cœur* of the WHO DG that 'I have ten seat belts on me and I cannot move an inch; [and] the bottom line is that the membership does not trust the secretariat'[12] reflects an all too common situation.

When the member states and the secretariats are, whether openly or not, divided, and where the former retain suspicions, there is likely to be immobility. The members cannot drive, they cannot do the secretariat's job, but they don't trust those who can. The secretariats, frustrated by a lack of direction from member states, develop their own themes and priorities, and thus exacerbate that suspicion. Institutions grind to a halt. These gaping holes of distrust imply that the gaps in the principal–agent relationships are real. Some members sometimes suspect the secretariat is shirking; secretariats are frustrated by the lack of direction or excessive intervention. Little can be achieved without endorsement and support of member states, or without the expertise

---

[12] Quoted in Xu Yi-chong and Patrick Weller, 'Understanding the Governance of International Organizations', in Patrick Weller and Xu Yi-chong (eds), *The Politics of International Organisations: Views from Insiders* (New York: Routledge, 2015), 1.

and input from the staff. Whether the initiatives come from the heads of IOs, the secretariats, or the membership is less important than the fact that both should have 'ownership' of what is being sought and want to make it work.

Organizational Legitimacy

The heads of IOs play a pivotal role in linking member states and the secretariat. If an IO needs the *legitimacy* created when it can combine authority and capacity, IO leaders are in the position to weave the disparate parts together. Whether appointed, selected, or elected, whether leading a relatively flat or hierarchical organization, these heads of IOs must be responsive to the member states as well as ICS. Leaders can make a difference in multilateral cooperation with their international standing, with the power and authority delegated by member states to IOs, and with their expertise, knowledge, and experience. Yet, not everyone was successful in facilitating multilateral cooperation and leaving their mark in IOs. That requires political, diplomatic, and organizational skills, a very difficult package for individual leaders to have.

* * *

The interplay between the three groups of players is illustrated in our three chapters (the representatives of member states (Chapter 2), the heads of IOs (Chapter 3) and the secretariats (Chapter 4), which examine the IOs in action as they determined agendas for the organization, allocated resources, and decided where staff and programmes would be located. All three provide caveats against too easy assumptions about the working of IOs and the allocation of power within them. They show that the IOs work differently from one another and over time.

Agendas for organizations' actions were never exclusively the prerogative of the rich and powerful member states. Creative small states, working both with developed states and with groupings of the like-minded, could place their issues on the agenda for multilateral cooperation that were at least taken seriously by the other members. On the other side of the coin, where larger states wanted their issues on the agenda, they had to work with other players and follow the rules and normative practices to persuade others to agree. The history of IOs is not one of dictation. As most IOs now prefer decisions to be made by consensus, or at least with the acquiescence of member states to ensure both the legitimacy and effectiveness of IOs, positive results are hard to achieve. Blocking new initiatives is much easier than taking an IO in new directions. How IOs decide what they do and how they pursue their objectives must be analysed by taking account of these complex political realities.

The same conclusion can be drawn on IO funding. Financial support for the IOs is shown to come from both assessed and voluntary contributions (some with conditions, but others without). To explain why the former covered less and less of the running costs of some IOs, we have drawn attention to the interests of all, not only the rich, players in the allocation of resources. The common arguments that IOs have financial problems because the rich countries are unwilling to pay or that IO bureaucracies have the tendency to ask for more from its stakeholders do not reflect how all IOs have approached their financing. At times, for instance, both IO leaders and the secretariat have asked member states not to increase the funding until the latter could agree on a clear set of objectives they expected the organization to achieve. Some IOs have had a good record in managing their funding and expenditures, while others have developed an organizational culture of deficit-driven budgeting. When private and public organizations, rather than states, increased their financial support to multilateral cooperation via the existing IOs, the working world of IOs became more complex. IO leaders had to balance the interests of both member states and donors while maintaining the principles of decision-making based on the sovereignty of states. These new sources of funding required IOs to go far beyond the traditional modes of nominal accountability to the governing bodies that had been regarded as a core component of IOs; they had to develop new institutional arrangements to reflect the changed circumstances. These developments need to be explained by examining how the participants acted and interacted without an initial presumption that funding problems of IOs were only a consequence of the unwillingness of the rich to pay and/or the demands of the poor for spending.

Location fragments the traditional modes of oversight as well as accountability. When IO secretariats have to adjust their working methods to take account of local demands and conditions, additional layers of the simple principal (member states)–agent (IOs) relationship are added. Now detailed projects are developed on the ground within the member states and are then sent to governing bodies for authorization. By that point the negotiations are effectively over, the client states are satisfied, and the budget is settled. Governing bodies have limited room to reject a project without causing disruption to IO operations. Of course, the secretariat and IO leaders try to ensure all substantive oppositions are cleared before major projects or programmes are even seriously considered, but the core dynamics have changed. Decentralized staff and actions subject the working of IOs to multi-level, multi-dimensional negotiations. There are across the world a great variety of modes of delivery and forms of relationships. Location was a key factor that shaped how different players puzzled through local problems and determined what was a rational solution to the dilemma. One size never fits all.

The interaction between member states, leaders, and staff lies at the core of any activity. Case studies of IOs in action, or analyses of single institutions, almost always come to the same conclusions.[13] They conclude (as we do) that the key to the success of any IO does not lie exclusively in the hands of any of the players. Asking how principals can assert their authority misses the point that leaders and bureaucracies need, and will always have, some level of discretion. Enhanced ability to improve the oversight capacity of member states may be desirable but is not enough. Nor is a more responsive and agile secretariat that can be both representative of its membership and dedicated to merit. If member states cannot agree, even an agile secretariat is left grasping at air. If IO leaders are selected on their talents—and certainly many have had distinguished careers outside the world of international organizations—that by itself does not provide any guarantee that they can transfer that success from a world of politics, academia, or banking to the world of international negotiation. We cannot find the answer to IOs' difficulties by looking at any of the three in isolation.

For an international organization (or its member states) to achieve these big targets requires at the very least the alignment of three components: the aspirations of member states to provide the sense of direction or, failing that, at least the authority to adopt proposals presented to it; the skills and cohesion of staff to provide the capability; the talent of IO leaders to meld those circumstances into an alliance that provides both legitimacy and impact. Given the pressures on all three players that we have documented, and particularly the divisions among member states about what IOs should do, it is no surprise that this combination is rare, even that it happens at all. We will never find, nor should we expect to find, perfect coherence and direction within an IO; they are complex institutions with multiple competing interests.

---

[13] See, e.g., Chwieroth, *Capital Ideas*, on the IMF; Craig VanGrasstek, *The History and Future of the World Trade Health Organization* (Geneva: WTO, 2013); Charles H. Weitz, *Who Speaks for the Hungry? How FAO Elects its Leader* (Uppsala, Sweden: DAG Hammarskjöld Foundation, 1997).

Select Bibliography

Abbott, Kenneth W., Genschel, Philipp, Snidal, Duncan, and Zangl, Berhard (eds), *International Organizations as Orchestrators* (Cambridge: Cambridge University Press, 2015).
Abbott, Kenneth W., and Snidal, Duncan, 'Why States Act through Formal International Organizations', *Journal of Conflict Resolution*, 42/1 (1998), 3–32.
Adams, Jim, 'Reform at the World Bank', in Patrick Weller and Xu Yi-chong (eds), *The Politics of International Organizations: Views from Insiders* (New York: Routledge, 2015), 58–81.
Albin, Cecilia, and Young, Ariel, 'Setting the Table for Succeed—or Failure?', *International Negotiation*, 12 (2012), 37–64.
Allison, Graham T., and Zelikow, Philip, *Essence of Decision* (New York: Longman, 1999).
Andresen, Steinar, *Leadership Change in the World Health Organization: Potential for Increased Effectiveness?* (Lysaker, Norway: Fridtjof Nansen Institute, 2002).
Baldwin, David (ed.), *Neorealism and Neoliberalism* (New York: Columbia University Press, ch1993).
Barnett, Michael, and Coleman, Liv, 'Designing Police', *International Studies Quarterly*, 49/4 (2005), 593–619.
Barnett, Michael, and Finnemore, Martha, 'The Politics, Power and Pathologies of International Organizations', *International Organizations*, 54/4 (1999), 699–732.
Barnett, Michael, and Finnemore, Martha, *Rules for the World* (Ithaca, NY: Cornell University Press, 2004).
Bauer, Stephen, 'Does Bureaucracy Really Matter'? *Global Environmental Politics*, 6/1 (2006), 23–49.
Bauer, Stephen, 'Bureaucratic Authority and the Implementation of International Treaties', in Jutta Joachim, Bob Reinalda, and Bertjan Verbeek (eds), *International Organizations and Implementation* (New York: Routledge, 2008), 62–74.
Beach, Derek, 'The Unseen Hand in Treaty Reform Negotiations', *Journal of European Public Policy*, 11/3 (2004), 408–39.
Bellmann, Charles, and Gerster, Richard, 'Accountability in the World Trade Organization', *Journal of World Trade*, 30/6 (1996), 31–74.
Benkimoun, Paul, 'How Lee Jong-wook Changed WHO', *Lancet*, 367 (2006), 1806–8.
Best, Jacqueline, *The Limits of Transparency* (Ithaca, NY: Cornell University Press, 2005).
Biermann, Frank, and Siebenhüner, Bernd (eds), *Managers of Global Change: The Influence of International Environmental Bureaucracies* (Boston: MIT Press, 2009).
Blavoukos, Spyros, and Bourantonis, Dimitris, 'Chairs as Policy Entrepreneurs in Multilateral Negotiations', *Review of International Studies*, 37/2 (2011), 653–72.
Bongang, Benn L., *The United States and the United Nations: Congressional Funding and UN Reform* (New York: LFB Scholarly Publication, 2007).
Bradford, Jr, Colin I., and Linn, Johannes F. (eds), *Global Governance Reform: Breaking the Stalemate* (Washington: Brookings Institution Press, 2007).

Brown, Archie, *The Myth of the Strong Leader* (New York: Basic Books, 2013).
Brown, Hannah, 'Profile: Margaret Chan: New is the Time for WHO to Achieve Results', *Lancet*, 369, 17 March 2007, p. 899.
Brown, Theodore M., Cueto, Marcos, and Fee, Elizabeth, 'The World Health Organization and the Transition from "International" to "Global" Public Health', *American Journal of Public Health*, 96/1 (2006), 62–72.
Burci, Gian Luca, and Vignes, Claude-Henri, *World Health Organization* (The Hague: Kluwer Law International, 2004).
Burki, Shahis Javed, 'World Bank Operations: Some Impressions and Lessons', in Indermit S. Gill and Todd Pugatch (eds), *At the Frontlines of Development* (Washington: World Bank, 2005), 121–50.
Burns, James MacGregor, *Leadership* (New York: HarperCollins, 1978).
Busch, Marc L., 'Overlapping Institutions, Forum Shopping and Dispute Settlement in International Trade', *International Organization*, 61/4 (2007), 735–61.
Busch, Per-Olof, 'The Secretariat of the Climate Convention', Global Governance Working Paper, no. 22 (October 2006).
Buzan, Barry, and Little, Richard, *International Systems in World History* (Oxford: Oxford University Press, 2000).
Cable, Vince, 'Foreword', in Fairtrade Foundation, *The Great Cotton Stitch-Up* (November 2010).
Callaghan, Mike, 'IMF Governance and Decision-Making Processes', in Patrick Weller and Xu Yi-chong (eds), *The Politics of International Organizations: Views from Insiders* (New York: Routledge, 2015), 119–25.
Carpenter, R. Charli, 'Setting the Advocacy Agenda', *International Studies Quarterly*, 51/1 (2007), 99–120.
Carpenter, R. Charli, 'Governing the Global Agenda', in Deborah D. Avant, Martha Finnermore, and Susan K. Sell (eds), *Who Governs the Globe?* (New York: Cambridge University Press, 2010), 202–37.
Chorey, Nitsan, *The World Health Organization between North and South* (Ithaca, NY: Cornell University Press, 2012).
Chow, Jack C., 'Is the WHO Becoming Irrelevant?' *Foreign Policy*, 9 Decembech. 5r 2010.
Chwieroth, Jeffrey, 'Principal–Agent Theory and the World Trade Organization', *European Journal of International Relations*, 17/3 (2013), 495–517.
Chwieroth, Jeffrey M., *Capital Ideas: The IMF and the Rise of Financial Liberalization* (Princeton: Princeton University Press, 2010).
Chwieroth, Jeffrey M., '"The Silent Revolution": How the Staff Exercise Informal Governance over IMF Lending', *Review of International Organizations*, 8/2 (2013), 265–90.
Claude, Inis, *Swords into Plowshares: The Problems and Progress of International Organizations*, 4th edn (New York: Random House, 1971).
Clift, Charles, 'The Role of the World Health Organization in the International System', Centre on Global Health Security Working Group Papers, Chatham House (February 2013).
Clift, Charles, 'What's the World Health Organization for?' Chatham House Report (May 2014).

'Controversy: Global Governance', *International Studies Quarterly*, 58/1 (2014), 207–24.

Copelovitch, Mark S., 'Master or Servant: Common Agency and the Political Economy of Lending', *International Studies Quarterly*, 54/1 (2010), 49–77.

Cornut, Jérémie, 'To Be a Diplomat Abroad', *Cooperation and Conflict*, 50/3 (2015), 385–401.

Cox, Robert W., 'The Executive Head', *International Organization*, 23/2 (1969), 205–30.

Cox, Robert W., and Jacobson, Harold K. (eds), *The Anatomy of Influence* (New Haven: Yale University Press, 1973).

Dahl, Robert A., *Democracy and its Critics* (New Haven: Yale University Press, 1989).

Day, Olivier, 'How Do Policy Ideas Spread among International Administrations?', *Journal of Public Policy*, 32 (2012), 53–76.

de Beer, Jeremy (ed.), *Implementing the WIPO Development Agenda* (Ottawa: Wilfrid Laurier University Press, 2009).

Dodd, Rebecca, and Lane, Christopher, 'Improving the Long-Term Sustainability of Health Aid', *Health Policy and Planning*, 25/5 (2010), 363–71.

Donnan, Shawn, 'World Bank Hit by Executive Departures', *Financial Times*, 7 November 2015.

Dove, Alan, 'Brundtland Takes Charge and Restructures the WHO', *Nature Medicine*, 4 (1998), 992.

Drake, William, and Nicolaidas, Kalypso, 'Ideas, Interests and Institutionalization: "Trade in Services" and the Uruguay Round', *International Organization*, 46/1 (1992), 37–100.

Dumont, Alberto J., and Fastame, Ines Gabriela, 'World Intellectual Property Organization Development Agenda', *Journal of Generic Medicine*, 6/2 (2009), 99–110.

Easterly, William, *The Whiteman's Burden* (New York: Penguin Press, 2006).

Elsig, Manfred, 'The World Trade Organization at Work', *Review of International Organizations*, 5/3 (2010), 345–63.

Elsig, Manfred, 'Principal–Agent Theory and the World Trade Organization', *European Journal of International Relations*, 17/3 (2011), 495–517.

Epstein, Susan B., Tiersky, Alex, and Lawson, Marian L., 'State, Foreign Operations, and Related Programs: FY2015 Budget and Appropriation', Congressional Research Service, 8 December 2014.

FAO, 'Report of the Independent External Evaluation of the Food and Agriculture Organization of the United Nations (FAO)', C2007/7A.1-Rev.1 (September 2007).

FAO, *Final Report Executive Summary: Office of Director General Review*, 19 March 2010.

FAO, 'Programme Implementation Report 2014–15', C2017/8 (2016), 75–6.

Finkelstein, Lawrence, 'What is Global Governance', *Global Governance*, 1/3 (1995), 367–72.

Foley, Michael, *Political Leadership: Themes, Contexts and Critiques* (New York: Oxford University Press, 2013).

Gailmond, Sean, 'Expertise, Subversion and Bureaucratic Discretion', *Journal of Law, Economics and Organization*, 18/2 (2002), 536–55.

Gailmond, Sean, and Patty, John W., 'Slackers and Zealots: Civil Service, Policy Discretion, and Bureaucratic Expertise', *American Journal of Political Science*, 51/4 (2007), 873–89.

Glaser, Charles L., 'Realists as Optimists: Cooperation as Self Help', *International Security*, 19/3 (1994–5), 50–90.

Godlee, Fiona, 'WHO in Retreat: Is it Losing its Influence?', *BMJ* 309/6967 (1994), 1491–5.

Godlee, Fiona, 'The World Health Organization: WHO in Crisis' (series of eight articles), *BMJ* 309 (1994), 1424–8, 1491–5, 1566–70, 1636–70, and 310 (1995), 110–12, 178–82, 389–93, 583–6.

Godlee, Fiona, 'The WHO: Interview with the Director General', *BMJ* 310 (1995), 583–6.

Godlee, Fiona, 'WHO Reform and Global Health', *BMJ* 314/7091 (1997), 1359–60.

Godlee, Fiona, 'WHO Director General Faces Leadership Challenge', *BMJ* 314 (1997), 993.

Graham, Erin R., 'Money and Multilateralism: How Funding Rules Constitute IO Governance', *International Theory*, 7/1 (2015), 162–94.

Grant, Ruth W., and Keohane, Robert O., 'Accountability and Abuse of Power in World Politics', *American Political Science Review*, 99/1 (2005), 29–43.

Grieco, Joseph M., *Cooperation among Nations* (Ithaca, NY: Cornell University Press, 1990).

Haas, Ernst B., *Beyond the Nation State*, 2nd edn (Stanford: Stanford University Press, 1968).

Haas, Peter M., 'Knowledge, Power and International Policy Coordination, Special Issue', *International Organization*, 46/1 (1992), 1–390.

Hallam, David, 'Turbulence and Reform at the United Nations Food and Agriculture Organization', in Patrick Weller and Xu Yi-chong (eds), *The Politics of International Organizations: Views from Insiders* (New York: Routledge, 2015), 184–207.

Harbert, Debora J., 'The World Intellectual Property Organization: Past Present and Future', *Journal of Copyright Society of the USA*, 54 (2006–7), 253–84.

Harbinson, Stuart, 'The World Trade Organization as an Institution', in Patrick Weller and Xu Yi-chong (eds), *The Politics of International Organizations: Views from Insiders* (New York: Routledge, 2015), 17–47.

Hawkins, Darren G., Lake, David A., Nielson, Daniel L., and Tierney, Michael J. (eds), *Delegation and Agency in International Organizations* (New York: Cambridge University Press, 2006).

Hawkins, Darren G., and Jacoby, Wade, 'How Agents Matter', in Darren G. Hawkins et al. (eds), *Delegation and Agency in International Organizations* (New York: Cambridge University Press, 2006), 199–288.

Heclo, Hugh, *Modern Social Politics in Britain and Sweden* (New Haven: Yale University Press, 1974).

Heclo, Hugh, and Wildavsky, Aaron, *The Private Government of Public Money: Community and Policy inside British Politics* (London: Macmillan, 1974).

Helfer, Laurence R., 'Regime Shifting: The TRIPS Agreement and New Dynamics of International Intellectual Property Law-Making', *Yale Journal of International Law*, 29 (2004), 1–84.

Hexner, Ervin P., 'The Executive Board of the International Monetary Fund: A Decision-Making Instrument', *International Organization*, 18/1 (1964), 74–96.

Hoole, Francis W., Job, Brian L., and Tucker, Harvey J., 'Incremental Budgeting and International Organizations', *American Journal of Political Science*, 22/2 (1976), 273–301.

Horton, Richard, 'Offline: Can WHO Survive?', *Lancet*, 380 (2012), 1457.

Huber, John D., and McCarty, Nolan, 'Bureaucratic Capacity, Delegation and Political Reform', *American Political Science Review*, 98/3 (2004), 481–94.

Hubloue, Luc, and Vongthieres, Orasa, 'Governance at Work at the International Monetary Fund', in Patrick Weller and Xu Yi-chong (eds), *The Politics of International Organizations: Views from Insiders* (New York: Routledge, 2015), 93–118.

IMF, 'Report on the External Evaluation of Fund Surveillance', 30 June 1999.

IMF, *Evaluation Report: IMF Performance in the Run-up to the Financial and Economic Crisis* (Washington: Independent Evaluation Office of the IMF, 2011).

'International Institutions and Socialization in Europe', *International Organization*, special issue, 59/4 (2005), 801–1079.

Jepperson, Ronald L., 'Institutions, Institutional Effects, and Institutionalism', in Walter W. Powell and Paul J. DiMaggio (eds), *The New Institutionalism in Organizational Analysis* (Chicago: University of Chicago Press, 1991), 143–63.

Joachim, Jutta M., *Agenda Setting: The UN and NGOs* (Washington: Georgetown University Press, 2007).

Johanson, Mark, 'How the US Lost UNESCO Voting Rights', *International Business Times*, 12 November 2013.

Johnson, Tana, 'Looking beyond States', *Review of International Organizations*, 8/4 (2013), 499–519.

Kahler, Miles, *Leadership Selection in the Major Multinationals* (Washington: Institute for International Economics, 2001).

Katzenstein, Peter, *Small States in World Markets* (Ithaca, NY: Cornell University Press, 1985).

Kavaksky, Basil, 'Pictures and Lessons of Development Practice', in Indermit S. Gill and Todd Pugatch (eds), *At the Frontlines of Development* (Washington: World Bank, 2005), 17–46.

Keck, Margaret, and Sikkink, Katherine, *Activists beyond Borders* (Ithaca, NY: Cornell University Press, 1998).

Keohane, Robert O., *After Hegemony* (Princeton: Princeton University Press, 1984).

Keohane, Robert O., 'Accountability in World Politics', *Scandinavian Political Studies*, 29/2 (2006), 75–87.

Keohane, Robert, and Nye, Joseph S., 'The Club Model of Multilateral Cooperation and Problems of Democratic Legitimacy', in Roger Porter et al. (eds), *Efficiency, Equity and Legitimacy: The Multilateral Trading System at the Millennium* (Washington: Brookings Institution Press, 2001), 264–94.

Killick, Tony, *Aid and the Political Economy of Change* (London: Routledge, 1998).

Kindleberger, Charles, 'Economists in International Organizations', *International Organization*, 9/3 (1955), 338–52.

King, Loren A., 'Deliberation, Legitimacy, and Multilateral Democracy', *Governance*, 16/1 (2003), 23–50.

Koremenos, Barbara, Lipson, Charles, and Snidal, Duncan, 'The Rational Design of International Institutions', *International Organization*, 55/4 (2001), 761–99.
Koremenos, Barbara, Lipson, Charles, and Snidal, Duncan (eds), *The Rational Design of International Institutions* (New York: Cambridge University Press, 2001).
Koremenos, Barbara, and Snidal, Duncan, 'Moving Forward, One Step at a Time', *International Organization*, 57/2 (2003), 431–44.
Kraske, Jochen, *Bankers with a Mission* (Washington: World Bank, 1996).
Krasner, Stephen D., 'Structural Changes and Regime Consequences: Regimes as Intervening Variables', in S. Krasner (ed.), *International Regimes* (Ithaca, NY: Cornell University Press, 1983).
Langrod, Georges, *The International Civil Service* (New York: Oceana Publications, 1961).
Lerner, Jack, 'Intellectual Property and Development at WHO and WIPO', *American Journal of Law and Medicine*, 34 (2008), 257–77.
Lesage, Dries, Debaere, Peter, Dierckx, Sacha, and Vermeiren, Mattias, 'IMF Reform after the Crisis', *International Politics*, 50/4 (2013), 553–78.
Levelle, Kathryn C., *Legislating International Organizations* (New York: Oxford University Press, 2011).
Lewis, Jeffrey, 'The Janus Face of Brussels: Socialization and Everyday Decision Making in the European Union', *International Organization*, 59/4 (2005), 937–71.
Litsios, Socrates, 'The Long and Difficult Road to Alma-Ata: A Personal Reflection', *The Politics of the World Health Organization*, 32/4 (2002), 709–32.
Lyne, Mona M., Nielson, Daniel L., and Tierney, Michael J., 'Who Delegates: Alternative Models of Principals in Development Aid', in Darren G. Hawkins et al. (eds), *Delegation and Agency in International Organizations* (New York: Cambridge University Press, 2006), 41–76.
McGregor, Alan, 'WHO again under Fire from External Auditor', *Lancet*, 343/8908 (1994), 1278–9.
McLaren, Robert, *Civil Servants and Public Policy: Comparative Study of International Secretariats* (Toronto: Wilfred Laurier University Press, 1980).
Mallaby, Sebastian, *The World's Banker* (New York: Penguin Books, 2004).
March, James G., 'Understanding how Decisions Happen in Organization', in J. G. March(ed.), *The Pursuit of Organizational Intelligence* (Boston: Basic Blackwell, 1999).
March, James G., and Olsen, Johan P., *Rediscovering Institutions* (New York: Free Press, 1989).
March, James G., and Olsen, Johan P., 'The Institutional Dynamics of International Political Orders', *International Organization*, 5/4 (1998), 943–70.
Marshall, Katherine, *The World Bank* (London, Routledge, 2008).
Martin, Lisa, 'Agency and Delegation in IMF Conditionality', paper for the Utah Conference on Delegation to International Organizations, 2002.
Martin, Lisa, 'Distribution, Information and Delegation to International Organizations', in Darren G. Hawkins et al. (eds), *Delegation and Agency in International Organizations* (New York: Cambridge University Press, 2006), 140–64.
Martinez-Diaz, Leonardo, 'Boards of Directors in International Organizations', *Review of International Organization*, 4/4 (2009), 383–406.

Mason, Edward S., and Asher, Robert E., *The World Bank since Bretton Woods* (Washington: Brookings Institution Press, 1973).
Maxwell, Simon, 'Food Security: A Post-Modern Perspective', *Food Policy*, 21/2 (1996), 155–70.
Mayhew, David, *Congress: The Electoral Connection* (New Haven: Yale University Press, 1974).
Mearsheimer, John, 'The False Promise of International Relations', *International Security*, 19/3 (1994–5), 5–43.
Mele, Valentine, Anderfuhren-Biget, Simon, and Varone, Frederic, 'Conflicts of Interest in International Organizations: Evidence from Two United Nations Humanitarian Agencies', *Public Administration*, 94/2 (2016), 490–508.
Milner, Helen, 'The Assumption of Anarchy in International Relations Theory', *Review of International Studies*, 17/1 (1991), 67–85.
Momani, Bessma, 'IMF Staff: Missing Link in Fund Reform Proposals', *Review of International Organizations*, 2 (2007), 39–57.
Momani, Bessma, 'Canada's IMF Executive Director', *Canadian Public Administration*, 53/2 (2010), 163–82.
MONAP, 'Food and Agriculture Organization (FAO) of the United Nations', vol. I, (December 2011).
Moraes, Henrique Choer, and Brandelli, Otavio, 'The Development Agenda at WIPO: Context and Origins', in Neil Weinstock Netanel (ed.), *The Development Agenda: Global Intellectual Property and Developing Countries* (New York: Oxford University Press, 2009), 33–49.
Morse, Julia C., and Keohane, Robert O., 'Contested Multilateralism', *Review of International Organizations*, 9/4 (2014), 385–412.
Mountford, Alexander, 'The Historical Development of IMF Governance', Independent Evaluation Office, IMF (BP/08/02) (May 2008).
Mouritzen, Hans, *The International Civil Service* (Aldershot: Dartmouth, 1990).
Nadelmann, Ethan A., 'Global Prohibition Regimes: The Evolution of Norms in International Society', *International Organization*, 44/4 (1990), 495–526.
Netanel, Neil Weinstock (ed.), *The Development Agenda: Global Intellectual Property and Developing Countries* (New York: Oxford University Press, 2009).
Neustadt, Richard, *Presidential Power and the Modern Presidents* (New York: Free Press, 1999).
Newmann, Iver B., 'To be a Diplomat', *International Studies Perspectives*, 6/1 (2005), 72–93.
Nielson, Daniel L., and Tierney, Michael J., 'Delegation to International Organizations: Agency Theory and World Bank Environmental Reform', *International Organization*, 57/2 (2003), 241–76.
North, Douglass C., *Institutions, Institutional Change, and Economic Performance* (Cambridge: Cambridge University Press, 1990).
O'Neill, Kate, Balsiger, Jörg, and VanDeveer, Stacy D., 'Actors, Norms, and Impact', *Annual Review of Political Science*, 7 (2004), 149–75.
OECD and FAO, *Synthesis of the Evaluation of FAO's Regional and Subregional Offices* (Rome: FAO, 2013).
Oye, Kenneth (ed.), *Cooperation under Anarchy* (Princeton: Princeton University Press, 1986).

Parizek, Michal, 'Control, Soft Information, and the Politics of International Organizations Staff', *Review of International Organizations* (2017); online first <https://link.springer.com/article/10.1007/s11558-016-9252-1> (accessed 1 January 2016).
Parker, George, 'Man in the News: Dominique Strauss-Kahn', *Financial Times*, 14 July 2007.
Patrick, Stewart, 'Prix Fixe and à la Carte: Avoiding False Multilateral Choices', *Washington Quarterly*, 32/4 (2009), 77–95.
Patz, Ronny, and Goetz, Klaus H., 'Managing Budget Conflicts in International Organizations', paper presented at the Panel, 'Bureaucratic Perspectives on International Organizations', ECPR General Conference, Montreal, 26–9 August 2015.
Paulson, Henry M., Jr, *Dealing with China* (New York: Twelve Hachette Book Group, 2015).
Peabody, John W., 'An Organizational Analysis of the World Health Organization: Narrowing the Gap between Promise and Performance', *Social Science & Medicine*, 40/6 (1995), 731–42.
Peretz, David, 'The Process for Selecting and Appointing the Managing Director and First Deputy Managing Director of the IMF', Backgrounder, IEO, IMF, BP/07/01 (2007).
Pierson, Paul, and Skocpol, Theda, 'Historical Institutionalism in Contemporary Political Science', in Ira Katznelson and Helen V. Milner (eds), *Political Science: The State of the Discipline* (New York: W.W. Norton, 2002), 693–721.
Pincock, Stephen, 'Hiroshi Nakajima', *Lancet*, 381 (2013), 1178.
Pitkin, Hanna Fenichel, *The Concept of Representation* (Berkeley and Los Angeles: University of California Press, 1967).
Pollack, Mark, 'Delegation, Agency, and Agenda Setting in the European Community', *International Organization*, 51/1 (1997), 99–134.
Prasad, Naresh, 'The World Intellectual Property Organization', in Patrick Weller and Xu Yi-chong (eds), *The Politics of International Organizations: Views from Insiders* (New York: Routledge, 2015), 134–62.
Princen, Sebastiaan, 'Governing through Multiple Forums: The Global Safety Regulation of Genetically Modified Crops and Foods', in Mathias Koenig-Archibugi and Michael Zurn (eds), *New Modes of Governance in the Global System* (Basingstoke: Palgrave Macmillan, 2006), 52–76.
Ravallion, Martin, 'The World Bank: Why It Is Still Needed and Why It Still Disappoints', *Journal of Economic Perspectives*, 30/1 (2016), 77–94.
Reinalda, Bob, and Verbeek, Bertjan (eds), *Decision Making within International Organizations* (London: Routledge, 2004).
Rhodes, R.A.W., and 't Hart, Paul (eds), *The Oxford Handbook of Political Leadership* (New York: Oxford University Press, 2013).
Rice, Andrew, 'How the World Bank's Biggest Critic Became its President', *Guardian*, 11 August 2016.
Rice, Andrew, 'Is Jim Kim Destroying the World Bank: Or Saving it from Itself', *Foreign Policy*, 27 April 2016.
Robbins, Anthony, 'Brundtland's World Health Organization: A Test Case for United Nations Reform', *Public Health Reports*, 114/1 (1999), 30–9.

Roeder, Philip G., *Red Sunset: The Failure of Soviet Politics* (Princeton: Princeton University, 1993).
Ruggie, John Gerard, 'International Regimes, Transactions, and Change', *International Organization*, 36/2 (1982), 379–415.
Ruggie, John Gerard (ed.), *Multilateralism Matters: The Theory and Praxis of an Institutional Form* (New York: Columbia University Press, 1993).
Ruggie, John Gerard, 'global_governance.net: The Global Compact as Learning Network', *Global Governance*, 7/4 (2001), 371–8.
Runciman, David, 'The Paradox of Political Representation', *Journal of Political Philosophy*, 15/1 (2007), 93–114.
Sachs, Jeffrey D., *The End of Poverty* (New York: Penguin Books, 2005).
Schlagheck, Donna M., 'The Political State of Administrative Reform at the United Nations', in Jerri Killian and Niklas Eklund (eds), *Handbook of Administrative Reform: An International Perspective* (Boca Raton, FL: CRC Press, Taylor & Francis Group, 2008).
Sell, Susan, *Private Power, Public Law* (New York: Cambridge University Press, 2004).
Shaw, D. John, *Global Food and Agricultural Institutions* (New York: Routledge, 2009).
Slater, Terry, *Strategic Organizational Review: Structure and Staffing Resources of the World Trade Organization Secretariat* (Geneva: WTO, 2001).
Snidal, Duncan, 'Political Economy and International Institutions', *International Review of Law and Economics*, 16/1 (1996), 121–37.
Sridhar, Devi, and Woods, Ngaire, 'Trojan Multilateralism: Global Cooperation in Health', *Global Policy*, 4/4 (2013), 325–35.
Stenson, Bo, and Sterky, Goran, 'What Future WHO?' *Health Policy*, 28/3 (1994), 235–56.
Stone, Randall W., *Controlling Institutions: International Organizations and the Global Economy* (New York: Cambridge University Press, 2011).
Strauss-Kahn, Dominique, 'My Vision for the IMF', *Wall Street Journal*, 21 September 2007.
Sykes, Alan O., 'Transnational Forum Shopping as a Trade and Investment Issue', *Journal of Legal Studies*, 37/2 (2008), 339–78.
Tallberg, Jonas, 'The Power of the Chair', *International Studies Quarterly*, 54/1 (2010), 241–65.
Thelen, Kathleen, 'Historical Institutionalism in Comparative Politics', *American Review of Political Science*, 2 (1999), 369–404.
Thelen, Kathleen, 'How Institutions Evolve', in James Mahoney and Dietrich Rueschemeyer (eds), *Comparative Historical Analysis in the Social Sciences* (New York: Cambridge University Press, 2003), 208–40.
Thomas, M. A., 'The Governance Bank', *International Affairs*, 83/4 (2007), 729–45.
Trondal, Jarle, 'The Autonomy of Bureaucratic Organizations', *Journal of International Organization Studies*, 5/2 (2014), 55–60.
Trondal, Jarle, and Veggeland, Fronde, 'The Autonomy of Bureaucratic Organizations: An Organization Theory Argument', *Journal of International Organization Studies*, 5/2 (2014), 55–60.
UN System, Standing Committee on Nutrition, *SCN Private Sector Engagement Report* (Geneva: SCN, 2004).

UNAIDS, *UNAIDS: The First 10 Years, 1996-2006* (Geneva: UNAIDS, 2008).
Urquhart, Brian, and Childers, Erskine, *A World in Need of Leadership: Tomorrow's United Nations* (Uppsala, Sweden: Dag Hammarskjold Foundation, 1990).
van de Graaf, Thijia, and Lesage, Dries, 'The International Energy Agency after 35 Years', *Review of International Organization*, 4/3 (2009), 293-317.
VanGrasstek, Craig, *The History and Future of the World Trade Organization* (Geneva: WTO, 2013).
Van Houtven, Leo, 'Rethinking IMF Governance', *Finance & Development*, 41/3 (2004), 18-20.
Vaughan, J. Patrick, Mogedal, Sigrun, Kruse, Stein-Erik, Lee, Kelley, Walt, Gill, and de Wilde, Koen, 'Financing the World Health Organization: The Global Importance of Extra-budgetary Funds', *Health Policy*, 35 (1996), 229-45.
Venediktov, Dmitry, 'Primary Health Care: Alma-Ata and After', *World Health Forum*, 19/1 (1998), 79-86.
Verweij, Marco, and Josling, Timothy, 'Special Issue: Deliberately Democratizing Multilateral Organizations', *Governance*, 16/1 (2003), 1-140.
Visser, Coenraad, 'The Policy-Making Dynamics in Intergovernmental Organizations', *Chicago-Kent Law Review*, 82/3 (2007), 1457-66.
Walt, Gill, 'WHO under Stress', *Health Policy*, 24/2 (1993), 125-44.
Weaver, Catherine, *Hypocrisy Trap: The World Bank and the Poverty of Reform* (Ithaca, NY: Cornell University Press, 2008).
Weiss, Thomas G., and Wilkinson, Rorden, 'Rethinking Global Governance', *International Studies Quarterly*, 58/1 (2014), 207-15.
Weitz Charles H., *Who Speaks for the Hungry? How FAO Elects its Leader* (Uppsala, Sweden: DAG Hammarskjöld Foundation, 1997).
Weller, Patrick, and Xu Yi-chong (eds), *The Politics of International Organizations: Views from Insiders* (New York: Routledge, 2015).
WHO, *Understanding Civil Society: Issues for WHO* (Geneva: WHO, 2002).
Williams, Douglass, *The Specialized Agencies and the United Nations* (London: C. Hurst & Company, 1987).
Woods, Ngaire, *The Globalizers: The IMF, the World Bank, and their Borrowers* (Ithaca, NY: Cornell University Press, 2006).
World Bank Independent Evaluation Group, *Trust Fund Support for Development* (Washington: World Bank, 2011).
World Bank Independent Evaluation Group, *The Matrix System at Work: An Evaluation of the World Bank's Organizational Effectiveness* (Washington: World Bank, April 2012).
WTO, 'Procedures for the Appointment of Directors-General' (WT/L/509), 2 January 2003.
WTO, *The Cotton Initiative*, and various documents at <https://www.wto.org/english/tratop_e/agric_e/negs_bkgrnd20_cotton_e.htm> (accessed 15 March 2015).
Xu Yi-chong and Weller, Patrick, *The Governance of World Trade: International Civil Servants and the GATT/WTO* (Cheltenham: Edward Elgar, 2004).
Xu Yi-chong and Weller, Patrick, 'Chrik Poortman: A World Bank Professional', *Public Administration Review*, 69/5 (2009), 868-75.

Select Bibliography

Xu Yi-chong and Weller, Patrick, *Inside the World Bank* (New York: Palgrave Macmillan, 2009).

Xu Yi-chong and Weller, Patrick, 'Agents of Influence: Country Directors in the World Bank', *Public Administration*, 88/1 (2010), 211–31.

Xu Yi-chong and Weller, Patrick, 'Understanding the Governance of International Organizations', in Patrick Weller and Xu Yi-chong (eds), *The Politics of International Organisations: Views from Insiders* (New York: Routledge, 2015), 1–15.

Youde, Jeremy, *Global Health Governance* (Cambridge: Polity, 2012).

Young, Oran R., *International Governance* (Ithaca, NY: Cornell University Press, 1994).

Yu, Geoffrey, 'What WIPO Should Do Next', *Managing IP* (July/August 2008), 24.

Yu, Geoffrey, 'The World Intellectual Property Organization: A Comment', in Patrick Weller and Xu Yi-chong (eds), *The Politics of International Organizations: Views from Insiders* (New York: Routledge, 2015), 163–9.

Yu, Geoffrey, 'The Structure and Process of Negotiations at the World Intellectual Property Organization', *Chicago–Kent Law* Review, 82/3 (2007), 1439–44.

Zhang, Shengman, *One Step at a Time* (先站住, 再站高) (Shanghai: Wenhui Press, 2006).

Index

Africa, Caribbean and Pacific (ACP) 51–2, 53
Azevêdo, Roberto 70, 71, 79, 89, 91

Black, Eugene 60
Bogsch, Arpad 74, 158–9
Brazil 42, 52, 151, 184, 193, 195, 211
Brundtland, Gro Harlem 59, 61, 62, 73, 95, 96, 98, 99, 122, 158, 189–90, 214, 224

Canada 22, 26, 52, 76
Chan, Margaret 59, 61, 74, 77, 79, 85, 86, 92, 96, 98, 144, 158, 167, 169, 191, 195–6, 214–15
Conable, Barber 66

Diouf, Jacques 59, 75, 220, 222, 235
Dunkel, Arthur 42, 68, 89, 95, 99

European Union (EU) 29, 45, 65, 152, 195; member groupings 50–1, 52

Food and Agriculture Organization (FAO) 1, 2, 54, 59–60; agenda setting 153–4, 155, 156–7, 162, 165; appointment of executive director 28; culture 132–3, 134; council 24; country delegations 220–2; elections 63, 65, 72–3, 75, 79; funding 182–7, 193, 202; Independent External Evaluation (IEE) 78, 122, 124, 138, 154, 155, 156, 194, 213, 239; leadership 78, 90; location 207–8, 212–13; mandate 142, 143, 145–6, 170; staff 35, 36, 37, 39, 42, 111, 114, 120, 122, 216–17; state representation 35, 36, 37, 39, 42; technical organization 32; tenure of directors general 36; World Food Programme 31, 35, 147; *see also* Doiuf, Jacques; Graziano da Silva, José; Prasad, Naresh

Gates Foundation 194, 197, 199, 202, 229, 239
General Agreement on Tariffs and Trade (GATT) 42, 61, 68, 71, 88, 131, 165, 231
Graziano da Silva, José 78, 79, 100, 207
Gurry, Francis 59, 61, 74, 75, 77, 79, 91, 98, 100, 134, 164, 167, 205

Harbinson, Stuart 91
Human Rights Council 52

International Civil Service 17, 224; agenda setting 147; bias 116; blame 129; characteristics 104–6; dual loyalties 127; expectations 112–17, 128, 237; policy communities 135–7, routines 125–30
International Fund for Agricultural Development (IFAD) 31, 147
International Monetary Fund (IMF) 1, 2, 3, 24; agenda setting 156, 161–2; appointment of executive directors 26–8, 30; culture 131, 132, 133, 134, 239; diplomatic role 81, 82, 83, 84; dual role of executive directors 39–40, 41, 42; funding 176–7, 192; leadership 60, 64, 65, 67–8, 82–3; location 205–6; mandate 142; proximity to USA 50; staff 113–14, 118–19; state representation 26, 33–4, 35, 36, 37, 44–50; *see also* Koch-Weser, Caio; Kohler, Hans; Lagarde, Christine; Strauss-Kahn, Dominique; Zhou, Xiaochuan 49
International Organizations (IO) agenda setting 140–2, 153, 155, 159, 160–1; Articles of Agreement or Treaties 23–4, 234; ambassadorships 46; cultures 130–5, 232–4; dual nature of state representation 39–44; hierarchies 218–19; leadership 59–60, 60–3, 63–77, 80–1, 81–4, 84–90, 90–100; location 204–10, 223–7, 230–1; mandates 142–7, 149–56, 161–5; member state groupings 50–3, 238; power of USA 53–4; rationalities of 230–1; staff profiles 107–10; staff expertise 117–24; state representation 25–33, 34, 38, voluntary contributions 191–6

Japan 26, 52, 184, 192

Kim, Yong Jim 60, 62, 67, 95, 98, 134, 159, 211–12
Koch-Weser, Caio 67
Kohler, Hans 67

Lagarde, Christine 98, 113
Lamy, Pascal 59, 60, 61, 69, 79, 80, 81, 82, 84, 87, 89, 91, 93, 95, 99–100, 123, 167, 178, 204
Lee, Jong-Wook 59, 61, 73–4, 98, 158, 214–15
Long, Oliver 68

McCloy, John 85
McNamara, Robert 60, 66, 99, 132
Moore, Michael 68–9, 102, 131

Nakajima, Hiroshi 83–4, 188, 189
Non-state players 165–9, 197–203, 241; funding of 173–5, 202

Obama, Barack 2, 27, 67, 82

Paulson, Hank 49, 84
Poortman, Chrik 95
Prasad, Naresh 91

Ruggiero, Renato 60, 83, 85, 87

Sanchez, Arancha 91
Saouma, Edouard 75, 78
Smith, Ian 95
State representation 14–15, 19, 234–6; appointments 25–33; difficulties of 54; interactions 22–3; member-state groupings 50–3, 54–5; qualities 22, 33–9; trustees or delegates 21–2
Stern, Ernest 95
Strauss-Kahn, Dominique 49, 61, 67, 68, 85, 177
Sutherland, Peter 61, 82

Trade-Related Aspects of Intellectual Property Rights (TRIPS) 44, 52, 159, 165, 166

United Kingdom 22, 26, 27, 152, 192, 195
United Nations 2, 3, 16, 26; Ambassadors 24; Human Rights Commission 3, 46, 52; state representation 29, 30, 43
United Nations Conference on Trade and Development (UNCTAD) 45, 46, 81, 157
United States of America 52, 65, 66, 72, 83, 88, 94, 144, 152, 173–4, 184, 192, 195, 196, 238, 239; power within IOs 53–4; proximity to IMF 50; state representation 26–7, 35, 49

Wolfensohn, James 41, 59, 61, 62, 66, 85, 87, 95, 98, 99, 146, 207, 211, 222, 224, 225, 235
Wolfowitz, Paul 49, 59, 66, 79, 87, 89, 95, 99, 100, 134
Wood, George 146
World Bank (WB) 2, 3, 24; agenda setting 156, 159, 161, 162; appointment of executive directors 26–8; culture 131, 132, 133, 134; dual roles of executive directors 39–40, 41; elections 63, 65; funding 176–7, 192, 199; leadership 58, 60, 64, 66–8, 81, 82–3, 84, 90; relationship with NGOs 136, 198; staff 114, 118–19, 206–7, 224–5; state representation 22, 28, 34; see also Black, Eugene; Conable, Barber; Kim Yong Jim; McCloy, John; McNamara, Robert; Poortman, Chrik; Stern, Ernest; Wolfensohn, James; Wolfowitz, Paul; Wood, George; Zhang Shengman; Zoellick, Robert
World Food Programme see Food and Agriculture Organization
World Health Organization (WHO) 1, 2, 3; agenda setting 158, 160–1, 164; culture 133; elections 65, 73–4, 75–7; funding 182–91, 194–6, 199, 200–1, 202; mandate 142, 143, 144–5; relationship with NGOs 136, 165, 169, 198–9, 200, 239; staff 113, 119, 208–9, 213–15; state representation 30, 35, 36, 37, 38, 39, 44, 46; technical expertise 32, 47, 120, 167; see also Brundtland, Gro Harlem; Chan, Margaret; Lee, Jong-Wook; Nakajima, Hiroshi; Smith, Ian
World Intellectual Property Organization (WIPO) 3, agenda setting 149–50, 151, 158–9; culture 131, 134; elections 65, 73–4, 79; funding 177–82, 192; location 204–5, 206; mandate 142, 143; member groupings 51, 53, 148; relationship with NGOs 165–8, 198; staff 114, 119; state representation 29, 30, 31, 35, 36, 37, 39, 44, 45, 46; technical organization 32, 47, 167; see also Bogsch, Arpad; Gurry, Francis
World Trade Organization (WTO) 2, 3; agenda setting 140; culture 130, 131, 132, 133; funding 177–82, 192; elections 63, 65, 68–71; diplomatic role 81, 82, 83, 84; leadership 58, 60, 64, 71, 90; location 204, 206, 211–12; mandate 142, 143; member groupings 51, 52, 53; relationship with NGOs 135–6; staff 112–13, 119; state representation 28, 29, 30, 34, 39, 42, 43, 45, 46, 51; technical organization 32, 167; see also Azevêdo, Roberto; Dunkel, Arthur; Harbinson, Stuart; Lamy, Pascal; Long, Oliver; Moore, Michael; Ruggiero, Renato; Sanchez, Arancha; Sutherland, Peter; Yeend, Tim

Yeend, Tim 91

Zhang, Shengman 87, 94, 95–6, 99, 225
Zhou, Xiaochuan 49
Zoellick, Robert 60, 82, 95, 99